THE ACADIANS

IN SEARCH OF A HOMELAND

JAMES LAXER

DOUBLEDAY CANADA

Doubleday Canada and colophon are trademarks.

LIBRARY AND ARCHIVES CANADA CATALOGUING IN PUBLICATION

Laxer, James, 1941–
The Acadians : in search of a homeland / James Laxer.
Includes bibliographical references and index.

ISBN-13: 978-0-385-66108-9
ISBN-10: 0-385-66108-8

1. Acadia—History. 2. Acadians—History. 3. Acadians—Ethnic

identity. I. Title.

FC2041.L33 2006   971.5004'114   C2006-904410-4

Jacket image (map): © Michael Maslan Historic Photographs/CORBIS
Book design and maps: Leah Springate
Printed and bound in the USA

Published in Canada by
Doubleday Canada, a division of
Random House of Canada Limited

Visit Random House of Canada Limited's website: www.randomhouse.ca

BVG 10 9 8 7 6 5 4 3 2 1

To Francis and Elaine

CONTENTS

—

Foreword   ix
Introduction: Acadie in Question   1

L'ACADIE

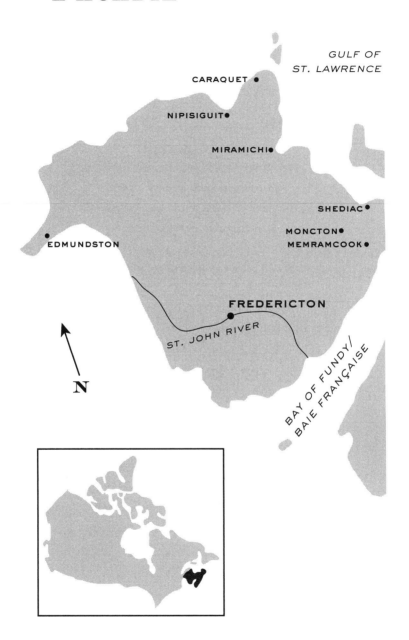

GULF OF
ST. LAWRENCE

CARAQUET

NIPISIGUIT

MIRAMICHI

SHEDIAC

MONCTON
MEMRAMCOOK

EDMUNDSTON

FREDERICTON

ST. JOHN RIVER

BAY OF FUNDY/
BAIE FRANÇAISE

N

GULF OF ST. LAWRENCE

CHETICAMP ●

PRINCE EDWARD ISLAND/
ÎLE ST JEAN

LOUISBOURG ●

● CANSO

NORTHUMBERLAND STRAIT   ANTIGONISH ●

SHEDIAC ●

● MONCTON
● MEMRAMCOOK
FORT ● ● FORT LAWRENCE
BEAUSÉJOUR ● BEAUBASSIN

BAY OF FUNDY/
BAIE FRANÇAISE

● GRAND PRÉ   ● CHEZZETCOOK

● HALIFAX

ANNAPOLIS ROYAL
● /PORT ROYAL

ATLANTIC OCEAN

● PUBNICO

—

WHEN I WAS ASKED TO WRITE the Foreword to this book, I immediately accepted. Having had the privilege of meeting James Laxer and discussing Acadian and Canadian issues with him a few summers ago, I was delighted to learn that he was writing a book about Acadie.

Since the 1990s, numerous works on Acadie and on Acadian studies have been written by both North American and European scholars in French, English and more recently in German. James Laxer's contribution to this impressive body of work is unique and is a witness to his excellent reputation established by his previous works. His analysis of Acadie's past and present is both pertinent and original through his examination of the historical and contemporary journeys of Atlantic Canada's Acadians and their Cajun cousins in Louisiana.

Another original contribution of James Laxer's work is in its view of contemporary Acadie. This book focuses on the Acadian community in New Brunswick, but the way in which Laxer examines the Acadian soul and the shifting identities in present-day Acadie can also be applied to the other Acadian communities of Atlantic Canada. Laxer has skillfully described the Acadian community's historical and contemporary quest for a homeland.

It is my wish that the great interest and pleasure I experienced by reading this book will be shared by others so that they can also discover one of North America's oldest societies whose resilient identity is a testimony to their *entêtement*.

Maurice Basque
Director
Études acadiennes
Université de Moncton

—

ACADIE IN QUESTION

IT WAS THE LAST DAY for the Acadians at Grand Pré, the last day for them to live normal lives in the community they had built over the past century. On the morrow the soldiers would arrive on British ships. Their commander had received instructions from Charles Lawrence, the acting governor of Nova Scotia, to forcibly remove the inhabitants, burn their houses, churches and mills and lay waste their fields. It was late September 1755 and much of the crop had not yet been harvested. But on the eve of the coming of the ships, the people of Grand Pré had no reason to fear the onset of winter. Over the generations, Acadians had learned the hard lessons of life in a new land whose winters were much more difficult than those in the region of France around La Rochelle from which many of the first settlers had come. Their homes were built for warmth, with wooden walls that were filled in with stone to provide insulation.

On their fertile marshland fields, close to the sea, the farmers of Grand Pré raised ample crops and livestock. To their diet, they added game and fish and wild berries. They were a largely self-sufficient people, although they conducted vigorous trade with New Englanders that provided them with goods they couldn't produce themselves.

Once the crops were off the lands, the Acadians could turn their minds to other things during the coming cold months. Most weddings in Grand Pré were celebrated between late October and February, the period when the demands of harvesting and planting were in abeyance. This was a time as well for preserving food, and making furniture, tools and toys for the children. It was a time for celebration and enjoyment. And it was just around the corner.

Grand Pré was the largest of the settlements around the shores of the Baie Française (Bay of Fundy), the homeland of a new and distinctive people. The original settlers had left France for Acadie for a variety of reasons. Ambitious ones had come with the hope of making it in the fur trade or the fishery. Others came in search of adventure in a new age that offered Europeans the means to emigrate. Some sought escape from the strictures of French society, and others wanted to be freed from the vicious religious wars that devastated La Rochelle and other parts of France in the early seventeenth century.

Like other Acadian settlements, Grand Pré was made up of numerous small hamlets, where the members of extended families lived close to one another. The Acadians had branched off from the society of their original French homeland and had developed a way of life that set them apart from the French of France, as well as from the French Canadians who lived along the banks of the St. Lawrence River. The Acadians of Grand Pré had developed close ties with the Mi'kmaq of the region and there was a considerable amount of intermarriage between the two peoples. In Grand Pré and other settlements, Acadian children, Mi'kmaq children and children of mixed race all played together.

Prior to the deportation, the word Acadie referred to a territory that was repeatedly fought over by the empires of France and England. (While some believe the name Acadie derives from the Greek Arcadia, which symbolized an ideal land, others think it comes from an aboriginal word, perhaps the Mi'kmaq word *Cadie*, or the Maliseet word *Quoddy*. Both words connote a piece of cherished land.)[1]

While the precise boundaries of Acadie were often in dispute, its broad shape was clear. Acadie included the territories of the present-day provinces of Nova Scotia (including Cape Breton Island), New Brunswick and Prince Edward Island. Lured by the warm summer weather into believing that all would be well, the French established their first settlement in what was to become Acadie in 1604 on the Île St. Croix, a small piece of land in the present-day state of Maine, located right next to the border of New Brunswick. The first winter was tragically disillusioning—over half of the men in the tiny settlement perished. The following year, the French expedition abandoned the island and moved across the Baie Française to the territory of present-day Nova Scotia, establishing the outpost of Port Royal.

Acadie has always been a tough territory on the northern edge of the temperate lands of North America, never an Arcadia, and vastly unlike the France from which the Acadians came. The new people developed their uniqueness in a morose and lonely setting, a land of dark green forests with only marginally decent agricultural prospects. Peninsular Nova Scotia, the homeland of most Acadians before the deportation, is a tough, unyielding, spiny territory that remains almost impassable in places, even in our time.

For the Acadians, the highway of hope, life, culture, song and freedom has always been the sea. The sea linked tiny settlements with one another, and the sea brought a good life for the Acadians, who soon grew into a people who mastered the fishery, the commerce of the region, and unlocked the way to farm the marshy lands next to salt water. But if the sea brought prosperity and communication, it was also the highway of war for those who often descended on Acadian communities to pillage and burn, and in the end to destroy their settlements and force them into exile.

The territory of Acadie was on the front lines of the clashes between the French and the English. In 1710, the bulk of Acadie was seized for the last time by the British. Under the Treaty of Utrecht of 1713, the British gained control of the territories of present-day New Brunswick and peninsular Nova Scotia, leaving only Cape Breton (Île Royale) and Prince Edward Island (Île St. Jean) in the hands of the French. For forty-five years, the Acadians lived uneasily under a British administration in a territory that the English called Nova Scotia. Repeatedly, they were pressured to swear an oath of allegiance to British rule. For the most part, the Acadians were willing to swear such an oath, but only if it included a caveat that they would not be required to take up arms against the French and the native Mi'kmaq in a future conflict.

A new struggle was playing out between the two empires, influenced crucially by the rising power of Massachusetts, with its appetite for Acadian farmland and for mastery over the fishery in Acadian waters. Against this backdrop, the relationship between the Acadians and the British administration in Halifax came to a crisis point. In the summer of 1755, Nova Scotia's acting governor summoned the representatives of the Acadians and demanded that they take another oath of allegiance to the regime, an oath that, this time, would be unconditional. When they refused, the Acadian representatives were arrested and imprisoned.

The expulsion commenced. About seven thousand men, women and children were herded on board British ships and from there they were transported to the Thirteen Colonies to the south. As the Acadians set out on their voyage of despair, many of them to die in shipwrecks and of disease, their homes, churches and mills were put to the torch.

The authorities who dispatched the ships and the soldiers were determined to remove the Acadians from their homeland and scatter them so they would cease to exist as a people. The goal was precisely to destroy the Acadians—not by killing them, although thousands were to die in the process, but by robbing them of their collective sense of themselves.

In 2004, four hundred years after the founding of the first Acadian settlement, two friends of mine are engaged in an animated conversation.

"You're not Acadian. You're Belgian," Elaine, a doctor who practises medicine in the town of Shediac, New Brunswick, tells her husband.

"I *am* Acadian," he insists. "My paintings are displayed in exhibitions of Acadian art." Francis is a professor at the Université de Moncton.

"You were born in Namur," she replies. "How can you be Acadian?"

"I've been here for thirty years. I've made a commitment to the Acadian project."

As for the skeptical wife, she is not entirely clear what is meant by "the Acadian project," and she is not sure she really qualifies as an Acadian herself. French is her primary language, and she speaks it 80 or 90 percent of the time, but she spoke only English until she was six years old. Her father was from a Quebec family but he was born in Saint John, New Brunswick. Throughout his life he spoke little French. Elaine's mother is French-speaking and the descendant of an Acadian family. One of Elaine's brothers speaks little French, while her other brother and her sister speak mainly French.

The conversation at the dining-room table of two friends, whose windows overlook the panorama of Shediac Bay, illustrates the complexity of what it is to be Acadian. The woman born in New Brunswick wonders whether she is Acadian, while her Belgian-born husband is sure that he is. It's an illustration of the quandary of today's Acadian identity and its shifting parameters.

While most peoples have a clearly demarcated territory they can call their homeland, this is not so for the Acadians. Not since *le Grand Dérangement*, the expulsion, has there been a territory that can unequivocally be called Acadie.

In the mid eighteenth century several thousand Acadians managed to avoid expulsion by hiding in the woods. Many of these people were to be among the founders of the New Acadie, which grew up in what would become the territory of New Brunswick. Hundreds more sought refuge on Île St. Jean (Prince Edward Island), but three years later, when this territory also fell into the hands of the British, they were expelled to France, and a large number of them died when the overcrowded ships on which they sailed went down in the stormy North Atlantic.

The years following *le Grand Dérangement* spawned the Acadian Diaspora, which persists to this day. Many Acadians ended up in other British North American colonies. Some, having been shipped to France, felt out of place and longed for the chance to depart for a part of the New World. About thirteen hundred Acadians made their way to Quebec in time for the British Conquest of New France. A few Acadians returned to Nova Scotia, and within a decade of *le Grand Dérangement* they were allowed to settle there again, although the lands from which they had been expelled were now occupied by new English-speaking settlers. Of the Acadians sent to the Thirteen Colonies, many returned to settle in the new Acadie, while thousands more, along with thousands who had been exiled to France, set out for Louisiana, where they established communities in a new homeland. These Cajuns lived under successive Spanish, French and American regimes. For generations they lived in largely French communities and retained French as their daily language. After the American Civil War, however, and especially during the twentieth century, the education of Cajun children in public schools, where English was the language of instruction, effectively killed French as a living language for them.

The heartland of the new Acadie was the eastern portion of what was to become New Brunswick. Memramcook, a settlement with roots going back to old Acadie, was one of the sites for the rebirth. In the north, as well, in what became known as the Acadian Peninsula, new settlements sprang up, with Caraquet taking on the role of a new cultural capital. While the new Acadie's stronghold would be in New Brunswick, over time sizable communities also took root in Nova Scotia, Prince Edward Island and Newfoundland.

Today, what makes Acadian identity elusive, even controversial, is that there is no clear Acadian territory, no Acadian state. Actually, there are three distinct ways of understanding Acadian identity, ideas that overlap but are also in conflict with one another. The first idea of Acadie is Diasporic, the notion of a people of wanderers without a homeland, a people tied together by family, blood, common customs and culture and a history whose central trauma is *le Grand Dérangement*, the expulsion of 1755. According to this conception, an Acadian is someone who is descended from one of the families expelled from Acadie by the British.

The second idea of Acadie, encountered increasingly in contemporary New Brunswick, is that Acadie is a land—not a land that constitutes a regional or national state, to be sure, but nonetheless a specific territory—and that the Acadians are the people who live in that land. This notion holds that anyone who is a French-speaker residing in this territorial Acadie is an Acadian. In this case, it does not matter who one's ancestors were. They may have come from Quebec, they may have been Irish or Anglo-Saxon, they may have been from France, the Middle East or North Africa—what creates a common bond is life in a French-speaking society whose widening sense of identity is no longer dependent on ethnicity.

The third conception of Acadie grows out of the second. The idea is that those who aspire to the Acadian cause—the Acadian project—on the Acadian territory are Acadians. This notion is narrower than the second and is voluntarist. It is tied to consciousness and activism. By definition, it is a notion that can have real meaning only for a rather limited number of people, most of them artists, academics or those who are involved in politics. This notion, like the second, is not limited to those descended from the historic Acadian families who experienced the expulsion.

Acadie, born of a shared inheritance and a shared history, whose central event was le Grand Dérangement, now exhibits a kaleidoscope of identities, some clashing, some fanned out in a rainbow of muted distinctions. The Acadians have never been stronger and more self-assured as a society than they are today. At the same time, they face monumental economic hurdles in the central Acadian homeland of New Brunswick if they are to prevent the Acadian project from being irreparably damaged.

At the beginning of the twenty-first century, the communities in the Acadian Peninsula, along the Gulf of St. Lawrence, confront very difficult times. The three basic industries on which they have relied—the fishery, forest products and farming—are all in decline. Together they are unable to provide the population with an assured livelihood. As a consequence, Acadian families and young people have sought out new homes and work in the more prosperous south-east, in the greater Moncton area. Moncton has become the Acadian metropolis, the centre where the Université de Moncton, established four decades ago, has been playing its indispensable role in educating Acadian professionals and Acadian intellectuals.

The Acadian story is that of a distinct people and their fate in the Diaspora in which they now live. It is as well a Canadian and a North American narrative of great significance, of the victims of a struggle between two empires. Finally, it is a story with universal resonance that shares elements in common with the experiences of many other peoples in the world of our time—of the determination of people to overcome a terrible fate and to survive with their way of life intact.

PART I

ACADIE

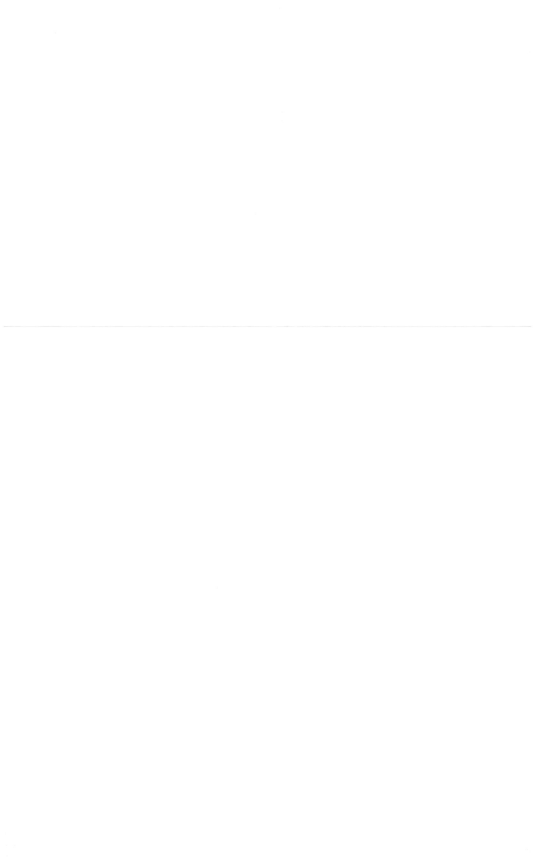

—

CHAPTER I

BIRTH OF A PEOPLE

ON APRIL 1, 1636, with seventy-eight passengers and eighteen crew members on board, the *Saint-Jehan* sailed out of the port of La Rochelle on the Atlantic coast of France. It is not fanciful to imagine that the migrants who were en route to Acadie watched as their ship edged past the twin towers at the narrow neck of the harbour. The towers—Saint-Nicolas, with its sculpted ramparts, and the domed Chain, both constructed in the late Middle Ages—are sentinels that watch over the approaches to La Rochelle still. Along with a third tower, the Lantern, which also served as a lighthouse and prison, these are the remains of the fortifications that once encircled the city.

Gazing back from the deck of the *Saint-Jehan*, the voyagers would have cast a sad and wistful eye on the gracious town. By that date, many of the houses and commercial establishments of La Rochelle were built of the pale beige stone that gives the city its light, almost ethereal beauty. For those on the journey to a New World, the last glimpse of their native land on this outward voyage would have been the sight of the offshore island of Ré, sinking slowly behind them. Twelve on board were women and about an equal number were children. While some of those on the ship were true colonists who were to remain in Acadie, most would eventually return to France.[1]

By the time the *Saint-Jehan* sailed, French explorers and merchants had been making the voyage across the Atlantic to what they called "New France" for over a century. New France was a sprawling, decentralized enterprise with multiple centres of authority and overlapping jurisdictions. During the seventeenth and eighteenth centuries, while their English rivals were establishing settlement colonies along the Atlantic seaboard, the French carved out a vast but much less populous empire that took the shape of a semicircle. It included Acadie and Canada (the name given to the settlements along the St. Lawrence River and the waterways that led to the continental interior). From their base in Canada, the French established posts down the Ohio and Mississippi rivers, leading to their base at New Orleans. Rounding out the semicircle were the French West Indian islands, where slave labour produced sugar and huge profits for French enterprises. (By the time the French holdings in the continental interior reached their greatest extent, Acadie had been lost to the British as a consequence of the Treaty of Utrecht of 1713.)

The French state tried, with varying degrees of success, to oversee its holdings in the New World and to insist that the monopolies and jurisdictions it established be respected. Especially during the religious wars in France in the seventeenth century, however, central authority was limited. In addition, the rivalry among the French ports along the Atlantic coast for advantage in the North American fur trade and the fishery added to the lack of centralized French control over the colonies.

If the state was one locus of authority, so too were the private companies that had the power to govern particular settlements, as well as to conduct commerce at these locations. While the French did not make use of joint stock companies in the manner of the English, a myriad of contractual arrangements were entered into between French companies so that they could pool their resources to undertake ventures. In addition, the government granted monopolies to companies to allow them to dominate commerce in particular places, to the exclusion of all others. Another locus of power was the Church. Rivalries between religious orders—for instance, between the Jesuits and other orders—and conflicts about the priorities of the Church in the colonies added to the jurisdictional complexity.

For the French state, the motivation for promoting transatlantic voyages was to join in the rush for colonies that had been sparked by the appearance of Spanish ships laden with gold and silver returning from Spain's ventures in the Americas. For wealthy French merchants, competing with one another for a state monopoly to enjoy the fruits of trade with a particular colony, the motive was profit. First the bountiful fishery off the banks of Newfoundland and later the trade in furs and the lure of other fisheries drew these capitalists. For adventurers, map-makers and geologists in search of minerals, the scarcely known lands on the other side of the Atlantic beckoned as places where fame and novel experiences could be had. For craftsmen, a voyage to the New World could be an excursion to practise their skills as roofers, masons or tile-makers and to earn money, before returning home to France after a specified period of time, usually from one to three years. Their service in the colony could improve their standing in the craft guilds to which they belonged in France. For some others, men, women and children, the idea was to settle in the colonies and never return to their homeland. For this latter group of people there was a myriad of motives—the desire to escape from family circumstances and obligations, the quest for a mate, the possibility of starting a new life in a completely new setting—the kinds of lures that have drawn millions of migrants to travel to new lands over the centuries.

The *Saint-Jehan* passengers would have anticipated a voyage of about seven weeks. Departing in early April, if all went well, they would have the advantage of good late-spring and summer weather ahead of them when they reached their destination. While the route from La Rochelle to the port of La Hève on the Atlantic south shore of Acadie (Nova Scotia) was well known by the 1630s, the vagaries of the North Atlantic, even in the most favourable seasons of the year, posed a monumental challenge. With luck, passengers travelling from France to Acadie in the spring might enjoy good weather, allowing them to spend their evenings promenading on the deck of their ship. But sudden storms and unfavourable winds were not uncommon. And even though ships that sailed to Acadie did not carry gold or silver, there was nonetheless the chance that they might be waylaid by pirates. Given the hazards, Atlantic crossings were not for the faint of heart in the 1630s.

Over the several years before the voyage of the *Saint-Jehan*, there had been a number of other sailings from France to Acadie. The first settlement in Acadie had been established by the French just over three decades earlier. What has made the *Saint-Jehan* especially interesting to posterity is that it is the only one of the sailings of the period for which a complete passenger list has been preserved. That list gives us an invaluable snapshot of the colonization of Acadie. Prior to the voyage of the *Saint-Jehan*, almost all of those who had journeyed from France to Acadie were men. With evidence of the inclusion of women and children on the *Saint-Jehan*, even though they were few, it becomes clear that the French endeavour in Acadie was becoming one of colonization. The goal was now to establish new and permanent settlements, rather than rely on transients who would work in the fur trade of the fishery and return to France one day.

The voyage of the *Saint-Jehan* has sometimes been compared to that of the *Mayflower*, whose passengers have been celebrated for the role they played in the story of America. In the case of Acadie, though, nothing has ever been that simple. Too many of the people on board returned to France to make this voyage a parallel to the sailing of the *Mayflower* to Plymouth, Massachusetts, in 1620.

The most socially prominent family on board the *Saint-Jehan* was that of Nicolas Le Creux, who came from Breuil, a town to the east of La Rochelle. Le Creux made the journey with his wife, Anne Motin, and two of her brothers, as well as his wife's sister Jeanne.

The *Saint-Jehan* reached Acadie just at the moment when the main base of the colony was being shifted from La Hève to the other side of the peninsula at Port Royal. The decision in favour of the move was made by Charles de Menou d'Aulnay, who had taken over the running of the colony after the death, in February 1636, of Isaac de Razilly. What gave d'Aulnay a strong personal interest in the arrival of the *Saint-Jehan* was the presence on the ship of his bride-to-be.

Le Creux's sister-in-law, Jeanne Motin, was twenty years old when she sailed on the *Saint-Jehan*. Her father was one of the directors of the Razilly-Condonnier Company, which oversaw the affairs of this part of France's Acadian venture. She married d'Aulnay, likely in Port Royal, shortly after her arrival and went on to have eight children with him. After her husband drowned in 1650, she married his archrival in the struggle for power in Acadie, Charles de la Tour, with whom she had five more children. None of the children she had during her first marriage were to have children of their own, but the offspring of her second marriage did, which makes Jeanne Motin one of the founders of a new people, the Acadians.

In addition to his relatives, Le Creux arranged for other migrants to be on the ship. These included a lumberman and an expert in the construction of mills, who was originally from Angers and who had lived in Paris for a time. Others among the passengers were farmers and craftsmen with specific vocations—a cooper, a cobbler, a master gardener, a gunsmith, a locksmith, four tailors, a tool-maker and a vintner. Nine of the men on the *Saint-Jehan* were carpenters from the Basque country, in the south-west corner of France, who were hired to build small sea-going ships and docks.[2]

The travellers' occupations illustrate the sophistication of the Acadian venture for its time. What impresses is the range of specialized crafts practised by the migrants. The Razilly-Condonnier Company, which mounted the voyage, was in business to earn a profit. Those on board had been carefully selected to carry out the tasks that would make the colony self-sustaining and eventually profitable. While a large number of those on the voyage were farmers, many were craftsmen from towns and cities, representatives of the rising merchant and capitalist interests that were fast transforming France. The migrants on the *Saint-Jehan* were not unskilled labourers fleeing wretched circumstances at home. Opportunity, and surely adventure, was in their minds as they set out on their odyssey.

The voyagers on the *Saint-Jehan* were leaving a country that was still locked in a social system in which kings ruled by divine right, aristocrats owned the land and the rural masses toiled as serfs. By the beginning of the seventeenth century, however, France was alive to the commercial changes that were pulsing through Europe from Spain, with its vast empire, to the prosperous and powerful Netherlands. Along the Atlantic coast of France, shipbuilders were constructing the vessels that sailed the North Atlantic in a quest for the cod that brought wealth to La Rochelle, Saint-Malo, Bordeaux and St. Jean de Luz. In all of Catholic Europe, the cod had become a staple of life. No wonder that the rival British fishermen often raised a glass of Jamaican rum to toast the Pope in Rome who watched over his fish-eating flock. In contrast to the vast fleets that sailed the North Atlantic in search of cod, the ships that carried migrants from France were few in number.

The migrants on the *Saint-Jehan* were on a journey that was only just within the technological capabilities of the age. But those en route to Acadie were not about to disappear into a wilderness, in which they would live in some sort of state of nature. Quite the opposite was true. When they reached their destination they would remain tightly leashed to France by networks of commerce, religion and instruments of state power. Changes of policy, shifting markets for furs and fish and developments in the hostile rivalry between France and Britain would vitally affect the prospects for the colony. Without profits from the fishery and the fur trade, these imperial enterprises would not have been established. For those with the greatest power in the mercantilist seventeenth and eighteenth century British and French empires, earning profits, in that odd combination of capitalism and plunder that characterized the age, was the ultimate point.

If opportunity drew the voyagers who sailed on the *Saint-Jehan* to the perils of a new world, there were plenty of good reasons why people would want to escape from the strife and warfare that had been the lot of France in recent decades. While foreign wars were common, what had embroiled the region from which the *Saint-Jehan* sailed was a vicious civil war that pitted the armies of Catholic France against the strongholds of the Protestant Huguenots. La

Rochelle had been a Huguenot city, and like other Protestant centres, such as Nantes, it was a city that was alive with the capitalist impulses of the day. La Rochelle and Nantes, centres of the country's Huguenots, were on the cutting edge of the new commercial ways. Among their number, in addition to bankers, they counted many skilled craftsmen and shipbuilders.

La Rochelle had its origins in the Middle Ages, in a time when natural fortresses were much prized. It was a time when the French monarchy was perennially in conflict not only with the English king, who fought for territory along the French seaboard, but with the feudal aristocrats who resisted the rise of a central power. A well-protected commercial city, like La Rochelle, could use conflict to its benefit, but a misstep could mean its doom. In this dangerous setting, La Rochelle rose to become a great centre for the export of wine and salt, harvested from its adjoining hinterland, to England. In 1224, however, when the city rallied to the side of the king of France against England, La Rochelle lost much of its English market to the advantage of its great rival Bordeaux.

Compensation for the loss of the English market came in the form of a growing commercial link with the Flemish and with the Germans. In 1360, during another episode in the perennial struggle between the kingdoms of France and England for control of France's Atlantic coast, the English seized La Rochelle. For the next twelve years the city was governed from London. While local leaders proclaimed their allegiance to the English monarch, opinion in the city was clearly hostile to the new rulers. For a time, the English, who ruled the city with a heavy hand, considered a scheme to rid La Rochelle of its disloyalty. They concocted a plan to seize the town's elites, lock them up and transfer them across the Channel to England. Then they would remove the local population and repopulate the city with English settlers. The idea, which bears an uncanny resemblance to what later happened to the Acadians, was never put into effect. In 1372, the gates of La Rochelle were thrown open to the army of the king of France and the time of English occupation came to an end.

La Rochelle's deep, long and narrow harbour made it the ideal place to construct a walled city. One look at the harbour and it is easy to see why it was so valued by the German navy during the Second World War. Indeed, as a consequence of its natural defences, La Rochelle was the last place in France to be liberated from the Germans. From the fourteenth century until early modern times, a metal chain linking the towers at the mouth of the harbour closed off the approaches to the town from interlopers.

The Huguenots suffered in the fierce wars of religion that wracked France during the Reformation and the Counter-Reformation. For a time, in the middle of the sixteenth century, La Rochelle became a Protestant stronghold, a centre for the propagation of reform Christianity throughout France. In the seventeenth century, though, in the tide of the Counter-Reformation, the Protestant power was overthrown in the city and Catholicism was reinstated. In 1628, eight years before the voyage of the *Saint-Jehan*, the city's days as an autonomous power centre came to a tragic end. La Rochelle was subjected to a lengthy siege by the Royal army. The defenders held out, despite the onset of famine within the walls of the city. The people of La Rochelle hoped that an English fleet would come to their rescue and raise the siege, but when the English ships did finally appear, they failed to drive off the ships and army of the French king. Recognizing that all was lost, the defenders opened the gates and the royal army occupied La Rochelle. Cardinal Richelieu, followed soon by Louis XIII, made a triumphal passage into La Rochelle. In the first days of the occupation, thousands more succumbed to the famine. As La Rochelle lost its liberty, France took a further step toward royal absolutism.

Well before the sailing of the *Saint-Jehan*, indeed throughout the sixteenth century, as French ships sailed each year in the quest for the fish of the Grand Banks of Newfoundland, other expeditions were undertaken that pointed the way to the eventual establishment of permanent settlements. The missions of Cartier and Roberval showed the French the way to the heart of the continent along the highway of the St. Lawrence River and introduced the French to the aboriginal peoples of the territory. When Jacques Cartier sailed to Newfoundland in 1534, there were already about one hundred French fishing vessels working in the waters near the island. These vessels hailed from Brittany, Normandy and the Basque Country, as well as from Bordeaux and La Rochelle.[3] But though colonization was on the agenda several times, and considerable parties of the French wintered in Canada, as far inland as the Island of Montreal, no permanent settlement resulted.

In 1600, therefore, after a century of exploring a vast realm in both North and South America already described by the French as a "New France," no colonists were in place. The knowledge acquired had been crucial for the future, though. The French had learned much about the geography of America, and their techniques for surviving in it had developed. Most important, they had concluded that only through interaction and co-operation with the aboriginal peoples could French colonization succeed.

The launching of New France took place right in the heart of the age of European mercantilism. The mindset of that historical period was very different from our own. We live with the assumption that commerce between nations can be beneficial to both sides in a trading relationship. Countries produce where they have a comparative advantage and sell to others, while buying from other countries the goods they produce most efficiently. The theory is that, as a result, all the participants grow richer. Mercantilists, however, believed that there was no such thing as a trading relationship that benefited both parties. One side won and the other lost, they thought. For them, trade was simply war fought by other means. The goal was to accumulate wealth for yourself—say, in the form of gold and silver from South America—and to beggar your neighbour. The French wanted an empire that would provide them with things they didn't have at hand: fish, furs, sugar and, if possible, gold, silver and diamonds. Colonies were not wanted to compete with the mother country, but to assist it in its commercial struggles with others. Colonists were needed to serve those ends. And those colonists could be dispatched to the New World either by the French state directly, or by private trading companies operating under the authority of the state.

The primary motive for founding colonies in this era was profit—profit from the fishery, profit from the fur trade or, always lurking in the minds of explorers, profit from fabulous mineral deposits. Well before the sailing of the *Saint-Jehan*, the fur trade in Acadie had become a highly profitable business. For instance, in a period of a dozen years following 1614, a major Huguenot firm based in La Rochelle oversaw the shipment of tens of thousands of beaver pelts to the French markets, the raw material for the production of the most fashionable style of men's hats.[4] The second major motivation for the seizure of territory by imperial powers in the age of mercantilism was strategic advantage. For instance, Île Royale (Cape Breton) became vital to the French, not only because of the fishery, but because it guarded the seaways to Canada. The third motive for the establishment of colonies was settlement, a goal that in various periods was foremost in French policy in Canada. Over the course of the seventeenth and eighteenth centuries, Paris became concerned about the vast population gap between New England and New France and at times made it a priority to finance and organize the sending of colonists.

Merchants and missionaries had roles from the start in the launching of Acadie. Around 1570, Samuel de Champlain was born in Brouage, near the Atlantic coast, not far south of La Rochelle. By the time he became involved in a venture to plant the first settlement in Acadie, he had already participated as a geographer and observer in an expedition up the St. Lawrence River as far as Montreal. The man in charge of the Acadian venture was Pierre Du Gua de Monts, a Protestant aristocrat from Saintonge. It is no accident that Champlain is the most famous of all the figures of New France while de Monts is known only to historians. De Monts was not on the scene for very long, and, as a Protestant, he could never have filled the position of father figure to what later came to be seen as the great Catholic enterprise that was New France. Champlain, on the other hand, was there at the start in Acadie, in a supporting role to be sure, and then played the central role in the founding and first decades in Quebec, until his death there on Christmas Day 1635.

Despite all the painstaking work of historians and other investigators into his past, many crucial facts about Samuel de Champlain remain shrouded in mystery. We have a clear picture of him only once he entered his Canadian phase. We do not know the exact year of his birth, although we know it was around 1570. It is not known whether he was born Protestant, although there are strong signs that he may have been. Brouage, at the time of his birth, was a Huguenot stronghold, and the name Samuel was a common Protestant name. What is clear is that by the time he came on the Canadian scene he was a Catholic, strongly committed to winning native people over to Catholicism. We also are not sure whether Champlain was a commoner or a nobleman. Sometimes he turns up in the records with the commoner's name Samuel Champlain, while in other cases he has the noble appellation Samuel de Champlain. Intriguingly, despite the large number of paintings and busts and statues of the man, we are not at all sure what Champlain looked like. One school of thought has it that Champlain was very plain, even unpleasant, to look at, and that as a consequence he had others sit for him as models for portraits and busts.

In the absence of a definitive storyline, many theories have been spun about Champlain, some of them with the feel of a detective novel about them. According to one explanation, Champlain was the son of a poor fisherman. Others have made the case that his father was a naval captain, and still others speculate that he was the illegitimate child of a noble father. One fanciful tale has it that Champlain was actually Guy Eder de La Fontanelle, a roguish thug who managed to escape a court order that he be broken on the wheel. According to this unlikely account, he later turned up in the guise of an honest man named Champlain.[5]

What we do know, and this has helped shape our conception of the man, is that he left lengthy journals, and commentaries on his travels and his life. We know, as well, that he was an extremely gifted map-maker and that his maps of seventeenth-century New France are of very high quality.

In June 1604, the two ships of the de Monts expedition sailed into the Bay of Fundy, which de Monts named the Baie Française. On board were no women. The party, which was surprisingly heterogeneous in its make-up, included artisans, Swiss mercenaries, two priests, a Protestant minister, a surgeon and a mining expert, as well as sailors. A man of North African origin who was a member of the expedition died during the voyage. Considering the dreadful fate that awaited so many of those who went with de Monts, the planning and provisions were by no means haphazard. On board were foodstuffs, tools, livestock and even a supply of building materials.[6]

Before making up their minds where to establish their base, de Monts and Champlain looked long and hard for possible locations. Had they chosen a location farther to the south, along the coast of New England, they might have altered the history of North America. In June and July 1604, de Monts, with Champlain among his party, set out along the coast of New England visiting such points as Baie des Îles (Boston Bay), Port Saint-Louis (Plymouth Bay) and Cap Blanc (Cape Cod). As they made their way, Champlain charted the coast with a set of maps so precise that historian Marcel Trudel concluded that "he deserves the title of first cartographer of New England."[7] During his voyages, Champlain was constantly on the lookout for promising mineral deposits. Deciding that none of the places they had seen was suitable for settlement, de Monts headed back to an island they had already considered, Île St. Croix, located in the St. Croix River, which forms the present-day boundary between Maine and New Brunswick. Here they came ashore and set up for the winter.

Viewed from the New Brunswick shore on the rainy afternoon of June 26, 2004, at the celebration held four hundred years to the day after the expedition landed on the island, Île St. Croix seemed graceful and lonely, but above all tiny. The mystery of St. Croix was enhanced by sheets of rain and bouts of fog that at times completely blanketed it from the view of the celebrants. At other times, only the tops of the trees were visible, and for a while the whole island could be seen. What is truly hard to imagine is a great European imperial power choosing this tiny piece of land for its first enclave on a vast continent.

To the explorers, an island felt like a secure location against the possibility of attack from native people, about whom little was known. In his journal, Champlain sang the praises of St. Croix:

> The island is covered with firs, birches, maples and oaks. It is naturally very well situated, with but one place where it is low, for about forty paces, and that is easy to fortify. The shores of the mainland are distant on both sides some nine hundred to a thousand paces, so that vessels could only pass along the river at the mercy of the cannon on the island. This place we considered the best we had seen, both on account of its situation, the fine country, and for the intercourse we were expecting with the Indians of these coasts and of the interior, since we should be in their midst. In course of time we hoped to pacify them, and to put an end to wars which they wage against one another, in order that in the future we might derive service from them, and convert them to the Christian faith.[8]

On the island, Du Gua de Monts established his "habitation." Champlain's positive sentiments about St. Croix turned out to be ill based, however. The winter of 1604–05 on the island was a disaster for the colonists. The little company that had been left, not to see a ship from France until the following June, was totally unprepared for what it was to endure. They had reached the island in June when the temperature was warm. The island was more or less at the same latitude as the region of France from which they had sailed. They hoped for a winter not much different from the relatively mild ones enjoyed by a place such as La Rochelle. It never occurred to them that the river around the island would freeze solid, cutting them off from easy water transit and fishing. They were not equipped with warm clothing. When winter came unusually early, with a savage blast at the end of October, they had to face six months of frigid weather before the thaw came at the end of April. To find fresh water during the freeze-up, men had to be sent across the ice to the mainland. Even the wine that had been brought from France froze solid and was sawn into pieces to be melted and consumed. Thirty-five of the seventy-nine men died from scurvy and cold. The following year the little colony moved to what seemed a more salubrious location, across the Baie Française, where Port Royal (so named by Champlain) was founded.

Mi'kmaq leaders welcomed the French at this new location. The Mi'kmaq, who lived in the territory the French called Acadie, dwelt during the summer in villages along the coasts of the Baie Française, the Atlantic and the Gulf of St. Lawrence. Their way of life centred on the sea, from which they acquired fish and shellfish. During the winter, the Mi'kmaq left the villages and divided into smaller hunting parties, pursuing game. They traversed the Baie Française and the Gulf of St. Lawrence in large canoes. With their mobility, the Mi'kmaq engaged in trade over a large area, including Newfoundland in the north and present-day southern New England.[9] It is likely that the Mi'kmaq were the first native peoples in North America to encounter Europeans. The encounters were not always friendly. In the 1520s, when Portuguese fishermen attempted to set up a permanent fishing station on Île Royale (Cape Breton Island), they were attacked by Mi'kmaq warriors.

For the Mi'kmaq, the first meeting with Europeans was, naturally enough, a hugely traumatic event, which is recorded in their oral tradition by a story that has been much repeated from generation to generation. No precise date can be put on the event. The story goes that on the very eve of the arrival of the first European ship, a young Mi'kmaq woman dreamed that her people were to be visited by strange men on a floating island. When Europeans—almost certainly fishermen who could have been French, Irish, Basque, Portuguese or English—did appear in a sailing vessel, the dream was recalled and it made a great impression on the Mi'kmaq. Its retelling is the sole record historians have of that momentous encounter.

It was by no means the norm for the French in their early efforts at settlement to meet with a friendly welcome from the population that lived in the territory. When the expedition of Jacques Cartier sailed up the St. Lawrence River in 1534, it met armed resistance from the native population. Again, when Quebec was founded in 1608, the first French residents met with a hostile reception from some of the native peoples of the area. That the settlers at Port Royal met with a warmer welcome may be because the Mi'kmaq had long traded with Europeans, and perhaps they had concluded that the Europeans did not plan to seize their land. Decades before the French established their settlement at Port Royal in 1605, the Mi'kmaq were trading with Europeans, likely selling furs in exchange for such goods as copper pots.[10]

The friendly relationship between the French and Mi'kmaq was to play a crucial role in the life of Acadie and in its troubled relationship with New Englanders and the English of the next century and more. During their second, and much warmer, winter, this time in Port Royal, the French received food and other assistance from the Mi'kmaq. An effort was made to maintain morale and a modicum of health through the creation of the Ordre de Bons Temps, the Order of Good Cheer, suggested by Champlain.

Du Gua de Monts sailed back to France before the second winter so he could influence the royal court in Paris, always a hotbed of intrigue. He needed to be there to try to fend off challenges to his trade monopoly in Acadie (with the exception of the fishery) from rival merchants. In the first years of the colonies in Acadie and the Valley of the St. Lawrence, there were constant struggles among merchants for access to commercial rights. The Crown was tempted to offer concessions and monopolies to merchants and companies in return for undertakings to promote settlement. When these commitments were not met, as often was the case, the French state undertook its own initiatives to promote settlement. Throughout this whole period, the French state was under constant financial pressure to deal with priorities that ranked higher than the North American colonies. In the seventeenth century, the French kings dreamed of making France the most powerful state in Europe. This meant it had to keep up a three-sided struggle against Spain to the south, the Austria of the Hapsburgs to the east and the English on the seas and in North America.

In 1607, with a squabble underway in France over political control of Acadie, the tiny post at Port Royal was actually abandoned and left in the care of natives who were pro-French. (With his departure from Port Royal, Champlain left Acadie for good. The next year he went on to found Quebec.) Three years later Port Royal was once again occupied by those who arrived as members of a new French expedition. The port had been kept in pristine condition by the natives who had cared for it.

In 1609, under pressure from the merchants of Saint-Malo, Dieppe, La Rochelle and St. Jean de Luz, Du Gua de Monts was stripped of his monopoly in Acadie. A major effort to colonize Acadie did not come until the 1630s. By then, Isaac de Razilly had been charged by the king to undertake a new effort to send settlers. Over the next few years, three hundred settlers from fifteen families made the voyage. These settlers, among them some of the migrants on the *Saint-Jehan*, were the true founders of the Acadian people.

—

CHAPTER 2

GROWTH
AND
UNCERTAINTY

WITH PERMANENT SETTLEMENT in Acadie underway in the 1630s, the colony was no longer simply a tiny outpost, with mostly male inhabitants. With more equal numbers of males and females, and a high birth rate, the Acadian population expanded rapidly. New settlements were established east of Port Royal along the Baie Française. In the Minas Basin, so named because of the copper deposits found there, Grand Pré was established, and at the eastern extremity of the bay Beaubassin was launched. Despite the continuing uncertainty of the larger world in which they found themselves, the Acadians developed their own society, with its own practices and rhythms.

While the fishery was important in the new settlements, as it was elsewhere in Acadie, it was agriculture, the cultivation of wheat and the raising of livestock, that flourished in Grand Pré and Beaubassin. In these settlements, the Acadians applied and adapted farming methods they had learned in the Poitou region of France aimed at bringing marshy lands along the sea under cultivation. The use of aboiteaux, dikes that prevented salt water from encroaching on the land while allowing fresh water to irrigate the crops, made this a novel and successful farming technique. The aboiteaux, a unique technological adaptation, took on a kind of personality and certainly helped shape the nature of Acadian communities and the way Acadians worked with each other and lived side by side. The aboiteaux were to promote the prosperity of Acadian communities. They were also to make others, principally the English of New England, envious of productive Acadian farmland.

When a French surgeon, Sieur de Dièreville, visited Acadie in 1700, he wrote the following description of the aboiteaux:

> Five or six rows of large logs are driven whole into the ground at the points where the tide enters the Marsh, and between each row other logs are laid, one on top of the other, and all the spaces between them are so carefully filled with well-pounded clay, that the water can no longer get through. In the centre of this construction, a Sluice is contrived in such a manner that the water on the Marshes flows out of its own accord, while that of the Sea is prevented from coming in.[1]

Up the Minas Basin, next to imposing cliffs that pointed the way toward the Baie Française, against the multi-layered tidal flats, was located the largest group of Acadian settlements, those that centred on Grand Pré. A high point of the achievement of Acadie before *le Grand Dérangement*, this is where the people, in a great collective effort, won the rich land of the tidal flats back from the sea. They began the task first on the higher ground, carving out a square of land from the tides and building their aboiteaux. From that first square of land, they pushed back the tides in similar pieces, square by square, until hundreds of hectares of excellent farmland had been painstakingly established.

On this highly fertile land, the farmers of Grand Pré raised ample crops of wheat, oats, barley, rye, peas and corn. In September, farmers gathered their grain and transported it to the local mills to be ground. In their gardens they grew cabbages and turnips, staples of the Acadian diet, as well as beets, carrots, parsnips and onions. They raised cattle and sheep, and around the settlements their pigs roamed in the nearby woods. The Acadians ate a lot of pork, mostly keeping their cattle for milk.

Acadian diets included cod, bass and salmon fished from nearby waters. Salt pork was a particular favourite. In winter, turnips, stored in cellars, and cabbages, left in the snow in the fields to be gathered when wanted, were important staples. Often in winter a hearty soup was served that could include beef shank, onions, beans, peas, cabbage, turnips and carrots. Acadians made use of black, cast-iron cauldrons for almost all of their cooking. Most foods were boiled, with foods requiring higher temperatures fried or baked. Fish were fried, often in bear oil, a practice that shocked European visitors. Bread was baked, and mixed-grain bread smothered in molasses, imported from New England, was often present at Acadian tables.

Apple cider, from the fine apples in Acadian orchards, and homemade wine were widely available, as was imported rum, often purchased illegally from Boston. A favourite beverage was a beer that was made from the sprouts of the spruce tree. The beer was an effective anti-scorbutic, effective in warding off scurvy.

From the earliest days of their settlements, Acadians, both men and women, were avid pipe-smokers. Mostly their clay pipes were imported from New England, although they fashioned some of their own, making use of local red clay. The tobacco Acadians consumed was all, or nearly all, imported.

Wool was used to make warm clothing suitable for the winters of Acadie. In addition, the Acadians grew small quantities of flax, from which they spun linen fibres to weave clothes for summer wear. Fabrics were often dyed red or black. Shirts with no collars, knee-length breeches and stockings were typical clothes for men, who also wore straw hats in summer and felt hats in winter. Women usually were attired in blouses with ankle-length skirts and stockings. Distinctive hooded capes, in a style common in an earlier period in France, rounded out the apparel of women, who pulled the capes over their heads and shoulders when they were out of doors. Both men and women wore moccasins, fashioned from the hides of moose or elk. When they were on boats or working in the marshy fields, the Acadians wore sabots, wooden shoes, usually made from willow.

The Acadians created a good life for themselves and their burgeoning families, achieving a standard of living that was undoubtedly higher than that of most people in France at the time. They built houses from the materials at hand, making use of Mi'kmaq insulation techniques to adapt European design to the harsher conditions of their new homeland. While a few affluent residents dwelt in two-storey houses built of wood and masonry, the kind of house that could be found in western France, most Acadians lived in one- or two-room log cabins or, alternatively, in dwellings constructed on wooden posts driven into the ground. Houses, in most cases, were minimally furnished. Storage chests customarily stood at the foot of beds. There was usually one table and a few chairs. For the most part furniture was built with cherry wood. Earthenware plates and saucers and a few cups and mugs rounded out the dishes.

The Acadian system of farming, through the use of aboiteaux in marshy lands adjacent to the sea, separated the land use of the Acadians from that of Mi'kmaq, which was a principal reason for the unusually good relationship between the two groups. From the viewpoint of the Mi'kmaq, the Acadians were creating new land to farm and were not encroaching on their territory. Of course, the extremely low population density in Acadie contributed to the amicable dealings between the two societies.

Royal authority was only rather lightly felt in the settlements of the Minas Basin, far from the capital at Port Royal. For the people of Grand Pré, rules that, in theory, restricted trade with the New Englanders meant little. Further up the Baie Française in the community of Beaubassin, a thriving if theoretically illegal trade with New England also prospered.

The number of French colonists who came to Acadie to stay was extremely small. In fact, while newcomers were added from time to time to the population pool, it was sixty families, migrating in the 1630s, who were the true founders of the Acadian population. Astonishing as it may seem, today's Acadian population is largely descended from as few as five hundred migrants from France.

Acadie grew because of the high birth rate of the Acadians, not because Paris was sending fresh migrants to the colony. It was normal for a second-generation Acadian woman to bear six or seven children. And because they ate well, and suffered relatively little from epidemic disease in comparison to peasants in France, the infant and childhood survival rates were high.[2]

Acadian society during this period relied for its cohesion on strong family relationships. Marriage was a central institution and one that involved not only couples but their families and the Church. The centrality of marriage is shown in the fact that, between 1702 and 1755, only 0.6 percent of the births in Acadie were illegitimate, a remarkably low proportion, lower than that in France during the same period. In fact, the number of illegitimate births peaked around 1710, during the time of armed struggle against Britain, when there was an influx of French soldiers to increase the strength of the garrison at Port Royal.

On average, couples in Acadie were younger when they married than couples in France. Under Catholic law at the time, girls were allowed to marry when they were as young as twelve and boys could marry by the age of fourteen. One study places the average age of Acadian females when they married at twenty years, five months. This encompassed a range of cases with fifteen as the youngest and thirty the oldest, the case of the thirty-year-old being a second marriage. Another study concludes that the average marrying age of Acadian women was twenty-one. Studies of the average age of marriage for women in Canada put the figure at between eighteen and twenty-two years. In France, the average was twenty-five or twenty-six.[3] The average age of Acadian males at the time of their first marriage was twenty-six. Before getting married, it was normal for young men to live in the home of their parents, where they provided a very important source of labour. At the time of their marriage, the practice was for the couple to establish their own ménage.[4]

Weddings in Acadie were never celebrated during Lent or Advent for religious reasons, and they seldom were solemnized during the months of spring planting and harvest.[5] Acadians valued the Church for the basic services it performed. Church records show that Acadians did indeed attend mass, baptize their children, have their marriages blessed and conduct their funerals in the church. But Acadian settlements were frequently without the services of a priest, for instance, during the time of English occupation of the colony in the mid seventeenth century. When a priest was not available, marriage unions were contracted, to be consecrated later when a priest was available, and a "dry mass" would be performed weekly by laymen.

While Acadians were staunchly Catholic, their relationship to the Church was not a matter of simple devotion and obedience. In France, La Rochelle and its surrounding region was at the centre of the struggle between militant Catholicism and the Huguenots. At the colony's start, there was a strong Huguenot influence that was extinguished following the victory of Catholicism in the homeland. The legacy of the Huguenot influence and the circumstances of the Church in Acadie meant that the Catholicism of the population was as practical as it was pious.

Just as their remoteness allowed Acadians to shape their communities and way of life without much interference from the state, it also coloured the way they approached the Church. From the point of view of an independent-minded frontier population, clerics were there to serve them, not the reverse.

The highest priority of the leadership of the Catholic Church in Acadie, however, was not to minister to the needs of the colonists for the sacraments but to convert native people to Catholicism, seen by the Church establishment in France as a more glamorous occupation. Not only did this alienate Acadians who felt the need for resident priests, it also created deeper concerns among the colonists. Warrior-priests who came from France to live among the Mi'kmaq were to add enormously to the tensions that existed between the Acadians and the British rulers following the Treaty of Utrecht.[6]

From the records of the time, we see a gregarious Acadian society whose members were fond of their celebrations, built around family gatherings, food, song and dance. Like other frontier societies in North America, despite the rigid class structure of France, theirs had a strong tendency toward egalitarianism. Individual actions and achievements counted in Acadie more than social background did. Mastering the arts of canoeing, snowshoeing, hunting and fishing, learning the lore of survival in the wilderness from the neighbouring Mi'kmaq—these were things that mattered more than formal education. In Acadian communities, there were many families whose children were the product of unions between French and Mi'kmaq partners, and this reinforced the good relations between the two groups. While the French influenced the Mi'kmaq, it is clear that the Mi'kmaq also influenced the French, contributing to their social outlook and way of life. The French founders of Acadie had assumed that the social hierarchy of an aristocratic order could be transferred to the New World. Within a couple of generations, a quite different society had emerged.

The Acadian economy involved contradictory elements—a fair degree of self-sufficiency side by side with commerce. Furs, fish and cattle were among the products sold externally, in places such as Boston, in return for items Acadians did not produce. Involved in commerce were merchants, as well as some fisherman and farmers who were wealthier than their neighbours. Ambition certainly drove a number of Acadians to accumulate for themselves and their families beyond their basic needs. Placing a brake on such materialism, however, was the Acadians' near self-sufficiency and the value they placed on their communities and families, as well as the work they did in common in fields that had been wrested from the marshlands.

Even though the fate of their society and much of its economic well-being rested on the decisions of others in Europe and America, the Acadians quickly developed a society with its own character. English and French outsiders alike could easily mistake the jovial lives of the Acadians for fecklessness, but the prosperity they had achieved was the fruit of immense effort and cultural adaptation. One reason Acadians grew closer to one another was the vast uncertainty of the world around them. Acadie was never free from the alarums that arose as a result of the highly strategic position their territory occupied in the imperial struggles between the French and the English. A glance at a map shows why this was so. The territory of Acadie jutted like a great anvil into the North Atlantic, a wedge between New England and Canada. Whichever imperial power held the land of Acadie would be well placed to threaten its opponent in the heart of its North American holdings.

Just as the French regarded the territory as vital to their interests, the English had designs on Acadie from the beginning. In 1613, acting on the orders of the governor of Virginia, Captain Samuel Argall sailed north with three ships, the warship *Treasurer* and two smaller vessels. The force laid waste the tiny Acadian settlement at Saint-Sauveur, then moved on to Île St. Croix, where the English destroyed the buildings that remained from the abandoned settlement there. Argall then raided Port Royal in the autumn, torched its buildings and stole or slaughtered the livestock, leaving the inhabitants, who had fled at the approach of the English ships, to fend for themselves over the coming winter.

In 1621, King James of England and Scotland granted a charter to Sir William Alexander to establish a colony in what was called New Scotland or Nova Scotia, a territory defined as comprising most of the land claimed by the French as Acadie. As it turned out, the Scottish colony went nowhere. After a few years, the small number of colonists who did get established in the vicinity of the ruins of Port Royal were withdrawn and sent back to Scotland. The claim to Nova Scotia by the English and Scottish did not go away, however.

As if external threats to Acadie were not enough, with the colony back in French hands, the fledgling Acadian communities were subjected to an internal struggle for power that erupted in a virtual civil war. When Isaac de Razilly died in February 1636, control of the affairs of the colony passed into the hands of Charles de Menou d'Aulnay. Soon there was bad blood between d'Aulnay and Charles de Saint-Étienne de la Tour, a headstrong figure in Acadie who had spent most of the previous twenty years in the colony, learning how to survive in its wilderness from the time he was a teenager. He grew up among the Mi'kmaq, spoke their language and acquired their hunting and survival skills.[7]

La Tour's father, Claude, had founded a small fort at Pentagouet at the mouth of the Penobscot River (in present-day Maine) that was captured by the English around 1626. The trouble started when

Razilly sent d'Aulnay to retake the fort in 1635. Razilly had assured d'Aulnay that he would have command of the fort. The problem was that the Company of New France (Compagnie de la Nouvelle-France, also known as Compagnie des Cent Associés), charged with overseeing the French commercial monopoly in Acadie, had planned to hand the fort back to Claude de la Tour. (With a monopoly granted by the French government, the company discharged state and security functions as well as engaging in commerce.) The fierce rivalry between d'Aulnay and Charles de la Tour was to degenerate into violence.

D'Aulnay, with his headquarters in Port Royal, faced la Tour, whose base of power was on the St. John River, across the Baie Française. Both men were associates of the Company of New France and they vied with each other for profits from the fur trade, Acadie's principal source of income. In 1640, not far from Port Royal, a sea battle erupted between the ships of the rivals. In this clash, d'Aulnay's naval captain was killed, but La Tour and his men were captured and held as prisoners. Following the battle, d'Aulnay went to France to seek the authority of officials there for his side in the dispute. La Tour was ordered to hand control of his forts over to d'Aulnay and to go to France himself, to justify his pugnacious behaviour. La Tour ignored the order. Faced with his rival's return from France backed up by four ships and the king's order for him to stand down, he fled to Boston. There he hired four ships of his own, fifty-four crew and sixty-eight volunteers, and with this private force he went after d'Aulnay and attacked Port Royal.

A battle erupted at a mill outside the fort. La Tour's men killed two supporters of d'Aulnay, wounded seven and took one man prisoner. They proceeded to burn the mill, kill the livestock nearby and make off with a ship laden with furs, gunpowder and other supplies. La Tour had the best of the fight, but his standing with the court in France was further weakened as a result, because he had turned to the English for recruits in his hour of need.

D'Aulnay gained the upper hand in the next round of fighting. With La Tour away in Boston at Easter 1645, d'Aulnay captured his rival's fort on the St. John River, the defence of the fort having been directed by La Tour's wife, Françoise-Marie Jacquelin. This time the victor left nothing to chance and proceeded to hang the members of La Tour's defence force, while his wife was forced to observe with a rope around her neck. Three weeks later, still under d'Aulnay's custody, she died.

It looked as if d'Aulnay's triumph was assured, but the wheel of fortune was to turn yet again. In May 1650, d'Aulnay's canoe overturned in the Annapolis River and he died of exposure as he clung to the capsized vessel. In his will, he had left everything to his wife, Jeanne Motin, for her use during her lifetime. While d'Aulnay did leave the settlement at Port Royal in good shape, with about three hundred French residents established there, his finances at the time of his death were not so rosy. He was massively in debt, and his principal creditor, Emmanuel Le Borgne, a La Rochelle merchant, moved to take control of d'Aulnay's holdings, sending an agent to Port Royal to seize furs and other assets there. D'Aulnay's widow fought back as best she could, but, finding herself in a battle she could not win, she then did the unthinkable and married her late husband's bitter rival, Charles de Saint-Étienne de la Tour.

In addition to attacks on Acadie mounted by British or colonial authorities and a private civil war in the colony, the settlers were also subject to attack by English freebooters acting on their own in a quest for plunder and profit. To make sense of this, it needs to be understood that the hallmark of the European empires of the sixteenth and seventeenth centuries was that the dividing lines marking off central government from local authorities, private actors from state actors and plunderers from merchants were not nearly as clear as we might imagine. It was common practice, for instance, for English privateers to sail into ports in Spanish America and to insist under threat of force that the local merchants and governor purchase their wares, which could be goods or slaves brought from Africa. If the locals refused to buy—Spanish law banned commerce with foreigners—then force was often used, and this included the torching of whole towns.

And the operations of privateers could tangle the affairs of the Acadians with those of the other French settlements in Canada. In the summer of 1628, privateers based in England learned that a French fleet was bringing supplies and several hundred colonists to New France. The privateers managed to cross the Atlantic ahead of the French fleet. Capturing the ships with their supplies and making prisoners of crews and passengers, the raiders demanded that Champlain surrender Quebec to them. Champlain refused and, with bravado, claimed that he had plenty of supplies. The next summer, however, when fresh supplies had not arrived from France, he was forced to capitulate and turn Quebec over to the privateers. The victors then sailed back to England with their booty and their prisoners. As part of a peace agreement between England and France, Quebec was restored to the French in 1632, and Champlain returned in the summer of 1633, after an absence of nearly four years, to resume command there.

In 1654, Port Royal and other settlements were seized by a military force from Boston that was led by Robert Sedgwick. The English capture of the colony was, as with so many developments in the history of Acadie, the consequence of distant events, this time in England. Although Sedgwick was a Massachusetts merchant and a Puritan, who led a force of one hundred New England volunteers in the attack, he also had with him two hundred of Oliver Cromwell's soldiers. These Roundheads, professional English soldiers, had honed their military skills in the English Civil War in the 1640s, the war that brought Cromwell to power and resulted in the execution of Charles I in 1649.

While the French defenders of Port Royal, who numbered about one hundred and thirty, did put up a fight, they could not hold out against the veteran Roundheads. Following their triumph, the militantly Protestant victors vented their spleen on a Catholic monastery that was under construction and on a new church in Port Royal. After vandalizing doors, floorboards and wood panelling, they smashed windows and brought their orgy of destruction to its climax by burning down the offending religious edifices.[8] The anti-Catholicism of the English invaders was to remain one source of the antagonism toward the French and the Acadians that would ultimately result in the deportation of the Acadians in 1755.

At the time of this English occupation, the Acadian population, of French origin, still numbered only about three hundred, mostly in the vicinity of Port Royal. Under the terms of surrender, the French soldiers and employees at the fort were sent back to France. The Acadian settlers were given the option of migrating to France. If they chose to remain, as most of them did, they were allowed to keep their lands and their right to practise their religion. English control continued until 1667, when Acadie was returned to French jurisdiction under the terms of the Treaty of Breda.

With the French resuming of control in Acadie, an effort was made to re-establish the enforcement of mercantilist rules to govern the trade of the colony. The Company of New France, which was disbanded in 1663, was replaced by the Compagnie de la Pêche Sédentaire, known at the Compagnie d'Acadie. Run by Claude Bergier, a Huguenot merchant from La Rochelle, the company seized a number of New England fishing and trading vessels operating in Acadian waters, which led to retaliation by New England privateers, who captured French ships. Acadians, who benefited from the trade with New England, were hostile to the attempt to reimpose a monopoly trade regime, an effort that had little effect, in any case.[9]

Renewed French control in Acadie did not provide a lengthy respite from the wars against the English. In the eighteenth century, the struggle between the two European powers was to reach its climax in America. The North American conflict between the British and French empires was strongly shaped by the major wars between them, but there was a local North American character to the struggles as well. The French and their Indian allies carried out devastating raids from Canada against isolated English settlements in New York and New England. In response, the English mounted assaults from their bases in these colonies against New France. And for the nascent metropolitan region of New England, there were particular reasons for striking out against Canada and Acadie that had little to do with the wider strategic concerns of the mother country.

In the spring of 1690, in reprisals for raids by the French against settlements in New England and New York, the English Admiral William Phips organized an attack against Acadie that resulted in the sacking of Port Royal and the English seizure of Acadian territory in what is now mainland Nova Scotia. Under the direction of Phips, an expedition from Boston that counted thirty-four ships and 2,300 men set out to attack Quebec, at the same time as an assault against Montreal was launched from New York with a force of 2,000 men. These expeditions came to naught, however. In 1697, the Treaty of Ryswick recognized all of the holdings of the French in North America.

This was to be the last time that Acadie would be saved for France, though. During the course of the War of the Spanish Succession that broke out in 1701, a new struggle erupted between the English and French in North America. In 1710, a British fleet seized Port Royal and renamed the town Annapolis Royal in honour of Queen Anne. This victory encouraged the British to mount a huge expedition whose goal was the conquest of Canada. Eighty-five ships and a force of twelve thousand were launched against Canada at a time when the French population of the colony numbered fewer than twenty thousand inhabitants. But the British fleet, as a consequence of fog and navigational errors, came to grief and the invasion had to be called off.

The terms of the Treaty of Utrecht of 1713, which concluded the war, were exceedingly harsh for the French. Under the treaty, France lost its foothold on Hudson Bay, its settlements in Newfoundland and Acadie, with the exception of Île Royale (Cape Breton Island) and Île St. Jean (Prince Edward Island).

As a colony, Acadie had always been something of a foundling. It had been ignored by France most of the time and it was often poorly administered. When the British acquired Acadie through the Treaty of Utrecht, there were only about 2,300 Acadians. Over the next forty-two years, to 1755, the date of the deportation, this number multiplied to approximately 13,000.

After the Treaty of Utrecht, Acadian settlements in peninsular Nova Scotia passed permanently into British hands. For the Acadians, over four decades of an uneasy existence under the British sovereign commenced. It was an era of great paradox for them. Their community, from its meagre beginnings, was burgeoning, with rapid population growth and rising prosperity. However, the tensions between France and Britain and between New France and New England did not abate. In a time before there was any concept of pluralism or of minority rights, the question of loyalty, of whether the Acadians had become faithful subjects of the British Crown, was always in the background, even during relatively peaceful periods.

The loyalty issue, the issue that would not go away and that ultimately was used by the British to legitimate the expulsion of the Acadians in 1755, had its roots in 1713. Under the terms of the treaty, the Acadians were allowed to keep their lands, provided they swore an oath of allegiance to the British crown. Since their position in the colony rested on the laws of Britain, the Acadians were allowed to own property. As Roman Catholics, though, they were not permitted to vote, hold public office or join the army. Over time, this restriction on the rights of Roman Catholics rose to paramount importance. Barred from participating in the governmental process in the colony, the Acadians were relegated, from the beginning of British rule, to an anomalous position. They were "in" but never "of" the colony.

The issue of the oath was critical to the fate of the Acadians. When colonial territory was transferred from one empire to another, it was standard practice for both the British and French to insist on an oath from inhabitants. In the British colonies, it was also the practice for a new oath to be taken when one monarch died and a new one came to the throne. Because the religious makeup of the populations in the Thirteen Colonies to the south varied considerably from colony to colony, the oaths had to be tailored to the particular locale. In the case of the Acadians, the British authorities sought an oath not from individuals but from Acadian communities. The Acadians elected their own representatives to negotiate and deal with the issue of the oath, which gave Acadian communities a collective political identity.

During the period from 1713 to 1755, a number of efforts were made to find a workable, long-term arrangement that would allow the Acadians to live peacefully in their settlements while the British exercised effective sovereignty over the territory. In the late 1720s, at a time of peace between Britain and France, and with a brief respite from tension, a compromise, of sorts, was achieved between the rulers of the colony and the Acadians. The death of George I in 1727 and the accession to the throne of George II created the opportunity for an affirmation of Acadian allegiance to Britain. What the leaders of the Acadian communities sought was a wording for the oath that would allow them to swear allegiance to the Crown while noting that they were exempt from taking up arms against the French or the Mi'kmaq in the event of a future war. Lieutenant Colonel Lawrence Armstrong, who had become the lieutenant-governor of Nova Scotia in 1725, a man detested by the Acadians, refused any such accommodation. Armstrong was a difficult, hard and unbending official who was unwilling to take any step to reach a compromise with the Acadians.

In 1729, however, a solution of sorts was found. The return of Governor Richard Philipps, a man of milder temperament who genuinely wanted peace with the Acadian settlers, created the opportunity for a deal to be struck. Philipps toured Nova Scotia, and everywhere he went he received a warm welcome from the Acadians. He returned to the thorny issue of the oath, known to the Acadians as *le serment*, and on this occasion a breakthrough was achieved. In December 1729, in the presence of Philipps, all the Acadian men aged fifteen and older in the settlements in the vicinity of Annapolis Royal signed the oath of allegiance. The men were required to put their names to the oath. In the frequent cases of those who were illiterate, the men made a cross and their names were appended.

The English text of the oath read: "I sincerely promise and swear in the faith of a Christian that I will be entirely faithful and will truly obey His Majesty King George the Second, whom I recognize as the sovereign lord of Nova Scotia and of Acadie. So help me God."[10]

The following spring, the same oath was signed by the men in the settlements around Grand Pré, Pisiquid, Cobequid and Beaubassin, again in the presence of the governor.

In return for the signing of the oath, the British authorities made a promise of their own. Sometimes this promise was written into the margins of the French translation of the oath and sometimes it was rendered verbally.[11] Alexandre Bourg, the notary at Minas, carefully kept a record of the concession made by the governor. His document, witnessed by priests from Grand Pré and Pisiquid, read:

> We . . . certify to whom this may concern that His Excellency Richard Philipps Esquire, Captain-in-Chief and Governor-General of the Province of His Majesty, Nova Scotia or l'Acadie, has promised to the inhabitants of Minas and other rivers dependant thereon, that he exempts them from bearing arms and fighting in war against the French and the Indians, and that the said inhabitants have only accepted allegiance on the promise never to take up arms in the event of war against the Kingdom of England and its government.

The notary kept one copy of this document for himself and forwarded another to French authorities.[12]

The Acadians had achieved the status they sought as the so-called neutral French. Having taken the oath, accompanied by the rider that they would not be dragged into British quarrels, the Acadians appeared to be in a position to thrive in what remained a strategic cockpit, the space between two empires, whose next quarrel might be only a few years away. For the time being, at least, the Acadians who were out of sight of the British garrison at Annapolis Royal could take advantage of recognition of their neutral status to trade with the French at Louisbourg as well as with the merchants of Boston.

While they lived under the British flag, British rule was, for the most part, lightly felt. There was an enviable balance in Acadian settlements around Grand Pré and Beaubassin between individualism, in which the head of the family fished and farmed for himself and his dependents, and collectivism, in which farmers worked together to sustain and extend the aboiteaux that won rich land for them from the sea. In the peculiar position they occupied, the Acadians had managed to escape from even the theoretical remnants of feudalism that had existed during the French regime prior to 1713. Acadian farmers enjoyed a position that farmers in France were not to enjoy prior to the revolutionary transfer of land from aristocrats to peasants that occurred in 1789.

The compromise—the "yes, but"—stood for a time and gave hope that a pacific way forward could be found. However, it always carried a certain lack of legitimacy in the eyes of many of the British authorities on both sides of the Atlantic, a lack of legitimacy that a crisis might quickly expose. And even in this hour of respite, shadows lengthened that would ultimately propel the Acadians toward disaster.

What endangered the relationship constantly was the strategic tension between Britain and France over the territory, a tension that never really went away. And this tension ate away at the possibility that the compromise of 1729 could endure. The French in Île Royale (Cape Breton Island) and in the Isthmus of Chignecto were forever trying to tempt the Acadians to work with them, or to decamp and relocate on French soil.

A man who played a key role in a continuing campaign to enlist the Acadians on the side of France against Britain was the Abbé Jean-Louis Le Loutre. From the time he first arrived in Louisbourg in 1737 until his death in 1772, Le Loutre was a warrior-priest who was determined to win converts to Catholicism among the Mi'kmaq, and who was never far from politics. His militant Catholicism and his loathing for the British regime in Nova Scotia inspired fear among British colonial administrators. In his fanaticism, Le Loutre brings to mind radical clerics of several faiths who have roiled the politics of our own time.

Born on November 2, 1711, in Morlaix in the Finistère region of France, Jean-Louis, with his four brothers and a sister, became an orphan at an early age. Raised in bourgeois ease by their maternal grandparents, who owned several paper-making enterprises, Le Loutre and his siblings received a solid religious education. At the age of twenty-one, Le Loutre entered the seminary of Saint-Esprit in Paris, and he was ordained as a priest in 1737.[13] Seized with the idea of becoming a missionary, Le Loutre was soon sent to Île Royale, where he arrived in August 1737. The plan was that he would go on to replace as priest the Abbé de Saint Poncy, whose departure had been engineered by Nova Scotia Lieutenant-Governor Lawrence Armstrong. Long concerned about the influence of the clergy at a time when most of the priests were trained in France, the British administration in Nova Scotia was about to meet up with the priest who was to dog their footsteps all the way to the deportation and beyond.

Under the guidance of the Abbé Pierre Maillard, also a graduate of the seminary of Saint-Esprit, who had served as a missionary to the natives, Le Loutre spent the winter at Louisbourg and learned the Mi'kmaq language. In September 1738, the young priest travelled to his mission in Chubenacadie on the Nova Scotia peninsula, where he supervised the construction of a church and began his work with the Acadians and the natives.

From the start, as he carried out his priestly duties, Le Loutre adopted an anti-British stance. On occasion, he and several other priests from France whose pastoral work was centred in eastern Nova Scotia threatened excommunication to Acadians who had taken up positions in the Nova Scotia administration. In one instance, they went so far as to deny the sacraments to an Acadian from Minas who had accepted a government commission. The priests influenced others in the community to have nothing to do with the man.[14]

Tension in the region exploded into conflict when a new war between Britain and France, the War of the Austrian Succession, broke out in the spring of 1744. In May, the Mi'kmaq joined forces with the French to seize the British fort at Canso. From there British prisoners were taken to Louisbourg. In October, the government of Massachusetts issued an official declaration of war against the Mi'kmaq, a struggle that was to be followed in the summer of 1745 by a New England–led assault on the fortress of Louisbourg. A few days after the declaration of war, the Massachusetts General Court established a bounty of one hundred pounds for the scalp of any adult male Mi'kmaq. The scalps of women and children were to be rewarded with a payment of fifty pounds. To make these bounties workable, Governor William Shirley of Massachusetts announced that the rewards would apply to any native person killed or captured east of the St. Croix River (in Acadie). Naturally, he exempted natives who were serving under his own military command.[15]

Born in 1694 in London, Shirley was the son of a merchant. Having trained as a lawyer in England, Shirley migrated to Massachusetts in 1731 and set up a law practice there. For a time he was Surveyor of the King's Wood, a post that required him to travel extensively in the colony and to become knowledgeable about its people and its communities. This put him in close touch with those in the north, in the lands of present-day New Hampshire and Maine, where sentiments against the French ran extremely high as a consequence of the butchery that had been practised in border skirmishes between New England and New France. Here was the origin of his strong antipathy for the French, which grew, over time, into a particular hostility toward the Acadians, whom he came to see as an obstacle to his dreams for the commercial expansion of Massachusetts. He fancied himself a man with talent for military leadership and military strategy. Shirley had an imperious personality and did not think much about the rights of those who were unlucky enough to be caught in his path. He was fortunate to marry well. His wife, Lady Frances, came from a wealthy and well-connected family, which helped her ambitious husband in his rise.

In the war against the Mi'kmaq, Le Loutre, whose mission at Chubenacadie was in an area of fierce native resistance, acted as the principal intermediary between the Mi'kmaq on British territory and the French at Île Royale. The Abbé passed on to the Mi'kmaq the plans of the French at Louisbourg to send a military force whose objective was to link up with the Mi'kmaq for a joint assault on the British garrison at Annapolis Royal. The Mi'kmaq, whose lives were now at stake, fell in enthusiastically with the French gambit. As far as they were concerned, the seizure of the British fort would mean the end of the British hold on peninsular Nova Scotia and would negate the menace that hung over their lives and those of their families. Three hundred Mi'kmaq warriors, accompanied by Le Loutre, their spiritual advisor, headed for Annapolis Royal, where they were supposed to meet up with a French regular force. Because the French failed to arrive at the appointed time, the Mi'kmaq siege of the fort was lifted.

At this critical juncture, Nova Scotia's acting governor, Paul Mascarene, appealed to Massachusetts to send a force to repel any renewed attack against Annapolis Royal. The authorities at Boston quickly assembled troops, supplies and armaments and dispatched them to Nova Scotia, where their presence helped turn the tide of the Mi'kmaq-French assault.[16] Although the French and their native allies renewed the attack on Annapolis Royal in September 1744, the siege was not pressed home to success and the chance for France to retake peninsular Nova Scotia, the heart of Acadie, slipped away. It may have come as something of a shock to the French that their assault on the British garrison at Annapolis Royal engendered so little support from the Acadians, who were not inclined to go over to the side of France in a new imperial war.

Open armed struggle between the Mi'kmaq and the French on one side and the British on the other placed the Acadians in a perilous position. They had taken the oath of allegiance to the British crown and did not want to lose their hard-won status as the neutral French. Nevertheless, in January 1745, Acadian deputies from eastern Nova Scotia took a petition to the provincial council raising their acute concerns about the bounty policy that offered rewards for Mi'kmaq scalps. The Acadians pointed out that a great many people of mixed Acadian-Mi'kmaq ancestry lived in their communities and that the bounty threatened their relatives, friends and the peace of their settlements. Moreover, many of these people had taken the oath of allegiance to the British monarch.[17]

Seized with the issue, the provincial council decided that the bounty policy would not apply to persons with Mi'kmaq ancestry who lived in Acadian settlements. Acting Governor Mascarene wrote: "In regard to the notion the inhabitants had amongst them that all who had any Indian blood in them would be treated as enemies, it was a very great mistake, since if that had been the design of the New England armed vessels it might very well be supposed that the inhabitants of this river, many of whom have Indian blood in them, and some even who live within the reach of the cannon, would not be suffered to live peaceably as they do."[18]

Just two weeks after the Acadians petitioned the provincial council on the issue of the bounty, a detachment of Canadian soldiers set out from Quebec to make another attempt to take back Annapolis Royal from the British. On the British side, moves were also being made. In January 1745, Governor Shirley of Massachusetts wrote to the Duke of Newcastle in England to propose an attack on the French at Louisbourg. Shirley made the case that the British needed to take Louisbourg to assure their hold on Annapolis Royal, on Nova Scotia as a whole and on the fishery in the Strait of Canso.[19]

The British force, whose manpower was raised mainly in New England—3,000 men from Massachusetts, 500 from New Hampshire and 500 from Connecticut, with cannons supplied from New York—set out for Canso, where they waited to be joined by Commodore Peter Warren, who arrived from Antigua with a force of 1,100 men and 192 cannons.[20] While the British were preparing to attack his fortress, Du Pont Duchambon, the French commander at Louisbourg, dispatched a shipload of munitions to aid in the Quebec-based assault on Annapolis Royal. But, as had been the case with the previous siege of the British garrison, the French force did not win the support of the local Acadians. And, like the previous attack, this one came to naught.

The British campaign—or, as it should be called, the Anglo–New England campaign—against Louisbourg had a dramatically different outcome. In mid May, the French commander whose small force was carrying out the siege of Annapolis Royal received an anxious message from Du Pont Duchambon, stating that Louisbourg was under assault and that he should come to the aid of the French fortress at once.

The fortress at Louisbourg on Île Royale had been the French response to the loss of peninsular Nova Scotia under the Treaty of Utrecht. The French government lavished resources on Louisbourg in a way they never had on Acadie before 1713. During its short but flamboyant life, Louisbourg was the *ancien régime* transplanted in the New World. With its clock tower, its busy streets and its seemingly impregnable ramparts, the ordered world of Louisbourg bustled with aristocrats and their families, tradesmen, carpenters, artisans, labourers and servants. Because of its prime location next to the waters of the North Atlantic fishery, Louisbourg did a booming business that exceeded that of all the ports of North America, with the exceptions of Boston, New York and Philadelphia.[21] Over the years only a small number of Acadian families from peninsular Nova Scotia took up the siren call of the French to come and settle in Île Royale. Those who did had to switch from farming to fishing, since Île Royale did not boast the fertile farmlands of the shores of the Baie Française. Some of the Acadians who settled for a time on the island ultimately decided to return to the old Acadie.

Louisbourg was well placed to serve as an entrepôt for the trade of the far-flung empire of France in North America, which stretched down the St. Lawrence River through Canada, and from there into the interior of the continent all the way to Louisiana in the south. The empire also including holdings in the Caribbean. Each year, dozens of ships from France, as well as ships from Canada and the Caribbean, were seen in the harbour at Louisbourg. That meant that furs from Canada and sugar and molasses from the Caribbean could be expected to be found at Louisbourg for transshipment to France. And fish could be found there, to be shipped to France and the

Mediterranean and to France's sugar islands in the Caribbean. Despite mercantilist trade restrictions, ships from New England came into the harbour, and officials at Louisbourg often looked the other way to allow trade with the New Englanders to flourish. New England merchants had much to offer, and the price was good for flour, wheat and other products. (At Canso, at the southern tip of Île Royale, in a more discreet setting away from the eyes of officials, there was also brisk trade between the French and the New Englanders. As for the Acadians, they benefited from the profitable commerce that tied Île Royale, Nova Scotia and New England together, no matter how much this trade violated the rules of both the British and the French.)

The French colony on Île Royale had grown quickly to a population of more than five thousand by the time the enemy bore down on it in the spring of 1745. The problem was that Louisbourg, for all its apparent solidity, was built on illusion, the most important being the illusion that it was impregnable. By the time the Anglo–New England force stood outside the fort, the British already knew a good deal about the problems the fortress faced. Fishermen and soldiers captured by the French at Canso, who had been set free in exchange for the release of French prisoners held by the British, had seen the inner workings of Louisbourg. They reported what they had seen to British officers. From this source, the attackers learned that the fortress, for all its grandeur, was short of food, and that ordinary soldiers were fed up with their poor treatment. Morale could be expected to be low in the face of the coming attack.

In the spring of 1745, Louisbourg was a decidedly alluring target for the British force composed mainly of New Englanders. William Shirley had gone to great lengths to recruit and equip an army for the attack. He assembled his own navy that included schooners and sloops, with pride of place going to Massachusetts's own newly built twenty-one-gun frigate.[22] Based on the intelligence they had gathered from the released prisoners, the New Englanders believed that if their largely amateur force struck quickly, before more soldiers and ships could arrive from France, they could prevail.

The New Englanders were driven not only by their desire to remove a strategic threat that hung over them and their fishery, but also by their hatred of the papacy and what they detested as the idolatry of Catholicism—twin pillars of their Puritan sensibility. One letter, addressed to William Pepperell, a merchant chosen by Shirley to lead the expedition, voiced the oft-expressed sentiment that the chance may have come to strike a blow at the papists: "O, that I could be with you and dear Mr. Moodey in that single church to destroy the images their sett up, and the true Gospel of our Lord and Saviour Jesus Christ, their preached." Samuel Moody, Pepperell's seventy-year-old chaplain, was outfitted with an axe that he intended to use to smash the idols that would be found when Louisbourg was taken.[23]

In a lighthearted note to his brother in Boston, Benjamin Franklin wrote from Philadelphia that so many prayers put on the scales "against the prayers of a few priests in the garrison, to the Virgin Mary, give a vast balance in your favour. If you do not succeed, I fear I shall have but an indifferent opinion of Presbyterian prayers in such cases, as long as I live. Indeed, in attacking strong towers I should have more dependence on *works*, than on *faith*."[24]

Despite the humour here, the religious fervour of New Englanders was deeply important in providing moral certitude in what was, in truth, an early but unmistakable expression of American metropolitanism. Though the British flag flew over their heads, theirs was an American cause.

On May 11, the expeditionary force, which included more than one hundred vessels and six hundred cannons, entered Gabarus Bay next to Louisbourg, where the troops were put ashore.[25] Because of the marshy ground that lay between the landing area and the fortress, the approach chosen for the attack left much to be desired. The British opened fire with their cannons on May 15. Two days later, Pepperell formally demanded the surrender of Louisbourg. The following day, Du Pont Duchambon displayed steely determination in his reply. The king of France had placed the protection of the town in the hands of the defenders, the commander declared, and the only reply to the British demand would come from the mouth of the French cannons.[26]

If the precise point chosen for the British landing was not without its disadvantages, the idea of a landing was nonetheless a good one. Du Pont Duchambon had always expected any attack on Louisbourg to be launched from the sea, not from the land. The plans for the defence of the fortress had been drawn up to repel a seaborne assault.

As the siege continued, the attackers made an agonizing effort to drag their cannons across the swampy terrain so they could bring the fortress under steady fire. The fort's defenders, composed of 560 French and Swiss soldiers and 900 militiamen, drawn from Louisbourg and neighbouring fishing stations, were heavily out-numbered by the New Englanders and the British.[27] Two days after the initial landing, British attackers seized the abandoned Grand Battery, a fortress that stood apart from the main ramparts of Louisbourg. With its twenty-eight forty-two-pounder guns, the Battery had been designed to direct fire at an enemy naval force in the harbour. It was, however, highly vulnerable to a land attack. The Grand Battery was taken without a fight, because the French had calculated that they did not have enough men to spare from the main fortress to hold it. The crucial mistake the French made was that, in their haste, they failed to move or effectively spike the big guns installed in the Battery. As a consequence, within a day of its capture, British gunsmiths repaired the French cannon and they were put to work, directing a withering barrage on Louisbourg.

While the defenders of the fortress were now under continuous fire from several directions, a British effort to seize another French strong point was repulsed with heavy losses. With this setback, the attackers lost their chance for a quick victory. Two outcomes were possible in what had become an extended siege. The French could be rescued by the arrival of supplies, armaments and fresh man-power from France or from the Canadian force that had unsuccess-fully attacked Annapolis Royal. Failing such a rescue, Louisbourg would fall.

A rescue from the outside came tantalizingly close to happening. In the end, however, the constant British battering won the day. On June 28, the British commanders accepted Duchambon's surrender.[28]

The aftermath of the fall of Louisbourg—and, along with it, of all of Île Royale—involved a menacing warning for what the future could hold for the Acadians of peninsular Nova Scotia, who, with a few exceptions, had clung to their status as the neutral French during the fighting. The British victors expelled to France not only the defenders of Louisbourg, but almost the entire civilian population of Île Royale as well—more than four thousand residents of the island, including nearly two thousand inhabitants, who were mostly Acadians. It was to be a forerunner of the mass expulsion of the Acadians a decade later. When France regained the island in 1748, only ninety-four of the pre-siege settlers remained.[29] When the inhabitants asked to be sent to Canada, the British refused, seizing the opportunity to deport a significant number of Acadians from the New World altogether.[30]

Having been named an admiral and the governor of the captured island for his role in the victory, Peter Warren was the key figure in expelling the French from Île Royale. Warren also wanted the French settlers removed from Île St. Jean, and he let it be known that he believed the Acadians of peninsular Nova Scotia should be deported and that their settlements should be burned and their lands flooded. [31]

William Shirley, who was later to play a pivotal role as a member of the triumvirate responsible for the deportation of the Acadians, now revealed his ambivalence on the issue of the future of the Acadians in the aftermath of the fall of Louisbourg. Like Warren, Shirley was rewarded for the victory with a promotion—to the position of colonel in the regular British army.[32]

In May 1745, when the Louisbourg assault was just getting underway, Shirley learned of the French attack on Annapolis Royal. He assumed that the Acadians had joined the expedition against the British position. In a letter at the time, he poured out his fury: "It grieves me much that I have not it in my power to send a party of 500 men forthwith to Menis [Minas], and burn Grand Pré, their chief town, and open all their sluices, and their country waste."[33]

This, however, was far from Shirley's last word on the subject. The capture of Louisbourg left him, for a time, in a better frame of mind on the subject of the Acadians. In 1746, Shirley weighed into the dialogue in official British circles about what should be the fate of the Acadians. He wrote: "After their having remain'd so long in the country upon the foot of British Subjects under the Sanction of the Treaty of Utrecht, to drive 'em all off their Settlements without further Inquiry seems to be liable to many objections. Among others, it may be doubted whether under the circumstance of the inhabitants it would clearly appear to be a just usage of 'em."

Shirley concluded that although the Acadian claim that they had a right to be neutral was objectionable, it was a notion that had had the official sanction of British governors. Considering that the Acadians had been "continuously plac'd between two fires," allowances needed to be made given their situation.[34]

At this stage, Shirley believed that, under a firm hand, the Acadians could be transformed into loyal subjects. They would have to take a new oath of allegiance, he believed, but he did not spell out what the oath would entail. The firm hand would be reinforced by the building of blockhouses to be manned by troops in the vicinity of Acadian communities. Shirley also favoured the establishment of English-language schools to transform the next generation of Acadians into English-speakers. And he wanted to see troublemaking French priests replaced with Protestant ministers in Acadian settlements. Acadians who would not take the new oath of allegiance should be expelled, in his opinion.

Shirley also had to pay attention to instructions from the British government not to enflame the Acadians by arousing their fears that they faced attacks and expulsion at the hands of New Englanders. In the spring of 1747, Thomas Pelham-Holles, Duke of Newcastle, secretary of state for the Southern Department, the minister responsible for North American affairs, wrote to Shirley raising concerns that the anxieties of Acadians had prompted them "to withdraw themselves from their Allegiance to His Majesty and to take part with the Enemy." "Proper Measures should be taken to remove any such ill-founded suggestions; and for that Purpose it is the King's Pleasure that you should declare in some publick and Authentick manner to

His Majesty's Subjects, Inhabitants of that Province, that there is not the least Foundation for any apprehension of that nature."[35]

The return of Île Royale and therefore of Louisbourg to France in the peace of 1748 reproduced the tense standoff between the British and French in the region. In 1749, the British decided to establish their own fort to offset Louisbourg. That fort was to be built at Chebucto Harbour. The British had not chosen to locate there before because the site was in the heart of Mi'kmaq territory, and building a fort could only be seen as highly provocative to the Mi'kmaq. Imperial anxiety about Louisbourg overcame concerns about the internal peace of the colony, however, and the British pressed ahead with the establishment of Halifax. With its excellent natural harbour, Halifax was to become a bastion of the British navy. The new town, which became the capital in place of Annapolis Royal, was populated with Protestants as a matter of high policy. Halifax was founded, among other things, to offset the weight of Acadian settlements on the other side of the peninsula along the Baie Française.

The British pushed ahead with the building of Halifax as rapidly as possible. A palisade was constructed in the new town to defend it against possible Indian attacks. British troops, who had been stationed at Louisbourg until that fort was handed back to the French, were relocated to Halifax. Some Britons who had been established in Louisbourg during the British occupation there moved to Halifax along with the garrison. And New Englanders, chary about locating in Nova Scotia with all its troubles, saw the founding of the new town as a positive sign, and some of them moved to the new community. Within two years, Halifax had amassed a population of over five thousand, although the numbers would decline for a time when some people who were fearful of Indian raids returned to New England.[36]

With their garrisons at Louisbourg and Halifax in place, the rival empires were readying themselves for the next round, the round that would see the Acadians deported and their communities put to the torch.

—

CHAPTER 3

LE GRAND DÉRANGEMENT

IN THE SPRING OF 1750, French troops and native warriors entered the Acadian settlement of Beaubassin at the head of the Bay of Fundy. The Abbé Le Loutre, always striving to win the Acadians to the French side, was at the centre of the affair. The French pressured the Acadians to leave their long-established settlement and to follow them to French territory on the northern side of the Isthmus of Chignecto. (The isthmus is the narrow neck of land that connects peninsular Nova Scotia to present-day New Brunswick. Controlling the isthmus was a high-stakes game for both the French and the British in their struggle for strategic advantage in the region.) In this tense situation, someone set fire to the village, possibly under the orders of Le Loutre, and one hundred and forty houses went up in flames. Their settlement destroyed, the homeless Acadians had little choice but to accompany the French and the native troops to nearby French-occupied territory.

In 1749, a French and Canadian force had arrived from Quebec in the area. Under the command of Chevalier La Corne, the French had begun construction of Fort Beauséjour and, at the other end of the isthmus, Fort Gaspereau. The uprooted Acadians established a new settlement next to Fort Beauséjour, and the question of their loyalty was inevitably raised. In 1751, the commander of the French troops at the fort asked the Acadians in his immediate area to swear allegiance to the king of France. Many Acadians, however, insistent on retaining their much-prized neutral status, refused, much to the chagrin of the Abbé Le Loutre.

Meantime, Le Loutre presided over the construction of a chapel in the Acadian community.

Things went miserably for the Acadians in their new settlement. In the spring of 1754, huge storm tides ruined the work they had been doing, under Le Loutre's direction, to reclaim the land for agriculture. Completely dispirited, a large group of the settlers petitioned French authorities to be allowed to return to where their former homes had been located—on the British side of the line. Furious because of what he saw as treachery, Le Loutre thundered his condemnation of those who had signed the petition. From the altar, he called on the signatories to "efface their crosses with their own saliva," warning that anyone who tried to return to British territory "would be shot."[1]

The British warily watched the burning of Beaubassin and the relocation of its Acadian community and had to decide what to make of it. Were the Acadians harried neutrals, victimized by the French, or were they their willing collaborators? For British officials, who had long been suspicious of, and hostile to, the Acadians, the chances of a sympathetic interpretation were slight.

The burning of Beaubassin and the resettlement of its people on French territory, along with the French creation of Fort Beauséjour, were to prove fateful for the Acadian population as a whole. From the point of view of the British, Fort Beauséjour posed a direct threat to their position in Nova Scotia. In addition to the major base at Louisbourg on Île Royale and Fort Beauséjour, there was now Fort Gaspareau, north of Beauséjour on the Isthmus of Chignecto. These installations put the French in a position to attack the British in Nova Scotia from two vantage points. The British retort to the return of the French to Louisbourg, under the terms of the Treaty of Aix-la-Chapelle of 1748, was the establishment of heavily fortified Halifax, their new capital. For its part, Fort Beauséjour also drew a British countermove on the strategic chessboard. Just a few hundred metres to the south-east of Fort Beauséjour, the British built Fort Lawrence. And at Grand Pré and farther east at Pisiquid they also constructed forts, both to counter the French buildup and to keep a watchful eye on the largest of the Acadian settlements. The cold war between the two imperial powers in Acadie was threatening to become a hot war in advance of the next general outbreak of hostilities between Britain and France. In 1749, when Colonel Edward Cornwallis was appointed governor of Nova Scotia, it was clear that the next showdown with the French was not far off.

As tensions rose, a hot war did break out in Nova Scotia between the British and the Mi'kmaq in the summer of 1749. Because of the long history of close relations between the Acadians and the Mi'kmaq, this conflict was bound to increase the negative attitude of Nova Scotia's rulers toward the Acadians. Conflict between the British and the Mi'kmaq had festered from the time of the Treaty of Utrecht of 1713. Indeed, from 1722 to 1725 an earlier war had flared between the two sides. In December 1725, representatives of a number of native nations, including the Mi'kmaq, met with the British in Boston to work out terms for peace. Under the terms of the treaties that were signed, the Mi'kmaq acknowledged British sovereignty, and in return they were accorded the right to govern their own affairs. The treaties did not provide the Mi'kmaq with clear boundaries for the territory they claimed as their own, however.[2] The British continued to regard Nova Scotia as theirs, to be governed as they chose. Their desire to bring the Acadians and the Mi'kmaq to heel one way or another had not changed.

In the summer of 1749, renewed hostilities between the British and the Mi'kmaq were triggered when a group of English-speakers, probably New Englanders, arrived at Canso to restart the local fishery. According to a later Mi'kmaq account of events, the English came upon a community of Mi'kmaq, whose men were away hunting and fishing, and killed twenty women and children. In September, in retaliation for this massacre, when another British ship arrived at Canso, Mi'kmaq warriors seized the vessel, taking twenty members of its crew hostage. Although the Mi'kmaq released the hostages, general fighting broke out between the British and the Mi'kmaq in the Isthmus of Chignecto, already a tinderbox of conflict between the British and the French. Skirmishes also occurred in the vicinity of Halifax, whose recent establishment by the British was a sore point for the natives, who regarded the location of the town as a flagrant intrusion into their territory.[3] Nova Scotia Governor Edward Cornwallis was determined to settle matters once and for all with the Mi'kmaq. He decided that if they did not come to terms quickly, they would be driven out of the territory. Once again, bounties were placed on the scalps of Mi'kmaq men, women and children by the British.[4]

In this highly volatile situation the position of the Acadians in Nova Scotia was gravely imperilled. Despite the fact that the Acadians had been successful in defining themselves as French neutrals who could stand aside when conflicts broke out between the French and the British, that position was anything but secure. The resettlement of the Acadians of Beaubassin in Beauséjour ignited paranoia in the minds of Nova Scotia's governors. The idea of solving Nova Scotia's problems through the expulsion of its entire Acadian population was back on the table. Deportation of the Acadians was a drastic solution that had been actively considered by influential British figures since 1713.

Decades before the deportation of the Acadians in 1755, a Scottish adventurer by the name of Samuel Vetch imagined a great imperial enterprise. He envisioned the conquest of Acadie and Canada and the expulsion of its French Catholic inhabitants. "The greatest part of the inhabitants being removed from thence is absolutely necessary," he wrote about the Acadians, both "for the security of our own people in case of an attempt by France to recover it, as [well as] to make the natives come over entirely to the interest and obedience of the Crown."[5] His idea was to expel the Acadians—forcing them to sail to Martinique in the West Indies in their own boats—and then to replace them with hardy Protestant Scottish colonists. His New Scotland would be inhabited by a race of people fit for a northern clime. For Vetch, this grand concept was inspired by the Act of Union of 1707 between England and Scotland. With the realization of his project, the English empire of the past would truly become a British Empire, with a distinct place in it for the Scots. What made Vetch more than an idle dreamer were his contacts in both New England and Britain. Vetch played a role in a number of efforts to conquer the territories of the French empire. He managed after the Treaty of Utrecht to become, for a time, the military governor of Nova Scotia. While his dream came to nothing during his day, it remained a deadly legacy for the future.

If Vetch never got the chance to expel the Acadians from Nova Scotia, the opportunity to do just that fell into the hands of two men who were ultimately more responsible than any others for the deportation of 1755. One was Massachusetts governor William Shirley. The other was Charles Lawrence. Lawrence, the man who was to order the expulsion in the summer of 1755, was born in Plymouth in 1709, the son of General Charles John Lawrence, who served under Marlborough in Flanders. Having received his military commission in 1727, Lawrence was sent to the West Indies from 1733 to 1737. Back in England, he became a lieutenant in 1741 and a captain in 1745. He was wounded in 1745 at the battle of Fontenoy. Two years later, Lawrence was a member of the English regular army that relieved the New England force that had been holding Louisbourg after the fall of the fortress in 1745. A tall, corpulent man with heavy jowls, Lawrence was noted for having an abrupt personality, for being arrogant and arbitrary and for treating his inferiors in insulting ways. He was a determined opponent of any move toward representative government. As governor, he delayed the implementation of steps in Nova Scotia to bring the colony into line with governing practices in Britain and in other British colonies in America.

By the time Charles Lawrence became acting governor of Nova Scotia in 1754, he had already developed a strong dislike for the Acadians, and for the French in general, and he had honed a particular loathing for the Abbé Le Loutre.[6] From his earliest days in the colony, Lawrence adopted a simple black-and-white attitude to its central dilemma. Either the Acadians should be required to swear allegiance to the Crown without equivocation or they should be deported. Lawrence's perspective on the Acadian question was influenced by a report submitted to the provincial council of Nova Scotia in 1753 by Charles Morris, an engineer, who had earlier carried out a survey of the eastern end of the Bay of Fundy on behalf of Massachusetts Governor William Shirley. The report contended that it was the Mi'kmaq who stood in the way of the successful British colonization of Nova Scotia, and that it was the Acadians who stood behind the Mi'kmaq, aiding and goading them in their hostility to the British. Thus, concluded Morris, the only way to solve the colony's problems would be to extract the root of the problem, the Acadians.[7] Morris concluded that the Acadian inhabitants were occupying the best land in the province. If the goal was to settle Protestants in the territory, much of this land would have to be confiscated from the Acadians. "Without that," he wrote, "I am sure it would be impossible any large number of Protestants can ever be settled in this country."[8] Morris's report reinforced the active interest of Shirley and his administration in the Bay of Fundy and its adjacent lands.

In the case Morris set out for the removal of the Acadians, there is a righteous tone that is customarily present in documents justifying the deportation of a people from their homes and communities. In an interview for this book, Gerald Caplan, a historian who is an expert on ethnic cleansing and genocide, explained that the righteous tone is the hallmark of the ethnic cleanser, that those carrying out such schemes genuinely believe that they are serving a higher purpose, that the removal of one people, invariably depicted as unworthy or evil, will open the way for a shining future for another.

The conclusions Morris reached were well known in British governing circles in Nova Scotia, Massachusetts and in Britain itself. In 1754, officials in London adopted the position that the Acadians should be made to sign an oath of allegiance to the Crown "without reservation" and that, in the event that they failed to sign the oath, they should be deprived of all rights to their property and deported.[9] This meant that, in principle, by 1754 London was prepared to contemplate the expulsion of the Acadians from Nova

Scotia. But there remained a long step between adopting that position in principle and acting on it. The British had not yet reached the threshold for action and were still prepared to vacillate, depending on the developing situation in the territory itself. Nonetheless, London's position was fateful because it was to serve as the basis on which Lawrence acted during the crisis of 1755.

In late April 1750, it was Lawrence who was dispatched to counter the French in the Isthmus of Chignecto. Indeed, it was the arrival of his force that triggered the French decision to compel the inhabitants of Beaubassin to abandon their settlement and move to French-controlled territory. With seven hundred men under his command, Lawrence had recently been appointed to the rank of lieutenant colonel. He found the French firmly established at Fort Beauséjour and realized that he could not seize the territory through a simple *coup de main*. He built his own fort immediately adjacent to the French fort. That fort, garrisoned with six hundred men, was named Fort Lawrence after the commander himself.

A rapidly rising career officer, who made it from major to brigadier in just a few years, Lawrence was in the right place to take over the administration of the colony when Governor Peregrine Hopson fell ill and sailed home to England in November 1753. From that moment, Lawrence was in charge of the Nova Scotia government, and he was sworn in as acting governor in October 1754. In addition to staking out the British position in opposition to the French in the Isthmus of Chignecto, Lawrence also played a vital role in establishing a colony of German settlers in Lunenburg on Nova Scotia's south shore. British authorities promoted the settlement as a way to offset the Acadian French-speaking Catholics with a new Protestant presence. German Lutherans were not the Nova Scotia government's first choice for settlers, but they were Protestants, and it had been proving difficult to attract New Englanders to the troubled colony.

Charles Lawrence and William Shirley had been nurturing their antagonism against the Acadians for a long time. It was, however, a third man who created the precise conditions that allowed

Lawrence and Shirley to act. That man was Colonel Robert Monckton. Unlike Lawrence and Shirley, who were administrators and planners as well as military men, Monckton, the youngest of the three, was a soldier first and foremost. Born in Yorkshire, England, in 1726, Monckton was the second son of John Monckton, 1st Viscount Galway, and Lady Elizabeth Manners. He was only fifteen years old when he was sent to join the 3rd Foot Guards in the British army. A year later, his unit was dispatched to the continent for action in the War of the Austrian Succession. The youthful Monckton saw action in the Battle of Dettingen in June 1743 and in the crucial Battle of Fontenoy in 1745. By the time he fought at Fontenoy, he had been commissioned a captain in the 34th Foot. In the early 1750s, Monckton's career continued to advance rapidly. He was elected to a seat in the House of Commons, not much of a challenge since his family controlled a parliamentary "rotten borough" (a constituency with very few voters), and he was promoted to the position of lieutenant colonel of the 47th Foot.

A high-ranking officer at the age of twenty-six, Monckton was sent to Nova Scotia in 1752, arriving in the colony just as the sixty-seven-year-old Peregrine Hopson reached Halifax and took over as governor. The young officer could have chosen to remain in England, where a political career was open to him. Instead, he opted for army life in a post that was on a far frontier of the British Empire, a frontier that was constantly alive to the danger of conflict with France.

After a short stay in Halifax, Monckton was dispatched to take command of Fort Lawrence. The following summer he was called back to the capital, where Governor Hopson appointed him to a position on the colony's Governor's Council. By the end of 1753, with Hopson's departure, Charles Lawrence had taken over the running of the colony and Monckton had become his most important military commander in the field. That position was solidified in December 1753, when the word reached Halifax that a rebellion had broken out in the German settlement at Lunenburg. Restive because of the miserable shacks in which they were housed and the poor food they had to endure, the recently arrived settlers became embroiled in conflict with the local British garrison. During an emergency meeting of the Governor's Council, Monckton offered to go to Lunenburg with a detachment of two hundred troops to restore order. The mission was a success. Monckton's quick pacification of Lunenburg heightened his reputation for effectiveness. Monckton's next assignment, in early 1754, was to take command of the British force at Fort Anne in Annapolis Royal.

In the summer of 1754, Shirley and Lawrence were co-ordinating plans to push the French out of the Isthmus of Chignecto and out of the lands on the northern side of the Bay of Fundy. Shirley anticipated the possibility of repopulating the isthmus with Protestant settlers from Ulster or New England, in particular the area around Beaubassin, site of the Acadian settlement, which by then had been abandoned.[10] In August 1754, in a dispatch to Lord Halifax, president of the Board of Trade, Shirley wrote of the views he shared with Lawrence:"From the experience he [Lawrence] hath had of the behaviour and spirit of the Acadians, he is of sentiment with me that the refusal of the revolted Inhabitants of Chignecto to comply with the terms upon which they had permission given to return ... is happy for the country, and even thinks it would be fortunate if a favourable opportunity should offer for ridding His Majesty's Government there of the French Inhabitants of the two districts of Minas and Annapolis River."[11] This dispatch makes it clear that a year before the capture of Fort Beauséjour and the launch of the deportation Shirley and Lawrence were thinking of using the critical situation in the Isthmus of Chignecto as the trigger for expelling all of the Acadians of Nova Scotia.

Both Shirley and Lawrence drew sustenance for their plans from identical dispatches they received in November 1754 from Sir Thomas Robinson, Britain's colonial minister. Robinson was responding to a report from Shirley the previous spring that a force of Acadians and Mi'kmaq had invaded New England territory. Robinson, who had no way of knowing that the report was faulty, had presented Shirley's alarmist dispatch to the king, who instructed the minister to direct the two governors to undertake such joint measures "as will frustrate the designs of the French." Shirley wrote to Lawrence to say that he regarded Robinson's dispatch "to be orders to us to act in concert for taking any advantages to drive the French of Canada out of Nova Scotia." While Robinson had been referring to what he thought was a threat from Canadian militia on the borders of New England, Shirley was treating this as a licence for much wider action. So, too, was Lawrence, who wrote Shirley underlining "the necessity of undertaking the Grand Project without waiting for any further sanction from England." Shortly thereafter Lawrence dispatched Monckton to Boston with a request to Shirley to raise two thousand volunteers for the purpose of carrying out an assault on Fort Beauséjour the following spring.[12]

In December 1754, just after the arrival of Monckton in Boston, Governor Shirley received a dispatch from Robinson. By then, the British government had heard the news of the defeat of a force of Virginia militia at the hands of the French and had decided that it was time to undertake a co-ordinated series of attacks against French positions in North America.

A few weeks later, in January 1755, Lawrence received a reply from the Board of Trade in London to his proposal that the Acadians should be removed from the Isthmus of Chignecto. The missive can hardly have been welcome to the Nova Scotia governor. It stated that no final judgment could be made "until We have laid the whole State of the Case before His Majesty and received his Directions upon it." While the Board of Trade was willing to agree that settling New Englanders on the lands of the "deserted inhabitants" would have "great utility," this could not be attempted until the French fortifications in the isthmus, Fort Beauséjour and Fort Gaspereau, had been taken. With the forts in British hands, the Acadians in the isthmus would be "driven to seek such an Asylum as they can find in the barren Island of Cape Breton and St. Johns and in Canada." "We could wish that proper Measures were pursued for carrying such Forfeiture into Execution by legal Process," the Board's letter continued, in obvious hesitation. Perhaps the refusal of the inhabitants could serve as the legal basis for the forfeiture of their property, but that was a question "which We will not take upon ourselves absolutely to determine," the Board's letter stated. Their missive concluded that Lawrence should consult on this matter with Jonathan Belcher, Nova's Scotia's chief justice.[13]

With Lawrence left dangling by London's equivocation on the matter of the Acadians, Shirley and Monckton made plans in Boston for the military assault on Fort Beauséjour. It was that mission, in the spring and summer of 1755, that was to create the strategic opportunity for the deportation. Shirley's vision for the region was to push for the achievement of British rule over the territory all the way to the south shore of the St. Lawrence River. He shared Lawrence's determination to push the French out of the Isthmus of Chignecto, where the hotly contested boundary ran along the Missiquash River, with the French at Fort Beauséjour on one side and the English at Fort Lawrence on the other. If the French could be driven out of the isthmus, Shirley reasoned, their position north to the St. Lawrence would be imperilled. Furthermore, he believed, if Fort Beauséjour were taken, the French could not long hold out in Louisbourg and Île Royale. While the French position in Louisbourg seemed strong, the fortress there was a constant drain of food and other products on an island that could never meet its own needs. While on a trip to England in 1753, Shirley pushed his vision on the British government. British Secretary of State Sir Thomas Robinson showed he had bought into that vision when he wrote to Shirley in Boston in July 1754 instructing him "forthwith to concert Measures for attacking the French Forts in Nova Scotia" in conjunction with Acting Governor Charles Lawrence in Halifax.[14]

Two battalions, one under the command of John Winslow and the other under George Scott, were raised in Boston. Under Monckton's overall command, the force was sent to Nova Scotia. As it turned out, the New Englanders, buttressed by 250 British soldiers, proved to be a fully adequate force to take on the small French complement at Fort Beauséjour. On June 16, 1755, after a siege of only a few days, the fort fell into Monckton's hands.

The fall of Fort Beauséjour dramatically shifted the strategic advantage in favour of the British, and in the bargain it also sealed the fate of the Acadians throughout Nova Scotia. Lawrence immediately recognized the strong hand he now held and he did not hesitate to play it. On July 18, 1755, in a letter to the Board of Trade, Lawrence set out his line of thought:

> As the French Inhabitants of the Province have never yet, at any time, taken the oath of allegiance to His Majesty, unqualified, I thought it my duty to avail myself of the present occasion, to propose it to them; and, as the deputies of the different districts in Mines Basin, were attending in Town upon a very insolent Memorial, they had delivered to the Council, I was determined to begin with them. They were accordingly summoned to appear before the Council, and, after discussing the affair of the Memorial, article by article, the oath was proposed to them; they endeavoured, as much as possible to evade it, and at last desired to return home and consult the rest of the Inhabitants, that they might either accept or refuse the Oath in a body; but they were informed that we expected every man upon this occasion to answer for himself, and as we would not use any compulsion or surprise, we gave them twenty four hours time to deliver in their answer; and, if they should then refuse, they must expect to be driven out of the country. . . . The next morning, they appeared and refused to take the oath without the old reserve of not being obliged to bear arms, upon which, they were acquainted, that as they refused to become English subjects, we could no longer look upon them in that light; that we should send them to France by the first opportunity, and till then, they were ordered to be kept prisoners at George's Island, where they were immediately conducted. They have since earnestly desired to be admitted to take the oath, but have not been admitted, nor will any answer be given to them until we see how the rest of the Inhabitants are disposed.
>
> I have ordered new Deputies to be elected, and sent hither immediately, and am determined to bring the Inhabitants to a compliance, or rid the province of such perfidious subjects. Your Lordships will see

our proceedings in this case at large, as soon as it is possible to prepare the minutes of Council.[15]

A week later, on July 25, 1755, the provincial council met again at the governor's house in Halifax. In his summary of the meeting, Governor Lawrence first reported the contents of a memorial received from the French inhabitants of Annapolis River. The memorial, which was signed by 207 of the inhabitants, stated:

> We have unanimously consented to deliver up our fire arms to Mr. Handfield, our very worthy commander, although we have never had any desire to make use of them against His Majesty's government. We have therefore nothing to reproach ourselves with, either on that subject, or on the subject of the fidelity that we owe to His Majesty's government. For, Sir, we can assure your Excellency, that several of us have risked our lives to give information to the government concerning the enemy; and have also, when necessary, laboured with all our heart, on the repairs of Fort Annapolis, and on other work considered necessary by the government, and are ready to continue with the same fidelity. We have also selected thirty men to proceed to Halifax, whom we shall recommend to do or say nothing contrary to His Majesty's Council; but we shall charge them strictly to contract no new oath. We are resolved to adhere to that which we have taken, and to which we have been faithful as far as circumstances required it; for the enemies of His Majesty have urged us to take up arms against the government, but we have taken care not to do so.[16]

In the dire circumstances they faced, the Acadians took their stand on loyalty and precedent, hoping that these would sustain them as they had in past crises. What they failed to understand was how the strategic situation had turned so markedly against them.

Lawrence had set the trap and proceeded to spring it, as his report shows:

They declared that they appeared in behalf of themselves, and all the other Inhabitants of Annapolis River, That they could not take any other Oath than what they had formerly taken, which was with a Reserve that they should not be obliged to Take up Arms, and that if it was the King's Intentions to force them to quit their lands, they hoped that they should be allowed convenient Time for their Departure.

The Council then asked them several Questions concerning the allegiance they so much boasted of in their Memorial, and the Intelligence which they say they have given the Government, of which they were desired to mention a single Instance whereby any Advantage had accrued to the Government, but this they were unable to do, on the contrary it was made very evident to them that they have always omitted to give timely Intelligence when they had it in their Power, and might have saved the Lives of many of His Majesty's Subjects, but that they had always secretly aided the Indians, and many of them had even appeared openly in Arms against His Majesty. They were then told that they must now resolve either to take the Oath without any Reserve or else to quit their Lands, for that affairs were now at such a Crisis in America that no delay could be admitted. . . . Upon which they said that they were determined One and All, rather to quit their Lands than to Take any other Oath than what they had done before.[17]

These meetings between the representatives of the Acadians, the provincial council of Nova Scotia and Governor Lawrence set the stage for the deportation, which was to begin within a few days. Governor Lawrence had removed the middle ground on which the Acadians had been able to stand in the past. As far as he was concerned, they could no longer be the "neutral French." The choice was a stark one: the Acadians could either back down completely and go over to the full position demanded by Lawrence or they would lose their lands and face expulsion. To finish the matter, Lawrence also added the clincher that should the Acadians fail to take the oath on this occasion they would never be permitted to do so again in the future. Lawrence's insistence that a forced oath would never do was the deft touch he needed to remove any ground on which the Acadians could stand.

On July 28, 1755, Governor Lawrence called a meeting of his council, including, on that day, Admiral Boscawen and Chief Justice Belcher. Waiting in abeyance outside the meeting were the deputies of the Acadian communities in Pisiquid, Minas and the River Canard. They had presented memorials stating that their inhabitants would take no other oath but the one that had been taken in 1729, which allowed them to retain their neutral status in the event of a new conflict between Britain and France. Having been called into the meeting, the deputies again refused to take the oath as demanded, and they were then placed in confinement. Governor Lawrence's report on the rest of the meeting stated:

> As it had been before determined to send all the French Inhabitants out of the Province if they refused to Take the Oaths, nothing now remained to be considered but what measures should be taken to send them away, and where they should be sent to.
>
> After mature Consideration, it was unanimously Agreed That, to Prevent as much as possible their Attempting to return and molest the Settlers that may be sent down on their Lands, it would be most proper to send them to be distributed amongst the several Colonies on the Continent, and that a sufficient Number of Vessels should be hired with all possible Expedition for that purpose.[18]

The conclusions reached at this decisive session of the council went beyond the plan to expel the Acadians and seize their lands. Also crucial were the decisions to rely on hired vessels to carry out the deportation and to send those deported to Britain's American colonies to prevent them from making a concerted effort to return and to challenge the newcomers who would replace them on their lands. There was nothing hot-blooded or last-minute about the decisions taken. These were carefully thought out plans that were sprung on the Acadians after the trap concerning the oath had been set.

The deportation, the evidence shows, was an operation launched by British commanders in North America. Governor Charles Lawrence played the critical role, conceiving the idea of the deportation when Monckton's successful assault on Fort Beauséjour placed a sudden strategic advantage in his hands. He sprang the trap, a trap he had long considered using when the time was right, by summoning the deputies of the Acadians and insisting that they take the oath of allegiance to the king. He knew they would refuse the oath without the reciprocal guarantee that they would not be expected to participate in a future war against France. That had been the consistent position of the Acadians since they had been offered that compromise in 1729. On that basis, they had constructed their fragile raison d'être. The Acadian position rested on a tragic sense of realism. They were well aware that they were located in an area of strategic struggle between the British and French empires. They didn't know when hostilities would resume and they didn't know which side would ultimately win. For them, the protection of their identity as the "neutral French" seemed the only conceivable course for self-protection.

Three days later, Governor Lawrence put the plan into effect in an order he sent to Colonel Monckton, who was in place at the crucial Isthmus of Chignecto in the aftermath of the fall of Fort Beauséjour. In his missive, he informed Monckton of the decision to expel the Acadians and issued instructions:

> . . . [A]s to those about the Isthmus who were in arms and therefore entitled to no favour from the government it is determined to begin with them first; and for this purpose orders are given for a sufficient number of Transports to be sent up the Bay with all possible dispatch for taking them on board, by whom you will receive particular instructions as to the manner of their being disposed of, the places of their destination . . .[19]

And then a deadly instruction to the Colonel:

In the mean time, it will be necessary to keep this measure as secret as possible, as well as to prevent their attempting to escape, as to carry off their cattle etc; and the better to effect this you will endeavour to fall upon some stratagem to get the men, both young and old (especially the heads of families) into your power and detain them till the transports shall arrive, so as that they may be ready to be shipped off; for when this is done it is not much to be feared that the women and children will attempt to go away and carry off the cattle.

To ensure that the women and children would be unable to flee and take their livestock with them, the governor instructed Monckton to secure "all their Shallops, Boats, Canoes and every other vessel you can lay your hands upon" and also to send out troops to the roads to intercept them. Since, under the expulsion order, the council had decided to expropriate all the land, homes and livestock of the Acadians, leaving them with only the "ready money" they had with them and their household furniture, the colonel was warned in the missive not to allow any sale of livestock by the condemned Acadians. The reason, Lawrence stated, was that their whole "stock of Cattle and Corn is forfeited to the Crown by their rebellion, and must be secured & apply'd towards a reimbursement of the expense the government will be at in transporting them out of the Country."

Lawrence informed Monckton that British officers commanding forts in Nova Scotia were also receiving similar orders to expel other Acadian communities. To assist in reducing these other communities, the colonel received an additional instruction. Fearing that the other Acadian communities might be successful in shipping their cattle to Île St. Jean (Prince Edward Island) and to Louisbourg by way of Tatmagouche (also spelled Tatamagouche), the governor ordered the colonel to send a detachment to Tatmagouche "to demolish all the Houses etc they find there, together with all the Shallops, Boats, Canoes or Vessels of any kind which may be lying ready for carrying off the inhabitants & their Cattle." As for the Acadians, during their coming deportation, they were to be provided with one pound of flour and half a pound of bread per day and a pound of beef per week for each person.[20]

The detailed plan for the expulsion, set down in the papers of British officials, in particular those of Governor Lawrence, is no less than an anatomy of British-style ethnic cleansing in the eighteenth century. All the mundane details are preserved. The expelled community was to lose everything it had worked to achieve over the previous century and more, and the deportees were, as much as possible, to pay for their own deportation. The record is dismal testimony to the proclivity of those who commit crimes against humanity to spell out their schemes in documents, noteworthy for their prosaic attention to detail and for their lack of any shred of human feeling.

As a prelude to the beginning of the mass deportation of the Acadians, Lawrence ordered that the parish priests at Minas and Annapolis Royal be arrested. Rounded up by British troops in the first week of August 1755, the priests were taken to Halifax. They were marched into the provincial capital in the company of a large detachment of troops. A crowd assembled at the sound of beating drums to witness and shout abuse at the captive clerics.[21]

The actual expulsion of the Acadians began under the direction of Colonel Monckton on August 11, 1755, at Fort Beauséjour, which had been renamed Fort Cumberland. Male inhabitants in the area were herded into the fort and confined there pending the arrival of ships to take them to the British colonies to the south. Having been ordered to assemble with no idea that they were to be confined, the prisoners had not brought food, blankets or additional clothing. They were locked inside dank quarters, where they slept on boards and were preyed on by vermin. Monckton, who had been meticulous in locking them up and preparing for their deportation, did nothing to take care of them. Not long after the Acadian men were confined, Monckton moved a number of them to nearby Fort Lawrence, which alleviated their misery somewhat. Having locked up the men, Monckton announced that they would be held until the ships arrived and then they would be deported. If the women and children did not report to join them on the ships, they would simply be left behind.[22] Following the removal of the deportees, their homes and settlement were put to the torch.

A month after the expulsions from the Isthmus of Chignecto, the deportation drama shifted to Grand Pré, the largest of all the Acadian settlements and the one best known to later generations, not only of Acadians, but of people around the world. The Grand Pré expulsion is best remembered not only because about 2,200 people were removed from the area between October and December 1755, but also because of the spotlight shone on this scene of deportation in Henry Wadsworth Longfellow's epic 1847 poem *Evangeline, Tale of Acadie.* A crucial source for Longfellow, who never visited Grand Pré, was the journal of Lieutenant Colonel John Winslow, the commander of the New England regiment stationed there, the man who oversaw the detention and expulsion of the Acadians and the destruction of their homes.

Winslow, a native of New England, was the great-grandson of Edward Winslow, one of the original settlers in Plymouth, Massachusetts. Before being selected by Governor William Shirley to serve in Nova Scotia in 1755, Winslow had been a captain of a Provincials regiment in a failed military expedition to Cuba in 1740, and later he became an officer in the British army and a major general of militia. Winslow commanded one of the two battalions that had been raised in New England for service in Nova Scotia. Shirley, who remained in Massachusetts, was colonel in chief of the force.

Lawrence's instructions to Winslow, sent from Halifax on August 11, spelled out one of his basic goals: "That the inhabitants may not have it in their power to return to this Province, nor to join in strengthening the French of Canada or Louisbourg: it is resolved that they shall be dispers'd among his Majesty's Colonies upon the Continent of America."

Lawrence informed Winslow that transports were being sent up the bay to Chignecto, where Monckton would load his detainees on board. From there, transports with additional space would head for the Basin of Mines, where the Grand Pré communities were located, to haul away some of the detainees. In addition, other vessels from Boston, with a capacity to hold one thousand people, were to sail directly to Grand Pré. Once the ships were loaded with their human cargo, they were to sail south, with five hundred detainees going to North Carolina, one thousand to Virginia and five hundred (or more, depending on the total) to Maryland. Lawrence warned the colonel that great care was to be taken to ensure that the Acadians did not secrete any weapons on their persons that they could use to try to wrest control of the vessels. To the same end, Lawrence included an instruction that during the voyages only a small number of Acadians be allowed "to be on the decks at a time." And the governor was stern in telling Winslow how he was to ensure that the Acadians were all rounded up and herded onto the ships. "If you find that fair means will not do with them," he wrote, "you must proceed by the most vigorous measures possible not only in compelling them to embark but in depriving those who shall escape of all means of shelter or support by burning their houses, and by destroying every thing that may afford them the means of subsistence in the Country."[23]

Lieutenant Colonel Winslow carried out the governor's instructions to the letter, but he was distressed by what was being done. He showed himself to be that poignant historical figure, the man who follows orders but can see their moral offensiveness. Such a man does not rise to the level of a hero who draws the line and says no.

Winslow ordered all the male inhabitants of Grand Pré aged eleven and older to assemble in the church, Saint Charles des Mines, at 3:00 p.m. on September 5. The colonel began his address to the residents, whose families lived in homes they had built, working lands they had won from the tides, for a century and more, informing them of the details of what he ominously called His Majesty's "final resolution to the French inhabitants" of Nova Scotia. "For almost half a century," he told them, His Majesty had granted them "more indulgence" than had been shown to "any of his subjects in any part of his Dominions."

Acknowledging briefly the enormity of what was happening, Winslow told his audience that "the part of duty I am now upon is what though necessary is very disagreeable to my natural make and temper as I know it must be to you who are of the same specia.... But it is not my business to annimedvert [animadvert]," he declared, and he proceeded to explain to what must have been a hushed and stunned assembly that all the French inhabitants of the area were to be removed, being allowed to take with them only their money and the household goods they could carry. He assured his listeners that he would do all he could to ensure that the goods they were taking would be secured by the deportees. "Whole families shall go in the same vessel," he promised. Acknowledging that "this remove . . . must give you a great deal of trouble," he expressed the hope "that in what every part of the world you may fall you may be faithful subjects, a peaceable and happy people." He concluded by informing the men present that from that moment they were to be held in custody by his troops.[24]

Having shown a modicum of compassion in his address to the men of Grand Pré, Winslow demonstrated a capacity for ruthless efficiency in the events that were to follow. For the five weeks following the meeting in the church, the Acadian men were kept under guard by Winslow's troops. During the day they were allowed outside in the fenced churchyard and at night they slept in the crowded confines of the church. Winslow had to deal with the problem of how to feed the prisoners, and the rest of the community, including his own soldiers, at a time when the wheat remained unharvested in the fields. The prisoners offered to go out and bring in the crop themselves, suggesting that they could leave twenty hostages behind to ensure their co-operative behaviour. Winslow turned down the offer and decided to let the women and the children, aged nine and under, do the work, pressuring them to do it by declaring that he had no intention of feeding the men being held under guard. If the men were to eat, the women and children would have to harvest the wheat to feed them. Winslow did decide that it was unrealistic to rely on the women and children to run the flour mill and allowed a few men to be allowed out, in shifts, to operate it.

With the men confined, some of Winslow's troops unleashed their fury against the women and children, pouring out their loathing for Catholics and Catholicism. Forcing women and children from their homes, the troops ransacked their personal belongings. They shouted anti-Catholic epithets at the terrified people, threatening them with death if they did not swear to abandon their religion and adopt the faith of the soldiers. Many decades after the event, a girl who had been nine at the time recalled the horrific scene: " . . . they made us line up while they loaded their guns with grapeshot. We were on our knees, our faces prostrate against the ground, offering our lives to God while waiting for the firing of the guns. I was only nine years old, and I too was prostrate beside my family. But suddenly the English changed their minds; they took all our goods and effects and left us nothing to cover ourselves."[25]

On the morning of September 10, Winslow, who had been concerned that he had only 300 soldiers to guard the 400 prisoners (an ample number, one would have thought), required the men to line up according to their ages, with the youngest among them all on one side. He then ordered 141 of the youngest to board a ship that would remain for a time in the harbour. In his diary, Winslow described the scene that followed:

[I] order[ed] the Prisoners to March. They all answered they would No go without their Fathers. I Told them that was a word I did not understand for that the Kings Command was be me absolute & should be absolutely obeyed & That I Did not Love to use Harsh Means but that the time Did not admit of Parlies or Delays and Then ordered the whole Troops to Fix their Bayonets and Advance Towards the French, and bid the 4 right hand Files of the Prisoners Consisting of the 24 men wch I told of my Self to Divied from the rest, one of whome I Took hold on (who opposed the Marching) and bid March. He obeyed & the rest followed. Thoh Slowly, and went off praying, singing and crying, being met by the women and children all the way.[26]

Conditions on board the deportation ships were atrocious. The vessels provided for the British at Grand Pré, rented from Boston, had been refitted along the lines of vessels used in the slave trade. The holds were divided into two or three levels, each level just over a metre high. No light, ventilation or sanitation was provided and food and water were meagre. Only a small number of the deportees were allowed on deck at a time to get some fresh air. The rest of the time the families were kept below deck in the foul holds.[27] On the *Endeavor*, one of the transport ships, which left the Minas Basin with 166 Acadians on board, only 125 survived the voyage to Boston. The *Ranger*, which departed with 263 deportees, reached Boston with only 205 still alive. The toll on the other four transports was less severe. At least these vessels arrived. Two of the vessels from the Isthmus of Chignecto, the *Boscawen* and the *Union*, with 582 Acadians on board, went down and all were lost.[28]

On August 11, 1755, the same day he wrote to Colonel Winslow, Governor Lawrence sent instructions to Major John Handfield, the commander of the British garrison at Annapolis Royal. Handfield had long served in Nova Scotia, having been appointed to the Governors Council in 1736. Rehearsing the decision he had conveyed to Monckton and Winslow that the government was sending away "the French inhabitants, and clearing the whole country of such bad subjects," the Governor informed the major that transports were being sent from Boston to Annapolis with a capacity to ship one thousand people. Since Annapolis was to be the last point from which the deportees were to be shipped, vessels with excess capacity from Chignecto and the Minas Basin were to call in there to take on board any Acadians still to be removed. Colonel Winslow, in the aftermath of the deportation of the Acadians from Grand Pré, following the torching and laying waste of the communities there, was to proceed on land with his troops to Annapolis Royal. En route, he was to round up any stragglers he encountered.

Lawrence instructed Handfield that from Annapolis the detainees were to be sent in the following numbers to the following destinations: three hundred people to Philadelphia; two hundred to

New York; three hundred to Connecticut; and two hundred (or more, if necessary) to Boston. The governor reiterated the baleful orders he had sent to Winslow regarding security, the need to use whatever means were necessary to round up the Acadians, to control them carefully on board the ships and then to lay waste their farms and put their houses to the torch.[29]

On August 11, the same day that he wrote the British commanders in Chignecto, the Basin of Minas and Annapolis Royal, Governor Lawrence addressed a circular letter to the British governors on the continent. He set out the case for the expulsion and asked for the co-operation of the colonies in receiving and making arrangements for the Acadians he was sending to their jurisdictions. Governor Lawrence's case for the expulsion rested on a litany of charges that, in his view, demonstrated what he called the "bad behaviour" of the Acadians. He reviewed the history of the British relationship with the Acadians since the colony passed into British hands. The Acadians "were permitted to remain in quiet possession of their lands upon condition they should take the Oath of Allegiance to the King within one year after the Treaty of Utrecht," he wrote. "With this condition," he continued, "they have ever refused to comply, without having at the same time from the Governor an assurance in writing that they should not be called upon to bear arms in the defence of the province."

Lawrence raised the thorny question of the oath that was, in fact, taken by the Acadians in 1729 when Richard Philipps was Governor of Nova Scotia. Acknowledging that Governor Philipps "did comply" with the Acadian request for the right not to fight in a future war, Lawrence dismissed the 1729 understanding, saying that it was a step of which "his Majesty disapproved and the inhabitants pretending therefrom to be in a state of Neutrality between his Majesty and his enemies have continually furnished the French & Indians with Intelligence, quarters, provisions and assistance in annoying the Government." He accused some of the Acadians of having "abetted the French Encroachments by their treachery," and others, he said, were guilty of "open Rebellion," and that "three hundred of them were actually found in arms in the French Fort at Beauséjour when it surrendered."

Despite this record of treachery, Lawrence wrote, "his Majesty was pleased to allow me to extend still further his Royal grace to such as would return to their Duty." He offered, he said, "such of them as had not been openly in arms against us" to retain their lands if they would take the oath of allegiance, "unqualified with any Reservation whatsoever." Their "audacious" and unanimous failure to do this had led him to conclude that "the inhabitants have forfeited all title to their lands and any further favour from the Government."

Having made his case for the obloquy of the Acadians, Lawrence wrote that since they numbered about seven thousand people, simply to drive them off to allow them to go where they pleased was not a viable option. Their removal in such a fashion would have "doubtless strengthened Canada." Not desiring this, he continued, "it was judged a necessary and the only practicable measure to divide them among the Colonies where they may be of some use, as most of them are healthy strong people."[30]

Lawrence's justification for the expulsion of the Acadians raised the difficult question of collective punishment. How could the large majority of Acadians who had played no active role in opposing the British regime be deemed guilty for the actions of the small number who had? Under British law, collective punishment was only sanctioned in cases of exceptional emergency.

The main Acadian deportations, commencing in 1755, dispatched the refugees from the communities along the Bay of Fundy to the Thirteen Colonies. There, the reception of these fellow British subjects by the local colonial regimes was hostile, even harsh. A number of colonial regimes sought to rid themselves of the unwanted French Catholics at the earliest opportunity. In some cases, Acadians who were inspired with the hope of returning to their original homeland were permitted to leave for neighbouring colonies by authorities who did not want to contribute to their upkeep.

At least two thousand people died during the ordeal of expulsion. The Acadian Diaspora was to scatter communities that endured to Canada, France, England and to many places in the Thirteen Colonies. Other colonial regimes deported the refugees as soon as they could to England or to France. Once the refugees reached England, many adult male Acadians were imprisoned, with some being kept in warehouses, in deplorable conditions, where large numbers succumbed to the plagues that frequently ravaged the deportees. In other cases, Acadian groups were allowed to live and gain a livelihood in an English town. Those who made it to France were only a little better off. There, the Acadians were forced into wretched peasant labour. Many of them were housed in barracks in seaports such as St. Malo, where outbreaks of smallpox took their toll. In the land from which their ancestors hailed, they remained a people apart. Their frontier and egalitarian ways did not fit in France in the last days of the old regime prior to the French Revolution.

The Acadians longed to leave France, and many did when they got the chance to migrate to French colonial locations in the Caribbean. Some relocated to the French island of Corsica. When, in 1785, the government of Spain hired vessels to transport the Acadians from Nantes to Louisiana, which had become a Spanish colony, many refugees decided to make that leap. The Acadians preferred anywhere in the Americas, as long as the English were not in charge, to Europe. Some families were divided, never to be reunited. Many journeyed directly to Louisiana from France. Others, who had remained in America, made their way along the coast of the Atlantic and around the Florida peninsula to this new Promised Land. And still others came there by way of Saint-Domingue, the present-day Haiti.

For many of the deportees, the ordeal of the expulsion went on for decades before they were finally able to find a place where they could sink new roots. Typical for many was the experience of one little boy, Pierre Vincent, whose family was expelled from Grand Pré in the autumn of 1755. Pierre was only seven when British officers commanded all the males ten years of age and older to gather in the church, where they learned of their impending deportation and the loss of their homes and land.

Along with his parents and his sister, Pierre was herded onto a ship that sailed for Virginia. But the British authorities there refused to allow the deportees into the colony. Smallpox ravaged the ships on which the Acadians were held and hundreds died. From Virginia, Pierre's ship sailed across the Atlantic to the English port of Southampton, where his father died in prison before the surviving members of the family were allowed to depart for France.

Pierre's family was dispatched to Belle-Île-en-Mer, a rocky island off the coast of Brittany, where they tried to scratch a living growing food in the stony soil. It was a barren, windswept place, where it was difficult to eke out even a meagre existence. The Vincent family found France a completely foreign land. Finally, in 1785, thirty years after he had been driven out of his home in Grand Pré, Pierre was one of 1,500 Acadians to set sail for Louisiana. His decades-long journey was only completed—after two marriages to women who died soon after—when he reached Calcasieu Parish in Louisiana. There he married a woman from Georgia named Sally Ryan. Together they reared their ten children on a homesite that is still known as the Vincent settlement.

That the decision made by Governor Lawrence, along with the members of Nova Scotia's Governor's Council, to deport the Acadians and lay waste their communities was not the choice favoured at the time by the British government in London was made clear in a missive from Secretary of State Sir Thomas Robinson to Lawrence from Whitehall, dated August 13, 1755. By that date, of course, although London was unaware of it, Lawrence was already setting in motion his plan to expel the Acadians. The gist of Robinson's message was that Lawrence ought not to proceed with precipitate action, that he ought to cool it: "It cannot therefore, be too much recommended to you, to use the greatest Caution and Prudence in your conduct towards these Neutrals [the Acadians], and to assure such of them, as may be trusted, especially upon their taking the Oaths to His Majesty, and His Government, That they may remain in the quiet Possession of Their Settlements, under proper Regulations."

Robinson informed Lawrence that the French ambassador had proposed to the British, in May 1755, that the French inhabitants should have three years to make good their departure from Nova Scotia with all their belongings. To the French proposal, the British government's reply had been as follows, Lawrence was informed: "In Regard to the Three Years Transmigration proposed for the French Inhabitants of the Peninsula, it would be depriving Great Britain of a very considerable Number of useful Subjects, if such Transmigration should extend to the French, who were Inhabitants there at the time of the Treaty of Utrecht, and to their descendants."[31]

The letter made it clear that the British government regarded the Acadian inhabitants of the province, for the most part, as useful subjects who ought to be kept in place in possession of their lands. The tone and substance of the message was very much at odds with the expressed views of Charles Lawrence on the subject of the Acadians. What the letter shows is that at the time of the triggering of the plan to expel the Acadians, Lawrence and his Governor's Council were acting on their own without the backing of Whitehall. The letter from Whitehall continued the interminable debate that had gone on since 1713 about what the ultimate fate of the Acadians ought to be. There had been those who had hoped to assimilate the Acadians by planting English and Protestant communities in the colony, with whom it was hoped that the Acadians would intermarry. There had been others, such as Lawrence, who believed that as long as the Acadians remained in Nova Scotia the colony would never settle down and English settlement there would be deterred. By the time the letter arrived from London, however, the time for debate in British circles had passed. The fateful decision to deport the Acadians had been taken.

It was not at all surprising, under the circumstances, that Whitehall and the British authorities in the colonies should have a very different view of things in the summer of 1755. While the European situation was extremely tense, peace still existed between Britain and France. It would be another year before the Seven Years'

War would break out. Meanwhile, in North America, conflict was already blazing.

If Lawrence was the point man in making the decisions in the summer of 1755, he could not have acted without the assistance and solid backing of Governor Shirley in Boston. The Massachusetts governor had long harboured the hope that Nova Scotia and the Bay of Fundy would become a reliable satellite region in his colony's commercial empire. Without New England muscle, the deportation would have been inconceivable, and Charles Lawrence was well aware of that. Most of the troops used to carry out the deportation were New England troops, and the ships used for the expulsion were hired from firms based in New England.

Shirley had attended a crucial meeting of governors of British colonies in mid April 1755 that was held at Alexandria, Virginia. Along with Shirley, the governors of Virginia, North Carolina, Maryland and New York had also been present. The figure around whom the council at Alexandria was organized was Major General Edward Braddock, the commander-in-chief of British forces in North America. Braddock had just arrived from England and was to have at his disposal two regiments of British troops, which were being sent over to add muscle to the British position vis à vis the French in North America. Despite the fact that Britain and France were nominally at peace, the British government and British colonial authorities feared a French military buildup on the continent. The intention of those at the council was to plan military assaults on strategic French positions.

Braddock did not have a positive view of the colonies and their troops. The English novelist and historian Tobias Smollett described him as "a man of courage, and expert in all the punctilios of a review, having been brought up in the English guards . . . naturally very haughty, positive and difficult of access, qualities ill-suited to the temper of the people amongst whom he was to command."[32] Braddock was the one who had handed out the military assignments at Alexandria. He had picked for himself the task of commanding the assault on the French at Fort Duquesne (Pittsburgh). Shirley was to lead a force against Fort Niagara, Colonel William Johnson was to attack the French at Crown Point, and Colonel Monckton was to lay siege to Fort Beauséjour.

For the most part, the attacks against the French had met with failure. Braddock set out with his force, deciding to take the direct route from Virginia to Fort Duquesne, refusing to take into account that this was difficult, mountainous terrain and that there were easier ways to get to his goal. While the British general's force slogged through the wilderness, the French at Fort Duquesne were preparing to meet him. They had carefully considered their ground and their fortifications, and had received arms from Canada with which to reinforce their native allies. When the British and French forces came upon each other not far from the French fort in an unexpected encounter for both sides, what began as a skirmish ended as a rout for the British. In a battle fought in ways entirely different from the classic affairs of Europe with which he was at home, Braddock lost his army and his life. Not only did the French capture Braddock's guns, they also came into possession of the late general's chest, which contained the British plans for its military assault on Fort Niagara.[33]

Attired in his new major general's uniform, Shirley proceeded to Albany where his troops were based. From there, he led his force toward Chouaguen on the south-eastern shore of Lake Ontario. En route he learned of Braddock's defeat and of his own son's death in the battle near Fort Duquesne. The loss of Braddock made Shirley the commander-in-chief of British forces in North America. Assessing the implications of the Fort Duquesne disaster, Shirley was inclined to go over to the defensive. He feared a French attack on Chouaguen from Fort Frontenac on the north side of Lake Ontario. Should he halt his attack on Fort Niagara to fortify his present position? In the event, Shirley remained at Chouaguen, short of provisions and with his troops losing their morale. To frequent desertions from his force Shirley responded by holding courts martial and ordering executions.

In late September, he followed the advice of his commanders and decided that the attack on Fort Niagara would have to be put off until the following spring.[34] Leaving his troops in winter quarters on the shore of Lake Ontario, Shirley headed back to Albany. From there he wrote to London, advocating an attack on Fort Frontenac the following spring. While Shirley was leading his troops on their failed expedition, the expulsion of the Acadians had been triggered by Lawrence and was being executed.

While William Johnson succeeded in driving back the French at Lake George, his attack on Crown Point did not result in any strategic advantage for the English. The one signal success in the co-ordinated series of attacks planned by Braddock came with the capture of Fort Beauséjour by the force of two thousand New Englanders commanded by Monckton.

Despite his key role in the deportation of the Acadians, Shirley was held responsible for the failure of his own attack on Fort Niagara. In 1756, he lost his position as governor of Massachusetts and was recalled to England. An inquiry into his role in British military defeats ended with Shirley's exoneration. In 1761, he was appointed governor of the Bahamas, a position he held until 1769 when his son took over the job. Shirley returned to Massachusetts, where he built a mansion for himself in Roxbury. He died there in 1771.

While Shirley was under a cloud for a time as a consequence of his failure at Fort Niagara, both Lawrence and Monckton were rewarded for their actions before the end of 1755. Lawrence was appointed governor of Nova Scotia, a promotion from his former position as acting governor. Monckton, who had not yet celebrated his thirtieth birthday, became lieutenant-governor.

In June 1756, the year following the start of the deportation, the war that had already begun in North America got officially underway in Europe. The Seven Years' War was to be yet another in the titanic struggles for supremacy between the British and French empires, a series of struggles that would not cease until the Battle of Waterloo in 1815.

In 1758, while Lawrence was sent as one of the commanders on the mission that would win him glory, the siege and capture of Louisbourg, Monckton remained on guard in Nova Scotia. And just as the fall of Fort Beauséjour had opened the door to the expulsion of the Acadians, the fall of Louisbourg made possible further expeditions to put the torch to the outlying Acadian communities that still remained. James Wolfe, soon to be immortalized for his victory over Montcalm on the Plains of Abraham, was sent up the coast of the Northumberland Strait to Gaspé, for the purpose of rousting out and destroying whatever French homesteads and communities he came upon. For his part, Monckton was sent on an equally unsavoury expedition. In command of 2,300 troops, he travelled seventy miles up the St. John River destroying the homes, livestock and crops of the Acadians who had settled there. The scorched earth policy that had been initiated three years earlier with the expulsion of the Acadians to diverse locations and with the torching of their homes and the flooding of their land was continued remorselessly three years further on. The goal was simple: there was to be nothing for the Acadians to return to should they ever be in a position to try.

The following winter, Monckton moved on to the next great military task. He was in New York working on the plans for the assault on Quebec. Along with Murray and Townshend, Monckton served as one of Wolfe's brigadiers in the attack. In the siege of Quebec in the summer of 1759, Monckton led one failed attempt to deposit troops on the Beauport shore next to the city on July 31. Six weeks later, he commanded the expedition that made the night landing at Anse au Foulon. The next day, in the Battle on the Plains of Abraham, Monckton commanded the British troops on the right flank. During the battle in which both Wolfe and Montcalm received fatal wounds, Monckton was also wounded, taking a shot that pierced his lungs. The wound was not serious, however, and Monckton took command of Quebec and the surrounding region shortly after the French surrender.

Monckton's role in the capture of Quebec opened the way for further advancement. In 1761, having been promoted to the rank of major general, he became governor of New York and commander-in-chief of the colony's military forces. In February 1762, he led the successful British assault on the French island of Martinique. The following year, Monckton left North America to return to England, where he had to answer charges made against him for alleged mistreatment of a dismissed officer. At his subsequent court martial, however, Monckton was exonerated.

In the relatively short span of eleven years, Monckton had played a prominent part in the British struggles against the French in North America. He was only thirty-seven years old when he returned to England, with twenty years of life ahead of him. In 1765, he was appointed governor of Berwick-upon-Tweed. In 1770, although no longer active as a military commander, he was still in the military and was named a lieutenant general. In his latter years, he sat in Parliament. Monckton died in 1782 and was buried in London, with full military honours.

Today, Robert Monckton's chief source of fame is that the city of Moncton was named after him. On the city's website, while the deportation of the Acadians is mentioned, Monckton's leading role in it is not. He is described merely as the British soldier "who led the capture of nearby Fort Beauséjour in 1755."[35] His fellow ethnic cleanser, Charles Lawrence, also had a Canadian town named after him: Lawrencetown, Nova Scotia. The town's website describes him as a governor of Nova Scotia and says nothing about the pivotal role he played in Acadie.

Lawrence, the man who triggered the deportation of the Acadians, did not long survive his deed. In 1758 he served as one of the three field brigadiers (the others were Whitmore and Wolfe) in the successful assault on the French fortress at Louisbourg. Returning to Halifax, where he once again administered the colony, Lawrence was much disappointed not to be included in Wolfe's operations against Quebec in 1759. Following a grand ball at Government House in Halifax in October 1760, Lawrence took ill and died.

The architect of the deportation, Lawrence had designed the operation so that the Acadians would be divided into small groups and dispersed throughout the British colonies along the Atlantic seaboard. That way, he calculated, as time passed the Acadians would lose their language and even the knowledge of their history. His goal was to extinguish the Acadian culture and identity through assimilation. Cleansed of their religion and their sense of themselves, these strong, healthy people, as Lawrence described them, would become useful and productive subjects of the Crown. Despite the scorched earth methods that were used, the deportation was a monumental failure. Over the long term, and continuing to this day, the determination of the Acadians to keep track of each other and of their families, throughout their Diaspora and in their central homeland in New Brunswick, has defied all possible expectations. From the very beginning, the deportation was the tragic fire from which the rebirth of the Acadians took flame.

—

CHAPTER 4

WHY WERE THE
ACADIANS DEPORTED?

AS WITH ALL GREAT HISTORICAL transformations, historians continue to argue about *le Grand Dérangement*. What caused the deportation of the Acadians? Who was responsible for it? These questions have long been asked and will not subside anytime soon. Even though the deportation of the Acadians occurred two and a half centuries ago, this is living history in the truest sense, still being played out, still being urgently assessed.

While the unearthing of documents heretofore unrevealed can continue to shed light on specific aspects of what happened, the bigger picture is clear enough. To explain what happened, both broad and immediate causes must be taken into account. The most general cause of the tragedy was the historic collision between the French and British empires in North America over the course of many decades. The whole life of Acadie up until the 1750s was caught in the vortex of the Anglo-French struggle. From the early seventeenth century until the deportation of the 1750s, both the French and the British pursued their claims in the region.

Immediate responsibility for the deportation rests with the triumvirate of British authorities in the region: Acting Governor Charles Lawrence of Nova Scotia; Governor William Shirley of Massachusetts; and Colonel Robert Monckton. In turn, they can be seen as the triggerman, the enabler and the enforcer. Lawrence had long displayed antagonism toward the Acadians. He believed that as long as the Acadians were present in Nova Scotia, their allies, the Mi'kmaq, would never be brought under control. And as a direct consequence, the colony could never attract the English Protestant settlers he wanted, in large numbers, to shape the character of Nova Scotia. The deportation was launched locally, without the knowledge of authorities in London, by Lawrence, who hatched the detailed scheme and sent out the instructions for it to be put into effect. But Lawrence was not acting in a vacuum.

It is not enough to say that the broadest cause of the deportation was the global struggle between the British and French empires. They were mercantilist empires, whose dominant interests were of a quite particular sort. The ultimate beneficiaries of mercantilist empires were the aristocrats and the wealthy who invested in monopoly enterprises that had the backing of the state. The idea—central to the capitalism of the nineteenth century and beyond—that countries could engage in mutually beneficial commerce with each other, the fruit of classical economics, had not yet been conceived. In the zero sum logic of the mercantilist era, it made sense that if one empire stood, the other must fall. That thinking was a powerful factor in determining the fate of the Acadians.

Within the logic of mercantilism, however, contradictions became apparent. Powerful new interests were emerging, and these had an impact on events in Acadie. By its very nature, a mercantilist empire was constructed to serve the interests of those at the centre. The colonies existed to supply staple products needed by the mother country. As a consequence, settler colonies posed a long-term threat to mercantilist logic. By the middle of the eighteenth century, the great British settler colonies on the eastern seaboard of America had evolved to the point at which that contradiction could no longer be ignored. New England had become a rising metropolitan power in its own right, whose own struggle for independence would flare into the open only two decades after the deportation of the Acadians.

New Englanders had their own interests at stake in the struggle over Acadie. Boston merchants had long coveted Acadian commerce. Indeed, they had perennially traded with the Acadians, both when Acadie was a French territory and later when it was a British territory. When the rules of mercantilism stood in the way of their trading relationship, Bostonians and Acadians regularly turned a blind eye and ignored the rules. From the seventeenth century, Acadie was a part of New England's rising commercial sphere. Long before 1755, William Shirley, the ambitious governor of Massachusetts, had expressed the view that the Acadians ought to be driven out. Then for a time he changed his mind and conjectured that, with British garrisons built close to their settlements and with Protestant settlers brought into Nova Scotia, the Acadians could be steered into becoming peaceful inhabitants of the region. Still later, as the crisis of the mid 1750s mounted, Shirley changed his mind again and became a crucial backer of the deportation. The Massachusetts governor had succumbed once again to the view that New England's commercial interests would benefit from the elimination of the Acadians.

If British authorities in the region, rather than the British government in London, launched the deportation of the Acadians, ultimate responsibility for the deed nevertheless rested with the British state. By the time the British government learned of Lawrence's plan to expel the Acadians and destroy their settlements, the scheme had already been put into effect. Would London have gone along with the deportation had it been consulted in advance? While that question can never be answered, what we do know is that London backed up the decisions that had been taken in Halifax. Lawrence and his cohorts were never disavowed or chastised for their actions. To the contrary, Lawrence was promoted to the position of governor of Nova Scotia by London, an implicit reward for his actions.

Beyond the British response to Lawrence's fait accompli, there is Britain's underlying responsibility for setting in train policies that marginalized the Acadians, placing them in an untenable position, so that a crisis was highly likely someday to lead to their expulsion. A dire long-term problem faced by the Acadians after 1713 was the absence of any conception of minority rights, or plurality, within the British Empire of the period. The Acadians had attempted to establish a "yes, but" allegiance to the British Crown, and that was not a status the British were prepared to recognize, at least not consistently, at the time.

France also played its part in the Acadian drama. In 1755, war between the British and the French was already flaring in North America, and soon the conflict would erupt in the decisive showdown of the Seven Years' War. France's involvement with Acadie, from the time of the first Acadian settlement and through the period of British sovereignty, was driven at the highest level by strategic concerns, as well as by commercial interests in the fur trade and the fishery. Rarely were the Acadians themselves in the forefront of the consciousness of the top authorities in Paris. After the loss of most of Acadie under the Treaty of Utrecht of 1713, the French chose Île Royale (Cape Breton Island) as the key to maintaining their position in the region. Louisbourg, whose fortification cost a great deal, was planned by Paris as the guardian both of the route to Canada and of the French fishery. In the end, Louisbourg turned out to be a gigantic failure as a fortress, captured twice by the British, in 1745 and again in 1758.

The Anglo-French struggle for control of Acadie had local features that set it apart from the broader global battle between the two imperial powers. One critical factor was the close alliance between the French and the native peoples of the region. Often the fighting between the British and French took the form of guerilla warfare. Raids against small frontier posts often resulted in killings, the taking of prisoners, the burning of buildings and other atrocities. While these ferocious episodes were triggered by both sides, frequently in revenge for earlier atrocities, the fear and loathing of New Englanders for the French—with distinctions between those in Canada and in Acadie regularly blurred—added fuel to the drive to expel the Acadians.

Religious enmity was also a factor in setting the stage for the deportation. Even though Acadie began as a venture in which both Catholics and Protestants were involved, New France, Acadie included, became, among other things, an expression of a reinvigorated Catholicism that was dedicated to seeking converts, notably among native peoples. And Puritan New England in the seventeenth and eighteenth centuries was deeply hostile to Catholicism and Catholics. The Acadians were always suspect in the eyes of New Englanders for that reason. Various personalities, among them the Abbé Le Loutre, played a crucial role in revving up the religious antagonism. Le Loutre was dedicated to preserving close ties between the Acadians and the Mi'kmaq. He was a militant on behalf of the French imperial cause who was determined to win the Acadians to France's side in the event of hostilities with the British. Le Loutre's machinations certainly fed the anti-Catholic phobia. The furtive Abbé was viewed with constant suspicion, much in the way Islamic clerics are viewed by some in the West today. He was arrested several times by the British but kept reinserting himself into the Acadian maelstrom.

In the eighteenth century, the wars of religion were not long in the past. The hatred between Catholics and Protestants that had played a role in early Acadie itself had also been important in stoking the antagonisms between Puritan New England and Catholic Acadie. From the time of the signing of the Treaty of Utrecht, the British goal in newly acquired Nova Scotia was to marginalize the Roman Catholic Acadians. The way to do this, the colonial rulers believed, was to entice more Protestant immigrants into the territory. They didn't care much what language the immigrants spoke— as was clear in the case of the Lunenburg Germans—as long as they were Protestants.

Religion mattered greatly in establishing the notion that the rights of opponents could be negated. For militantly Protestant New England, Catholic Acadie was not merely an obstacle in the way of economic expansion and a source of raids and strife—it was the base of the Antichrist. For the New England that had spawned the Salem witch trials, the France that had launched vicious oppression against the Protestants of France with the revocation of the Edict of Nantes was the embodiment of evil. For Charles Lawrence and William Shirley, contemplating the idea of expelling thousands of people and destroying their communities was more palatable because the people in question were Catholics. That fact allowed the decision-makers to marginalize the Acadians in their thinking, to conceive of them as a hostile mass, as members of a collective who had no individual rights. Contributing to the notion of the Acadians as the "other," as a people who could not make a claim to the same treatment as Englishmen or Protestants, was the relationship between the Acadians and the Mi'kmaq. The English rulers could never rid themselves of the idea that the Acadians and the French priests had a special hold on the Mi'kmaq, and that the relationship between the two would mean that the colony would be permanently threatened with chaos. And that led them back to the original proposition that without peace, orderly settlement could never occur.

What about the behaviour of the Acadians themselves? Were they loyal to the British Crown? While the depth of their loyalty can be questioned (and why should it have been more than perfunctory?) the effort of the Acadian leadership to pursue a correct path with respect to the British sovereign was reasonably consistent. The Acadians, however, were far from unswerving in the positions they adopted. Some co-operated with the British when that was convenient and then worked with the French when they were locally in the ascendancy. With their proclivity for seeing the Acadians as the "other" and holding them collectively responsible for the actions of the few, the British were inclined to see examples of Acadian aid for the French as evidence of the treachery of them all.

When all the possible causes of the expulsion of the Acadians are considered, what becomes apparent is that the event itself was triggered by what might be described as a "perfect storm." In that sense, the deportation was an event very much of its time. Only a few years later, little thought was given to the idea of expelling the French Canadians following the British Conquest of Canada. In part, this was a matter of sheer scale. While the deportation of the Acadian population of about thirteen thousand people was doable, the deportation of ninety thousand French Canadians would have been enormously more difficult. In the case of the French Canadians, the British soon concluded that they could concede some recognition, including the right to practise their faith, to a conquered people. Moreover, with the fall of New France, France had lost its strategic ability to challenge the British in North America.

With the Acadians, the British had struggled awkwardly with the idea of reaching an accommodation, but in the end they had turned to force. The expulsion of the Acadians was tragic not least because it was so unnecessary and within a relatively short period of time would have been unthinkable. It was one of those important historical events that was not inevitable in some large sense, and indeed was unusually subject to the decisions and whims of particular individuals.

On August 9, 1755, an anonymous correspondent wrote to Boston from Halifax, announcing the expulsion of the Acadians to New Englanders. In subsequent weeks, the letter was published in a large number of colonial newspapers:

> . . . We are now upon a great and noble Scheme of sending the neutral French out of this Province, who have always been secret Enemies, and have encouraged our Savages to cut our Throats. If we effect their Expulsion, it will be one of the greatest Things that ever the English did in America; for by all Accounts, that Part of the Country they possess, is as good Land as any in the World: In case therefore we could get some good English Farmers in their Room, this Province would abound with all Kinds of Provisions.[1]

It is hard to conceive of a more concise exposition of the case for ethnic cleansing than this.

To what extent was the deportation of the Acadians deliberately undertaken to deprive the Acadians of their lands? There is plenty of evidence that the English rulers, and the New Englanders as well, were all too aware of the achievement and the success of the Acadian settlements along the shores of the Bay of Fundy. The Acadians were uniquely successful in expanding the rich acreage they had won from the marshes and the sea. On the spiny, mountainous, largely inhospitable peninsula of Nova Scotia, they occupied the most desirable farmland. On this land, they had succeeded in creating a good life for themselves and their families. A sign of their prosperity, which was uppermost in the minds of the British authorities, was the rapid growth of the Acadian population and consequently of the area occupied by their settlements. Far from being marginalized in the colony, the Acadians were holding their own as a proportion of the population. Ironically, the most successful era enjoyed by the Acadians in Nova Scotia was the one that followed the Treaty of Utrecht. Their very success made them, in the eyes of the colonial rulers, a mounting threat to be dealt with when the opportunity presented itself.

Were there precedents for the expulsion of the Acadians? That the British were prepared to expel entire populations in the aftermath of a military victory was already abundantly clear following the capture of Louisbourg in 1745. With Île Royale and Île St. Jean in their hands, the British speedily deported the population of Île Royale, sending its people to France. In the case of Île St. Jean, the British agreed at the capitulation of Louisbourg in 1745, in exchange for the return of six hostages by the French, not to expel the inhabitants for one year. The Acadians on the island were fearful that deportation would not be long in coming. The British, likely because of the logistical problems involved, did not carry out the expulsion on that occasion.

Île St. Jean was to meet its own terrible fate in 1758, when Louisbourg once more fell into the hands of the British, this time for good. Following the deportation of the Acadians from mainland Nova Scotia in 1755, about two thousand of those who had escaped expulsion managed to reach Île St. Jean, which was still in French hands. Even before 1755, Acadians from the mainland had sought the island as a haven from which they hoped they would not be deported. In the last years of the colony, the people of the island were in dire straits. The population, swollen with the arrival of refugees, had increased to about 4,400 people, up from under 1,000 a decade earlier. There was not enough food to meet the needs of the population.

With Louisbourg secured, the British quickly dealt with the French on Île St. Jean, rounding them up for deportation to France. About three thousand people were expelled from the island by the British. Most of the rest managed to flee to the Baie des Chaleurs or Quebec, while a few remained hidden on the island. About seven hundred of those deported who had been crowded into two ships, the *Duke William* and the *Violet*, died when the ships went down in a storm. A large number of those on ships that made it to France also died in the miserable conditions endured in the transatlantic crossing. Those who did reach France had not come to the end of their wretched journey. Most opted in the following years to leave. A few actually made it back to Acadie, but the largest number found their way to Louisiana.[2]

While the deportation of the Acadians was still being actively pursued, the British captured Canada. Quebec fell in 1759 and Canada was ceded to Britain with the Treaty of Paris in 1763. Under that treaty, the British acknowledged the right of the people of Canada to retain their property and to practise their religion. With the Treaty of Paris, as well, the British brought the deportation of the Acadians to an end. In subsequent years, under carefully controlled arrangements, they allowed some Acadians to return to their former homeland, but not to reacquire the lands they had lost.

The next great upheaval in North America following the Treaty of Paris was the American Revolutionary War from 1776 to 1783. In that war, the British were the losers, and the colonials, who had participated in expelling the Acadians, were the winners. In 1783, the peace settlement between Britain and the newly established United States of America was followed by the departure, partly voluntary, partly forced, of tens of thousands of Loyalists from their homes, many to Britain and many to British North America.

From the moment the Acadians were taken from their homes and scattered, a fierce debate has waged about the meaning of the deed. Through all their struggles to come, from that day to this, the Acadians have never been free from that debate.

CHAPTER 5

ACADIAN RESISTANCE

IT IS DUE IN LARGE MEASURE to the epic poem *Evangeline, Tale of Acadie*, by Henry Wadsworth Longfellow, that the Acadians have been blessed—or cursed, depending on your point of view—with an enduring image as religious, long-suffering, passive people who endured *le Grand Dérangement* without offering much resistance. By and large, the ethnic cleansers who masterminded the deportation succeeded with their duplicitous strategy of disarming the Acadians and taking possession of their boats before moving to expel them. For this reason, it is true that the deportation proceeded in most places without much violent resistance. There were exceptions to this, however, and resistance to the deportation took a number of forms.

The deportation transformed some people, whose lives up to then had held little clue that they possessed such qualities, into heroic and determined leaders. One of the most remarkable of the lives transformed by the deportation was that of Jacques Maurice Vigneau, who was born in Port Royal in 1702.

The son of a fisherman, Jacques Vigneau grew up in the family home within view of the French fort at the heart of the community. As a child at the hub of French officialdom in Acadie, Jacques witnessed the comings and goings of French ships and military units. As a child, his playmates included not only Acadians but Mi'kmaq children as well. Not only was he educated to read and write—by no means a certainty in the Acadie of the period—he also learned to speak Mi'kmaq and English, in addition to his native French.

Jacques was eight years old when the English captured Port Royal in 1710. His father, Maurice, faced the same pressure as other men in the Acadian community to swear an unconditional oath of allegiance to the British monarch. At first he refused. But in 1717, the British military at Annapolis Royal threatened to block fishermen from putting out to sea if they failed to swear the oath. Faced with ruin if they could not fish, the senior Vigneau and a number of other fishermen backed down and swore an unconditional oath to King George. Having gained official permission to embark, Vigneau then boarded his family onto his fishing vessel and, under the guise of going fishing, set sail for Île Royale, which remained under the control of France. The family established a new home on the Gulf of St. Lawrence, not far from peninsular Nova Scotia.

In the 1720s, Jacques Maurice Vigneau left Île Royale to settle, marry and raise a family in Beaubassin, the thriving Acadian community at the head of the Bay of Fundy on the Isthmus of Chignecto. Vigneau became a successful merchant, acquiring a ship and transporting goods between Acadian villages in Nova Scotia and Île Royale.

When the British and the New Englanders seized the French fortress at Louisbourg in 1745 and deported the French inhabitants of Île Royale to France, the strategic situation in the region was completely transformed. Some members of the Nova Scotia Governor's Council favoured the expulsion of the Acadians, but this idea was shelved on grounds of practicality. In the aftermath of the fall of Louisbourg, Vigneau showed his moderate, or opportunist, colours by offering to assist the British governors at Annapolis Royal. In 1746, he transported men, provisions and information for the British from Annapolis Royal across the Isthmus of Chignecto and by sea from there to Louisbourg, which was then in British hands. On an earlier occasion, however, Vigneau had hosted a commander of the French army at his home in Beaubassin. At that time, the French reported that he had offered their forces the use of his ship for their projected attack on Annapolis Royal. And later in the war, when the French military returned to Beaubassin, Vigneau once again offered them his services.

Vigneau was present in Beaubassin in the spring of 1750 when French troops and native warriors took control of the settlement and pressured the Acadians there to move to French-controlled territory. In the aftermath of the burning of the town, Vigneau was compelled to move, along with the others from the settlement, to Fort Beauséjour. Like other Acadians who had lived in Beaubassin, Vigneau was vocal in expressing his resentment. Still possessing his ship and able to function as a merchant, however he was better off than most. For the most part, the Acadians at Beauséjour were reduced to tending cattle, draining marshes and establishing new farms. In 1751, when the French commander asked the displaced Acadians to swear allegiance to the King of France, Vigneau refused.

As tensions mounted in Nova Scotia, Vigneau presented himself as willing to co-operate with, or even to aid, the British. In the spring of 1753, a delegation of British soldiers from Halifax set out to negotiate an understanding with Mi'kmaq leaders on a range of issues. On his return, Anthony Casteel, a member of the British party, reported that the Mi'kmaq had ambushed the British soldiers, killing all of them except himself. Taken captive, Casteel was spirited across Nova Scotia to Beauséjour, where he met Vigneau, who was prepared to negotiate his release in return for the payment of a ransom. Casteel testified before the Governor's Council that Vigneau cast himself as friendly to the British and claimed that he had negotiated ransoms of this sort in the past. A French officer put this behaviour in a different light when he compared Vigneau to a slave-trader, cynically observing that he appeared to have been profiting from hostage-taking and the extraction of ransoms.

In 1753 and 1754, Vigneau served the British by carrying sensitive information between Halifax and Beauséjour and passing messages to British officers at their fort on the Isthmus of Chignecto. In the summer of 1755, while some Acadians fought alongside the French troops in the brief defence of Fort Beauséjour, Vigneau welcomed the British. With the fort in his hands, Colonel Robert Monckton

summoned the Acadian dwellers to seek from them an unconditional oath of allegiance to King George II. The residents, Vigneau
included, refused to do this without assurance that they would not
be required to take up arms against France. Local inhabitants
offered to help the British in others ways, with gifts of eggs, milk,
chickens and strawberries.

When the order to expel the Acadians that had been issued by
Nova Scotia's acting governor Charles Lawrence reached Monckton,
Vigneau was herded onto a ship, the *Prince Frederik*, which set sail
for Savannah, Georgia. With him on the voyage were his wife and
sixteen children and grandchildren. Upon the arrival of the *Prince
Frederik* in Georgia, Vigneau immediately took the lead in pressing
the authorities to allow him and his family to leave the colony.
Georgia's governor was not favourably disposed toward the Acadian
refugees and had only allowed them to come ashore when he was
told that they were ill and low on food. Vigneau asked the governor
not for the right to return to Nova Scotia but for permission to
leave Georgia with the members of his family. When his request
was granted, his "family" grew and he left Georgia with ninety-eight
dependents.

The strange party left by canoe and headed up the Atlantic coast
to Charleston, South Carolina. In April 1756, the governor of South
Carolina granted Vigneau and his "family" the right to quit his jurisdiction and proceed to North Carolina. After being held under
arrest for a time in North Carolina, Vigneau soon succeeded in convincing the authorities there to allow him and those with him to
continue their northward journey up the coast. In mid summer
1756, Vigneau and his group reached New York, where again they
were briefly detained. Yet again, Vigneau convinced the provincial
governor to let his party proceed on its way.

Vigneau and his flock made it to the vicinity of Cape Cod,
Massachusetts, where they entered Barnstable Bay and were sighted
and then surrounded and detained by community residents. When
the local sheriff learned that a party of Acadians had fallen into his
hands, he transferred them to the custody of the sheriff in Boston.

After the whole group had been kept in Boston for several days, Vigneau's persuasiveness worked once more. This time, he and his actual blood relatives were granted permission—through the passage of a bill by the colonial legislature—to remain within ten miles of Boston.

In September 1756, released from close custody, the Vigneau family moved north across the Charles River to Charlestown. The selectmen (town councillors) of Charlestown warned the legislature in a formal letter about the folly of allowing the Vigneau family to remain so close to the coast, from which they could easily escape. Yet another special bill was then passed by the legislature that directed the Vigneau family to settle near Worcester, further inland. The rest of the members of Vigneau's party were directed to other locales, most of them not far from the sea.

Vigneau was unable to support his family in this latest location to which their odyssey had led them. Town authorities, not anxious to sustain them on the public rolls, petitioned the legislature to move the Vigneaus again. In 1758, the Massachusetts legislature moved the family to Brooksfield, where at first they could not find employment. In 1759, Vigneau petitioned the provincial government to compensate him for the seizure of his canoes. He was granted seven pounds, eight shillings and two pence.

At some point over the next four years, Vigneau managed to obtain a seaworthy vessel, which he named the *St.-Jacques*. In 1763, after the signing of the Treaty of Paris, which granted Acadians the right to move to French-ruled territory, Vigneau set sail with his family for Miquelon, a tiny island off the cost of Newfoundland, which, along with St. Pierre, remained in the hands of the French. They travelled in a convoy with other ships, the whole party numbering 110 Acadians. Vigneau, who travelled at least once to Nova Scotia to bring other Acadians to Miquelon, resisted the idea of relocating to Cayenne in the Caribbean—an idea taken up by some Acadians—because he believed that this would be too hot a climate for Acadians to endure. In 1767, the governor of Miquelon decided to send all the Acadians on the island to France. Vigneau and the others were transported to Nantes. A year later, though, he returned to Miquelon, where he died in 1772.

Vigneau did not start out as a heroic character. Prior to 1755, he was prepared to co-operate with both the French and the British depending on which way the winds of fortune were blowing. Once deported with members of his family, however, he displayed fierce determination to return to Acadie, no matter how long that took.

Although Vigneau's dream of a return to the old homeland was never realized, others were successful. The return of solitary individuals and small groups of deportees is an extraordinary chapter in the Acadian story. When they reached the territory from which they had been expelled, they discovered that their settlements had been eviscerated, their farms laid waste, their homes burned. Together with the several thousand people who had hidden in the forests or had stayed in remote locations and escaped deportation, they became founders of the new Acadie.

While Vigneau's example is not one of armed resistance, there are such stories. The most notable figure in the Acadian resistance was the charismatic Joseph Broussard, who came to be known as Beausoleil, a man who carried out his great exploits when he was in his fifties. Broussard was born in Port Royal in 1702, the place and year of Vigneau's birth.

The future guerilla fighter, displayed in a portrait in later life as tall with an open face and a broad nose, was disputatious from an early age. Not at all like Vigneau, who seemed able to get along with everyone, Broussard was notorious for getting into scrapes. In 1724, when Louis Thibault, a relative newcomer to Annapolis Royal, brought charges against Broussard for threatening and harassing him, the authorities summoned Broussard to appear before them. When he failed to do so, he was ordered a second time to appear, and he was charged as well with having been involved with Mi'kmaq warriors who had attacked the fort at Annapolis Royal. When he finally did appear to face these charges, he sought a pardon, which was turned down, and the young man was incarcerated. Luck then intervened for Broussard. He was released from his imprisonment because the authorities simply did not have the facilities and manpower to keep people behind bars. The understanding was that Broussard would be watched over by the local Acadian community, which would be responsible for ensuring that his troublesome ways did not persist.[1]

As a young man, Broussard, who spoke the Mi'kmaq language, had learned much about how to survive in the wilderness from his Mi'kmaq acquaintances. For the British authorities his close relationship with the natives marked him from an early date as a man to be watched carefully. Not long after his first encounter with the law, he was accused again, this time of consorting with the Mi'kmaq—always cause for concern among the British—and for not keeping the authorities informed about the activities of Mi'kmaq in the region.[2]

Not long after these early incidents, Broussard, along with his brother Alexandre, became involved in a territorial dispute with another Acadian family over tracts of land that they claimed for themselves. And then in 1726, Broussard, who by then had married, was charged with having fathered an illegitimate child. Despite his protestations of innocence, the young man was again locked up by the authorities. In this dispute, a certain Marie Daigle, the wife of Jacques Gouzil, appeared before His Majesty's Council at Annapolis Royal to make the case that Broussard was indeed the father of her daughter Mary's baby. She charged that Broussard was guilty of "committing fornication" with Mary, "who being brought to bed of a daughter had laid the same to the said Broussard, and he refusing the child maintenance and denying himself to be the father prayed relief."

In the case, which was argued before John Doucett, the lieutenant-governor of Nova Scotia, the midwife who had delivered the baby testified that, during the most painful part of her delivery, Mary had cried out that Broussard was the father. The court, ruling in favour of the complainant, ordered Broussard to pay support of three shillings and nine pence a week until the child was eight years of age. Concerned that the order would be ignored, the court demanded that

Broussard put up security to demonstrate that he intended to obey the court ruling. Faced with jail in the event that the security was not forthcoming, Broussard was saved from again being placed behind bars by two local inhabitants, who came forward and posted bonds of a hundred pounds each to assure his freedom.

Even then, the unseemly affair was not at an end. Two months after the court order had been handed down, Joseph Broussard's mother, Catherine Richard, appeared before His Majesty's Council and succeeded in having the level of support for the child reduced to five shillings a month. At this point, other members of the community became involved. One woman offered to look after the baby for five shillings a month. Mary Daigle, the child's mother, did not want to lose her baby, and she decided she would care for her daughter even without Broussard's support. Broussard's brother-in-law, Charles Landry, offered both support and shelter for the mother and baby for a year. This proposal was agreed to and the affair was finally settled amicably.[3]

The case sheds light not only on the character of the man who was to take on the British during the crisis of the deportation but also on the workings of society in eighteenth-century Acadie. Noteworthy is the role played by the women, who took a leading part in the settlement of disputes and in the community's ability to come up with its own solutions rather than relying on the rulings of the council.

Around 1740, the members of the Broussard family again demonstrated their adventurous nature when they moved to the very frontier of settled Acadie and established a tiny hamlet on the Petitcodiac River, only a few kilometres from present-day Moncton. This remote place where only family members settled was called Village-des-Beausoleil. In 1747, when Britain and France were at war and most Acadians were adhering to their position as "French neutrals," Broussard provided assistance to the French troops who fought the British in the Battle of Minas. As a consequence, Governor William Shirley of Massachusetts declared Broussard and eleven others "outlaws." A British reward of fifty pounds sterling was proclaimed for the capture of each of these culprits.⁴ The crisis passed and Broussard was able to rejoin Acadian society.

In June 1755, when the British attacked Fort Beauséjour, Broussard again took up arms on the side of the French. This time he led a force of irregulars in skirmishes against the British outside the fortress. Unlike the French army regulars, whose defence of the fort was far from heroic, Broussard and his comrades succeeded, in one daring encounter, in capturing a British officer. On June 16, the day the French fort surrendered, Broussard, with sixty men, both Acadians and Mi'kmaq, raided a British encampment. For him and his followers it was the start of what was to become a guerilla war against overwhelming odds. Over the next few years, Broussard conducted a campaign against the British on both land and sea. When he was at first imprisoned in Fort Lawrence with a number of the more militant Acadian men in the autumn of 1755, Broussard managed to escape from the fort with eighty-six fellow insurgents in an intrepid escapade. During a violent thunderstorm in the hours before dawn on October 1, the imprisoned fighters exited the fort through a tunnel they had dug beneath the prison wall, utilizing spoons, knives and other implements smuggled in by their female relatives, who were supposedly bringing them food and clothing.⁵

Beausoleil's escape from the fort so alarmed the British that they decided they had to heighten their security against the threat posed by the guerillas. Alexandre Broussard, the brother of Beausoleil, and twenty-one others were imprisoned and taken on board the British gunboat *Syren*. Under the orders of Charles Lawrence, these high-risk prisoners were to be deported as far from Acadie as possible. The Acadian resisters were shipped to Charleston, South Carolina, where they were taken in shackles to Sullivan's Island. Despite special efforts to guard the prisoners, Alexandre, along with four others, managed to escape. Having taken provisions they found in the house of an absent planter, the five trekked north, making it back to present-day New Brunswick, where they were reunited with Beausoleil and his band of insurgents.

Operating from Chipoudy, on the north shore of the Bay of

Fundy just west of the mouth of the Petitcodiac River, the Broussard brothers, their seven sons and their followers mounted a continuing armed struggle against the British. Both Joseph and Alexandre Broussard lost their eldest sons during the campaign, and Beausoleil also lost his mother, wife and other children.

At Chipoudy, another key figure in the resistance, a young Canadian officer, Charles Deschamps de Boishébert, helped organize Acadian refugees and assembled a guerilla force that included Mi'kmaq and Maliseets to fight the British. In late August 1755, having laid waste the Acadian settlements on the Isthmus of Chignecto, Colonel Monckton dispatched two hundred New Englanders aboard two armed sloops to destroy Acadian settlements near Chipoudy. Under the command of Major Joseph Frye of Massachusetts, the British force torched and ransacked small Acadian settlements along the Petitcodiac River. On September 2, they were meting out the same treatment to an abandoned settlement, burning homes and setting fire to a chapel, when they were suddenly attacked by three hundred men, who fell on them, firing muskets and screaming a blood-curdling war cry. The New Englanders broke ranks and ran for the riverbank. With the tide going out, Frye had trouble landing more men to aid his fleeing troops. Twenty-three of his men lay dead and eleven more were seriously wounded by the time the rest of the troops made it back on board the ships.[6]

The counterattack organized by Boishébert struck fear in the hearts of the British troops, who learned at their cost that the Acadians could strike back. The insurgents did not stop the British from undertaking more raids, however. In November 1755, a British expedition under the command of Major George Scott destroyed the Village-des-Beausoleil, the hamlet established by the Broussard family.[7]

Broussard's fighters carried out daring raids on British military detachments and on their posts. In the winter of 1756, a band of guerilla warriors ambushed a British force that was en route from Shediac to Fort Cumberland (Fort Beauséjour), killing two soldiers.

Not long after, a force of Acadians and natives burned two British ships at Baie Verte on the Northumberland Strait, and during the ensuing melee they killed seven British soldiers and took one prisoner. Their exploits made it extremely difficult for British troops to venture outside their fortresses.

Like all wars between guerilla fighters and regular forces, this one was ugly and brutal. In November 1758, determined to stamp out the resistance, the British sent an expedition to the Petitcodiac region of present-day New Brunswick. They laid waste the countryside and burned all of the Acadian settlements. The government placed a bounty on the heads of Acadians in the region. In response to it, many Acadians were killed and a number of them, including women and children, were scalped. In another foray against the insurgents, the British sent a sloop up a river, hoping to lure Acadian fighters to attack the vessel; meanwhile British troops hid in the woods. When the Acadians took the bait and appeared, the British killed three men, scalped them, and took nine men prisoner. Fourteen guerilla fighters chose to brave the river rather than be captured. As the men fought to survive in the swirling waters, the British shot ten of them dead and the other four escaped.[8]

The fall of Fort Louisbourg to the British in July 1758 cut off the supply of arms and provisions that had helped keep the Acadian resistance alive. The following year, Quebec fell, and it became clear that the insurgency of Beausoleil and his band of fighters was doomed to failure. In mid November 1759, the Broussard brothers made their way to Fort Cumberland in response to the offer of an amnesty that had been made the previous month to the Acadian insurgents by General Edward Whitmore, the British governor at Louisbourg. In a document setting out his terms, Beausoleil offered to surrender, but with the caveat that the insurgents be allowed to remain in the territory and be permitted to practise their religion. According to one version of events, Alexandre Broussard was left in the hands of the British as a hostage while Beausoleil departed to parlay with his men. Beausoleil, fearing that the British were planning to spring a trap on them, moved north with the small number of remaining insurgents. The following summer, he and his men surrendered to a British force at the mouth of the Restigouche River. Another group of Acadian insurgents, about seven hundred strong, also surrendered.[9] One defiant holdout against the surrender was another of Beausoleil's brothers, Jean Baptiste Broussard. In the dead of winter, to avoid falling into the hands of the British, he undertook an overland trek across present-day New Brunswick to Quebec, where he joined up with French resistance fighters there in May 1760. During the gruelling journey, his wife, his mother-in-law and two of his children perished. With his surviving son and daughter, he eventually went to France.[10]

Once the Acadian resisters were taken into custody, the British offer of an amnesty vanished into thin air. The guerilla fighters, Beausoleil among them, were marched to Halifax and imprisoned in the fortress on George's Island. As Acadian fighters were rounded up and added to the numbers already incarcerated there, the British authorities grew concerned that Beausoleil's presence among them could lead to a new attempt at armed resistance. In the summer of 1762, Beausoleil, his son Joseph and his brother Alexandre's son Anselme were transferred to Fort Edward in Windsor, Nova Scotia. The following spring, deciding that Beausoleil was a threat no matter where he was located, the British moved the Acadian leader back to George's Island, where he was held under the tightest possible security. While the leader of the resistance was imprisoned on the island, many of the other Acadian prisoners there were allowed to go to work for the immigrants the British had brought in from New England to settle on the land that had once been held by the Acadians.

In 1764, with the war against France over, the British authorities decided to allow Beausoleil to leave Nova Scotia with a number of his followers. Using the money they had earned working for those who had taken their land, the Acadians hired ships to take them to Saint-Domingue (present-day Haiti). Under the leadership of Beausoleil, 193 Acadians left Halifax, first for Saint-Domingue and then the following year for the Attakapas region of

South Louisiana.[11] On October 20, 1765, shortly after his arrival in Louisiana, Beausoleil succumbed to one of the plagues that were the curse of the Acadians on the run. He was buried near the present-day town of Broussard, named in his honour. In the Acadian museum in nearby St. Martinville, the most prized possession is a wall-sized painting of the arrival in Louisiana of Broussard and his followers.

Broussard and his guerilla warriors were not the only Acadians to resist *le Grand Dérangement* with force. Noel Brassard, a prosperous farmer from Petitcodiac, was one of those driven out his home, along with the members of his family, during the deportation. Hiding in the woods from the British, overwhelmed by hunger, cold and illness, Brassard lived the hell of watching his aged mother, his wife and eight of his children die. Brassard, who survived the ordeal, was left with an implacable hatred for the English, and he decided to exact his own personal revenge. Armed with his gun, he stalked English farmers, sliding through the forest and pouncing on them one by one when he saw his chance. Over a five-year period, he shot and killed twenty-eight of his hated foes in his one-man vigilante campaign.[12]

Armed resistance was one sign of the resilience of the Acadians in the response to the assault on their communities. Another and much more enduring one was the creation of two new homelands, the first of them in the Maritimes, on the doorstep of the original Acadie.

PART II

REBIRTH

CHAPTER 6

ACADIE: A NEW BEGINNING

Only Grand Pré remained deserted, solitary, mute, like some ancient temple haunted by the gods . . .

Like the wheel of a cart, like the helm of a ship, the new Acadie had spread the spokes of its compass points to the four corners of the country, without knowing it. Playing blind man's buff with Destiny, Acadie had, in the long run, reopened all its fields and replanted roots everywhere.

Without really meaning to.

—ANTONINE MAILLET, *Pélagie: The Return to Acadie*

WITH THE CONCLUSION of the Seven Years' War, Acadians were accorded the right to return to Nova Scotia. This right, however, was subject to severe restrictions that made those who returned second-class subjects of the Crown, both legally and as a result of the dire circumstances to which they had been reduced. Acadians were forbidden to resettle on the lands from which they had been deported. The colonial regime in Halifax was determined to reserve the best lands in Nova Scotia, including the fertile farming regions along the Bay of Fundy coast, for immigrants from New England. Not only were Acadians forbidden to occupy lands their families and communities had wrested from the sea over the previous century and more, they were limited to settling in small groups in separate locations. Colonial authorities did not want Acadians to reconstitute themselves in large enough numbers that they could assert themselves as a people. In addition, until June 1768, a Nova Scotia government regulation formally stipulated that grants of blocks of land in the colony would be made only to persons who undertook to settle the land with Protestant inhabitants. To relax, if not abolish, this regulation, British authorities announced that in the colonies, unlike Britain itself, Catholics could own and inherit land. This stance opened the door to the return of Acadians to Nova Scotia, even though the law that prohibited Catholics from owning or inheriting land was not repealed until 1783.[1]

The Acadian return from exile took place slowly and over a period of many years, from many locations in the Thirteen Colonies, England and France. And then there were the Acadians who had escaped deportation by heading into the interior of what was to become New Brunswick. Most Acadians in exile lived together in groups that varied in size from a few individuals to hundreds of people. It took time for the exiles to learn that they would be allowed to return. And it took more time for groups of Acadians to decide that it was safe and to work out the ways to travel back to Nova Scotia. Some returned by boat and some actually made the journey overland.

Those who returned were required to swear an oath of allegiance to the Crown. The plan of the authorities was to keep the Acadians on the margins of society throughout the Maritimes, in Nova Scotia, Cape Breton Island, Prince Edward Island and in New Brunswick, once it was established as a separate colony in 1784. Immigration of English-speaking settlers was key to marginalizing the Acadians. By 1763, twelve thousand migrants from New England had settled in Nova Scotia.[2]

There is a tragic irony in the fact that some Acadians were hired by the new settlers to assist them in restoring the aboiteaux that had been essential to the success of Acadian farming in the days before the deportation. The wanton destruction of Acadian communities had not only involved the burning of houses and churches, it had resulted in the wrecking of much of the system of water management on the marshy soil that had been reclaimed from the sea. To make the aboiteaux operational again, the New England settlers, who were not schooled in this form of agriculture, soon realized that they needed advice and assistance from former Acadian farmers.

Acadians returning to Nova Scotia sought new land to occupy. By the end of the eighteenth century there were about four thousand Acadians living in Nova Scotia. The largest number of these settled on the Bay of Fundy coast, west of the territory of old Acadie, in the area that lies between Digby and Yarmouth, at the tip of the peninsula. Although the new land was picturesque, affording spectacular views of the sea, its scrubby soil and rocky outcroppings forced the Acadians to turn to the sea for their livelihood. Just as the original Acadians, many of whom had been townspeople, had mastered the art of transforming marshy soil into rich farmland, the resettled farmers had to learn to become fishermen. For over two centuries, since their settlement in this part of Nova Scotia, Acadian fishermen have sailed out of their tiny ports in search of scallops, lobster, shrimps and codfish.

The decision of the British Board of Trade in 1764 to permit some Acadians to resettle in Nova Scotia was prodded along by a Huguenot fish merchant who hailed from the English Channel island of Jersey. Jacques Robin, who was setting up long-term fishing posts on Cape Breton Island and on the Baie des Chaleurs, regarded the Acadians as especially useful because of their vast experience in the territory, and also because their close relationship with the Mi'kmaq could add a fur-trading component to his commercial ventures.[3] A letter from the Colonial Office to Governor Wilmot in Halifax showed that, while the imperial authorities did not object to the return of Acadians to work in the fishery, London continued to regard the Acadians as a threat to the tranquility of Nova Scotia. " . . . [W]e see no objection to their [Acadians] being accommodated with small lots of land amongst the other settlers," the letter stated, "provided they take the Oath of Allegiance and that great care is taken to disperse them in small numbers that it may not lie in their power to disturb and annoy that Government, which was in its first establishment obstructed and brought into so great danger by their rebellious and turbulent disposition."[4]

The heartland of Nova Scotian Acadie after the return was in the province's south-west, between Digby and Yarmouth, centred on the present-day township of Clare. In addition to those settlements, there were six other regions in Nova Scotia (using present-day boundaries) where Acadians settled in significant numbers: Argyle (Yarmouth County); Minudie, Nappan, and Maccan (Cumberland County); Cheticamp (Inverness County, Cape Breton); Île Madame (Richmond County, Cape Breton); and Chezzetcook (Halifax County). In the settlements in Cumberland County and close to Halifax, the use of the French language has almost entirely disappeared. Meanwhile, in Clare and in Cheticamp, where large Acadian settlements grew up in isolation from English-speaking communities, the French language and culture have remained vibrant.[5]

One of those who found his way to the new Acadian settlements in Cape Breton Island, a few kilometres west of Cheticamp, was Paul-Marie Doucet. His remarkable journey began when British soldiers launched the deportation of the Acadians from the Isthmus of Chignecto in August 1755. Paul-Marie was only eight years old when Colonel Robert Monckton's troops rounded up the Acadians in the region and herded them onto ships. For some reason, while his parents and his brothers and sisters were deported, the young boy was not among those captured. What happened to him on that fateful summer day is not known. He may have been playing in the woods or he may have been fishing. One can imagine the paroxysm of fear that must have overtaken him when he returned to find his home, indeed the whole village, in flames, with his family and his neighbours gone. He may or may not have seen the ships carrying the deportees away.

What is known is that the members of Paul-Marie's family ended up among the Acadian refugees who stayed for a time outside Nantes, France. His parents died there, but his surviving brothers and sisters migrated from France to Louisiana. What had become of Paul-Marie, the boy who had "escaped" from the British, remained shrouded in mystery until 1767. That year, one of the little boy's brothers contributed a declaration to a set of papers that recorded what had happened to some of the Acadians who had migrated to Louisiana. "My brother Paul-Marie Doucet, born at Beaubassin in the month of January 1746," he reported, "is presently living at Miramichi." By the time this declaration was made, the Miramichi region had become the location for hunting camps as well as camps devoted to the cod fishery. It is likely that Doucet was earning a living in the camps that were home to many Acadians who had escaped deportation.

Three decades after he had been left behind, Paul-Marie Doucet showed up in the Acadian settlement at Cheticamp, Nova Scotia. With him was his wife, Félicité-Michele, who may have been Mi'kmaq, and their three sons. Early in the nineteenth century, when a missionary visited the small Acadian community of Grand Étang, just west of Cheticamp, he compiled a list of the people living in the community. Included on the list was the family of Simon Doucet, his wife Scholastique and their ten children. Simon was the son of Paul-Marie, the boy who had been left behind.[6]

In 1769, what had been Île St. Jean under the French regime was renamed Prince Edward Island and was constituted as a separate British colony. As they had been in Nova Scotia, Acadian communities were re-established on Prince Edward Island in the years following the Treaty of Paris. The expulsion of most of the settlers there had occurred in 1758, three years after the main expulsions from Nova Scotia, with most of those expelled sent to France. In the first years following the deportation, only a small number of Acadian families, living in severe poverty, were left on the island.

The first significant act of the British government following the establishment of Prince Edward Island as a colony was to divide the island up into sixty-seven giant lots. Ownership of these lots was handed over to wealthy aristocratic friends of the government. The consequence was that the island was saddled for more than a century with absentee British landlords. Only when Prince Edward Island became a Canadian province in 1873, and the government of

Canada bought out the remaining landlords, did the island end its era of tenancy. In addition to the crushing problems they already had, the Acadians who remained on the island in 1769 suffered the additional hardship of becoming tenants on land they had previously owned.[7]

In 1764, a visitor to the island observed that the few Acadian families he saw lived in tiny cottages in the woods. These people were reduced to a meagre diet of fish and game. A few years later, almost all of the Acadians in Prince Edward Island toiled for British companies operating in the fishery. While some Loyalists were given free land on the island, the authorities took the position that Acadians had to buy or rent land. The consequence was that a number of Acadians chose to move to Cheticamp in Nova Scotia, where they had an easier time acquiring land of their own.[8]

While the old Acadie had been centred on lands along the Bay of Fundy in Nova Scotia, the largest part of the new Acadie was established farther north in what would, in 1784, become New Brunswick. In the eastern extremity of the region, the only part of the original Acadian homeland that had not been occupied by English-speaking settlers was the land around Beaubassin, in the region of Pubnico and along the left bank of the Petitcodiac River. Here there was a base where the old and the new Acadie overlapped.

The isthmus that connects New Brunswick and Nova Scotia included some original settlements, such as Memramcook, now regarded by Acadians as the cradle of the new Acadie. The returning Acadians sought out unoccupied land they could farm and, in many cases, access to the sea, so they could support themselves and their families as fishermen. Most of the Acadians settled in the strip of territory along the coast of New Brunswick stretching north from Shediac to take in what is called the "Acadian Peninsula," and beyond to Bathurst, all the way to the Quebec border. Among the first of the settlements along this coast were Grande-Digue (across the bay from Shediac) and Cocagne, advantageously situated where the Cocagne River empties into the Northumberland Strait. There were Acadian settlements farther north in Caraquet (which came to be regarded by many as the cultural capital of the new Acadie) and Nipisiguit as early as 1760.

In the distant north-west on the upper reaches of the St. John River, far from the sea, Acadians settled in Saint-Basile in 1785. This was the first settlement in what was to become the Madawaska region, today a key Acadian area, whose largest city is Edmundston. The Madawaska region quickly developed its own identity. It became a meeting point among New Brunswick, the state of Maine and the province of Quebec. While many of those settling in the region were Acadians who had been driven out of the lands of the lower St. John River and the area around Fredericton in a so-called "second expulsion" when the Loyalists arrived, the Madawaska territory also drew migrants from the adjacent regions of Quebec, along the St. Lawrence River, Kamouraska and Temiscouata. Remote though it was, the Madawaska region became embroiled in boundary disputes. The dispute between New Brunswick and Maine, which came close to provoking war between Britain and the United States, was ultimately resolved with the Webster-Ashburton Treaty of 1842. The final boundary between Quebec and New Brunswick was drawn in 1885.

The new Acadie was poor. Indeed, for many decades Acadians were the poorest British North Americans, and later Canadians, of European descent. The Acadians worked farms on substandard land, spent their winters in the bush toiling for the forest products industry and fished the waters along the coast. Most remained poor, while only a very few got rich. When Jacques Robin, the Jersey Island merchant, lobbied for the right of Acadians to return to Nova Scotia to work in the fishery, he started what became a decades-long system in which traders from Jersey, with their access to credit and markets, controlled the livelihoods of Acadian fishermen, whose toil left them perpetually indebted.[9] The system closely resembled the operations of a company town, with the Jersey traders providing credit and goods to the fishermen whose income was never high enough to repay them. In effect, they were reduced to the status of indentured labourers.

To appreciate the full extent of the trauma they suffered, it must be considered that the Acadians had gone from having an independent, relatively prosperous and largely self-sufficient society, to living on the margins of a dominant social order. They had no option but to earn their living in the few ways open to them, and most of them lived in poverty.

The new Acadian communities, certainly those by the sea, had a distinctive look and feel that persists even today in Acadian communities along the Northumberland Strait. The sea is the front door of these towns and villages. In places like Pointe-du-Chêne, Shediac, Cocagne and Bouctouche, a large wharf juts out into the sea. Moored to it are fishing boats, rising and falling with the tides, and on top of the wharves are boats undergoing repairs alongside the skeletons of boats beyond repair. From the wharf, in good weather and bad, the fishermen venture forth in their quest for lobster, shrimp, crab and, in earlier days, cod. In modern times the wharf is a place where people assemble to enjoy a sunset, to watch sailboats on a summer evening, to eat fast food, and, for the young, to drive their cars up and down in search of the admiration of others. People also gather, as they have for over two centuries, to await the return of the fishing boats with their bountiful or paltry catch, which in good times fetches a decent price and in bad times brings little more than it costs to operate and maintain the vessels. The sea is the source of life, just as it is, on infrequent and unforgettable occasions, the purveyor of tragedy, when loved ones do not return. Shipwrecks, drownings and terrible storms are scarred into memory, just as happy memories recall the boats being decked out with flags and bunting when they go out to sea for the first time in spring, from harbours like that of Cocagne, after receiving the blessing of the bishop.

The Acadian towns have an unmistakable look as well, with their small, white clapboard cottages (now mostly covered with aluminum siding) and their front doors set high above the ground and painted deep-sea blue. Along the coast there are, as well, the much larger clapboard homes of the relatively wealthy.

In their new communities, having lost so much in the deportation and the return, the Acadians were reduced to a struggle for survival. They had little capital and were dependent on others to find work as fishermen and in the forest products industry. Most of the Acadians were illiterate, and the establishment of schools in their communities was a long and slow process. For the most part, it was priests from Quebec who became the anchors in the new Acadian communities. The priests played a critical role in keeping the language, culture and faith alive and ultimately in inspiring learning among the Acadian young, from whom the educated elites of the future would ultimately come.

Political rights came slowly to the Acadians who had resettled in the Maritimes. While Acadians acquired the right to vote in Nova Scotia in 1789, they were not enfranchised in New Brunswick until 1810, and they won the vote in Prince Edward Island only in 1830.[10] The acquisition of formal political rights was important, but with few leaders, the survival of the Acadians for many decades was more a matter of perseverance on the part of individual men and women. Dispossessed and poorly educated, Acadians were often ill prepared to defend their rights with respect to property. The consequence was repeated cases of further loss of lands on which they had settled.

It would be a long time before there would once again be an Acadie, as such. Acadian communities during these decades had few links with one another and, apart from the Church, had no institutions that sought to advance their broader collective interests. Individuals often played an outsize role in nurturing the new communities.

Madeleine LeBlanc arrived in Pointe-de-l'Église in Nova Scotia in the early 1770s when the Acadian community there was just being established. She is reputed to have taken an axe in hand as a symbol of fortitude and determination to urge on her parents and friends to demonstrate pluck in the task ahead. She became the mother of many children and lived to be ninety-eight. A storyteller, she ended many of her tales with the proposition, intended to raise morale, that "poverty never killed anyone."[11] Acclaimed

Acadian writer Antonine Maillet, in her novel *Pelagie: The Return to Acadie*, tells the tale of a widow who leads her followers out of exile and back to Acadie. The theme of the indomitable woman who comes to the aid of her people is a powerful one in Acadian culture. Stories such as that of Madeleine LeBlanc give this theme a solid historical foundation.

Playing a role in the Church in these perilous times following deportation and resettlement was Joseph Mathurin Bourg, who had been born near Grand Pré in 1744 and expelled with his family, first to Virginia in 1755 and then to Britain, where he stayed from 1756 to 1763. Following a period of study in France, Bourg set out for Canada, where he was ordained as a priest in 1772. Thought to have been the first priest to return to Acadie following the deportation, he served as vicar general for Acadian missions between 1774 and 1795.[12] Bourg travelled widely through the scattered settlements in his domain, bringing the sacraments to people who had long been without them, at a time when the Acadians were beginning to re-establish themselves.

Instrumental in shedding light on the life and times of Acadians in the early decades of resettlement was Venerande Robichaux, who was born at Port Royal in 1753 and was deported as an infant with her family to Boston. She emigrated from Boston to Quebec in the 1770s where she remained until her death in 1839. From there she maintained a lengthy correspondence with members of her family who lived in the Miramichi region of northern New Brunswick. Her writings on political questions, family affairs and the conduct of business were first published in 1887 in the Acadian newspaper *L'Évangéline*.[13]

Despite the traumas faced by the Acadians, their communities grew both in number and in size. In the last years of the eighteenth century, important Acadian communities were established in the south-east of New Brunswick, including Barachois, Bouctouche and Richibouctou, and in the north-east, including Neguac, Tracadie, Shippagan and Petit-Rocher. A religious census taken in 1803 revealed that by that date the Acadian population of New Brunswick had reached 3,700 people.[14]

While more Acadian settlers were to arrive, what drove the growth of population in the settlements was a high birth rate that made for a more rapid growth in the Acadian than in the anglophone population in New Brunswick. By 1867, the year of Confederation, just under 45,000 Acadians constituted almost 12 percent of the province's population. By 1971, the province's 235,000 Acadians made up 37 percent of the New Brunswick total.[15]

The project for British North American union in the 1860s drew mixed reactions from Acadians, as it did from English-speaking residents of the Maritimes. There was certainly no general enthusiasm for Confederation. In elections in New Brunswick in 1865 and 1866, most Acadians voted for members of the legislature who opposed Confederation, and accusations were made in the legislature that the priests in the Acadian parishes had urged their parishioners to oppose the new federal union. One voice in favour of Confederation was *Le Moniteur Acadien*, the Acadian newspaper published in Shediac, New Brunswick, whose publisher, Israel Landry, hailed originally from Quebec. The paper made the case that it would be advantageous for Acadians to be in a political union that included French-speaking Quebec.[16]

In the closing decades of the nineteenth century, a new Acadian leadership emerged, much of it within the Church, to found new Acadian organizations and provide Acadians with potent symbols of identity. In 1880, the Société Saint Jean Baptiste of Quebec held a congress, to which they invited Acadians. Dozens attended, and the following year the Acadians convened a national congress of their own in Memramcook, New Brunswick, at which they undertook to affirm themselves as a people.

The congress was held at the Collège Saint-Joseph. The college, a crucial vehicle for the education of a new Acadian elite in the late nineteenth century, had been established in 1864 by Father Camille Lefebvre, a member of the Holy Cross Fathers Congregation. It was the first French-language degree-granting institution in Acadie. Other such colleges were to follow: the Collège Saint-Louis in Saint-Louis-de-Kent, New Brunswick, in 1874; the

Collège Sainte-Anne in Pointe de l'Église, Nova Scotia, in 1890; the Collège du Sacre-Coeur in Caraquet, New Brunswick, in 1894; and the Collège Saint-Louis in Edmundston, New Brunswick, in 1946.

While five thousand people attended the critically important meeting at Memramcook, only a few hundred took part in the discussions. The issues addressed were those that were of broad concern to Acadians. One of these, to be addressed again at future congresses, was the threat to Acadian communities posed by the emigration of large numbers of their young to work in the mill towns of New England. On the agenda, as a way to counter emigration, was the promotion of rural colonization within New Brunswick, an idea that was very popular during the same period among influential circles in the Church in Quebec, where religious leaders tried to discourage the emigration of French Canadians to the United States and of rural Québécois to Montreal. As well as discussing economic issues of concern to Acadians, the congress focused on other questions that were to be perennial topics for the future: education; how to assert a growing role for Acadians in the Church; and the promotion of Acadian journalism. The congress chose Our Lady of the Assumption as the patron saint of the Acadians and picked Assumption Day, August 15, as the date for their national holiday.

In attendance at a second national congress in Miscouche, Prince Edward Island, were two figures of immense importance to the revival of Acadie, not just as a collection of individual communities but as a wider entity with a collective consciousness. Marcel-François Richard was descended from ancestors who left France to settle in Acadie in 1649. Following the deportation, members of the Richard family settled in New Brunswick, where the grandfather of Marcel-François founded the hamlet Saint-Louis de Kent in 1789. Born in 1849, the youngest of ten children in a family that was far from wealthy, Marcel-François completed his basic education in 1860 and then studied at St. Dunstan's College in Charlottetown. From there he went to Montreal, where he continued his studies at the Grand Séminaire and became a priest. In 1874, the young priest founded the Académie Saint-Louis, which he conceived as a counterweight to the Collège Saint-Joseph in Memramcook. As a consequence of struggles within the Church, where the new college was seen by some as too strongly nationalist, Richard's college was closed in 1882. Throughout his life, Father Richard was instrumental in promoting the building of schools, convents and churches in Kent and Northumberland counties in New Brunswick, with their large Acadian populations.[17]

The other towering personality in attendance at the Miscouche congress was Pascal Poirier, who was born in Shediac, New Brunswick, in 1852. He attended the Collège Saint-Joseph and studied law in Ottawa. In 1885, he was appointed to the Senate by Prime Minister John A. Macdonald, the first Acadian to become a member of the upper chamber. Involved in the major questions of concern to Acadians during his long career in public life, Poirier was strongly involved in the struggle within the Church in favour of the appointment of an Acadian bishop, an issue of great importance since the Church was the one institution that all Acadians shared. It was, moreover, a difficult issue because of the persistent opposition from New Brunswick's Irish community, with its entrenched position in the Catholic hierarchy, to the idea of a stronger position in the Church for Acadians.

Poirier wrote about the history of the Acadians and he authored two important works in linguistic studies, *Le Parler franco-acadien et ses origines* and *Glossaire Acadien*. In these books, he set out to demonstrate that the French spoken by Acadians closely resembled the linguistic usage of western France in the seventeenth and eighteenth centuries and was not, therefore, a bastardized patois, a charge not infrequently heard in Poirier's day and since.[18]

At the congress in Miscouche, an Acadian flag was devised. It was the French tricolour, with a gold star in the blue area. The gold star, in addition to depicting a star of the sea that promised safe passage to sailors, represented Our Lady of the Assumption, and since gold is the papal colour, it symbolized devotion to the Church.[19] In addition, the question of a national anthem for the Acadians was raised at Miscouche. Some suggested "La Marseillaise," but when

Father Richard rose and sang "Ave Maris Stella," those in attendance joined in. Pascal Poirier suggested this song become the Acadian anthem, and the idea was adopted.

The period of Acadian national assertion at the end of the nineteenth century has been called the "Acadian renaissance," and it is no exaggeration to understand it in those terms. For the first time since *le Grand Dérangement* over a century earlier, the Acadians were emerging as a whole people. During this time, the Church was critical to the quest for a renewed identity. Since Acadians had no state to call their own, and little recognition from any state of their collective existence and needs, the Church was the only powerful institution that bound them together, the only institution whose elites could act on their behalf. The consequence, as in the case of other peoples in similar straits, was the elaboration of a conservative, Catholic, nationalist Acadian identity.

The national congresses were held against the backdrop of a rising Acadian population, especially in New Brunswick, and the establishment of new Acadian institutions. In 1887, Valentin Landry founded the newspaper *L'Évangéline*, publishing it first as a weekly in Digby, Nova Scotia, and later in Weymouth. In 1905, he decided that the paper would do better if he moved it to Moncton, which was already emerging as a crucial Acadian centre. In Moncton, the paper tended to concentrate on issues of interest to Acadians in southeastern New Brunswick, but it continued, as well, to cover news about the Acadians in the Maritime provinces.[20] In 1903, Acadians in Massachusetts founded La Société Mutuelle l'Assomption, and this insurance company, which was to grow into a major enterprise, moved its head office to Moncton in 1913. During the same period, the long-term Acadian effort to obtain the appointment of an Acadian bishop bore fruit with the appointment of Monsignor Édouard-Alfred LeBlanc in 1912 as bishop of the diocese of Saint John. Two years later, an Acadian parish was created in Moncton.[21]

Along with the rise of Acadian nationalism during the last decades of the nineteenth century, there is evidence that some prominent Acadians, despite the tragic history of their people, supported Canada's place in the British Empire as a setting under which Acadians had achieved political rights and stability. Some among them hoped that Britain could play a role in finding an accommodation between Catholics and Protestants in Canada. In 1887, when enormous celebrations of Queen Victoria's Golden Jubilee were organized throughout the empire and across Canada, *Le Moniteur Acadien* joined in the festive mood, expressing a fondness for the monarch and other members of the royal family. The newspaper reported that Acadian merchants and other townspeople were prominently involved in organizing local celebrations in Shediac for the royal birthday. Floats in the town's procession mixed pro-royal sentiment with advertising for local businesses. The local militia, which may have included Acadians, gave a twenty-one-gun salute. Local games were held and Queen Victoria was loudly cheered.[22]

The Acadian renaissance had succeeded in re-establishing Acadie as a collectivity. An educated elite had emerged and significant institutional gains had been made. But for the vast majority of Acadians, life was hard in the last decades of the nineteenth century and the first decades of the twentieth. As fishermen and loggers, many Acadians remained virtually the indentured servants of fishing and forest products enterprises. Despite the expansion of schools, and the rise of a cohort of Acadian women teachers who played a crucial role during this epoch, illiteracy was all too frequent.

Conditions were not the same everywhere. Among the Acadians in south-western Nova Scotia standards of living did rise, and this was also true in south-eastern New Brunswick, where many Acadians found work that paid relatively well in Moncton in the Canadian National Railways yards. In north-western New Brunswick, the city of Edmundston rose during the 1920s to become a major pulp and paper centre that provided employment for many. However, in New Brunswick's north-east and in the Acadian centres in Prince Edward Island, poverty remained the norm.[23]

While the first decades of the twentieth century were mean enough, the Great Depression that began in 1929 made matters even more difficult. Jobs were scarce, and both the fishery and the forest products industries suffered. In some ways, Acadians, who were already used to bad times, may have endured the Depression better than those in newly settled regions of the country who had known boom times in the recent past. With their large families, and customs that gave meaning to the concept of the extended family, Acadian communities were resilient during periods of sharp economic contraction. Suicide rates and feelings of personal worthlessness were much worse in Alberta, for example, with its history of boom and bust and its greater social dependence on the more fragile base of the nuclear family.

A rather narrow elite, educated in the outlook that had been promulgated during the period of the Acadian renaissance, continued to dominate Acadian life. By the end of the Second World War, it was becoming ever more apparent that this elite had made its contribution to Acadians and was now becoming a stumbling block in the way of further advance. The next generation of Acadians would have to move outside the confines of the Church to make use of the state to create opportunities on a much wider front. New strategies would have to be conceived to move forward, and in the more prosperous times of the post-war decades, with new ideas in the air, not only in Acadie but throughout the industrialized world, new ways and new leaders were found.

—

CHAPTER 7

THE LOUIS MAILLOUX AFFAIR
THE STRUGGLE FOR ACADIAN SCHOOLS

CONFEDERATION IN 1867 brought with it the hope that religious minorities—Protestants in Quebec and Catholics, including Acadians, in the other provinces—would be protected should provincial governments assault their educational rights. The first major challenge to this constitutional regime came in New Brunswick. In April 1871, the government of Premier George E. King introduced Law 87, The Common School Act, the purpose of which was to overhaul the province's system of education. The act established free primary school education, created new school districts and provided for the construction of schools. The act also decreed that all schools in the system would be non-confessional. It barred the teaching of the Catechism in public schools, required nuns and priests to have a school teaching certificate from the government, prohibited them from wearing religious habits in school and banned the display of religious symbols in classrooms.

Prior to 1871, the education of Acadians in New Brunswick was rudimentary. The first schoolhouses were built in Acadian areas of the province in the 1850s. Prior to that time, teachers travelled from community to community and boarded with local families. These itinerant educators tried to pass on the basics of reading, writing and arithmetic to their pupils before moving on to another town or village. Most Acadian centres had a schoolhouse and a teacher after the 1850s. Many families were too poor to send their children to these schools, however, and had to keep their sons and daughters at home to help out with chores there, or to work on the family farm.

The schools had few books available to them, and those that existed were treasured and handed down from pupil to pupil. A favourite tool of education in these schools, in place of notebooks, was the small slate board on which pupils wrote with a slate pencil, before wiping it clean with a damp cloth. Many of the instructors in Acadian schools were teaching nuns.

The New Brunswick Common School Act posed a frontal challenge to the province's Roman Catholics, two-thirds of whom were Acadians and about one-third of whom were Irish. In practice, the act forced Catholic parents in New Brunswick who wanted to send their children to a Catholic school to pay twice. Under the previous system, there had been a separate school tax in the province. Now the funding of schools was to be covered by the property tax. Catholics protesting against the new school regime were forced to support the province's public schools when they paid their property tax in addition to paying fees for a private Catholic school.[1] Acadians saw the law as an attack on their culture, their language and their religion.

Resistance to the act was mounted by both French- and English-speaking Catholics in New Brunswick. Because of their stronger social position in the cities at the time, much of the leadership of the struggle fell to the Irish, despite their smaller numbers. (In later school disputes in Canada, such as the one in Ontario in the early twentieth century, the Irish and the francophones were on opposite sides, since the issue was perceived to be about French language rights.)

For four years following the passage of the act, a fierce struggle was waged in opposition to its provisions. Many Catholics refused to pay the school tax. While the main battleground was in New Brunswick, there were serious skirmishes as well in Ottawa and Quebec. The Roman Catholic hierarchy in Quebec, with its very close ties to the federal Conservative government of John A. Macdonald, demanded that Ottawa use its constitutional powers to negate the New Brunswick school law. The British North America Act gave the federal government the power to pass remedial legislation to restore school systems for minorities should those systems be negated by a province. The power of remedial legislation was meant to offset the authority granted to provinces to administer their own educational systems. What limited the scope for remedial legislation, however, was the caveat that minority rights were protected in the BNA Act only to the extent that they had existed at the time the province entered Confederation. And since most provinces had very rudimentary systems of education when they entered Confederation, this weakened the protection the federal government could provide. Nonetheless, the arrangement between Catholics and Protestants was a cornerstone of Confederation, one that would be at least as important as linguistic arrangements.

Quebec Conservatives, however, were not keen to become involved in any constitutional fight. Central to their thinking was that if Ottawa acted to uphold the rights of Catholics in New Brunswick, someday the federal government could end up interfering with Quebec's control of its educational system. Macdonald's trusted lieutenant in Quebec, George-Étienne Cartier, made exactly this appeal to the people of that province in an address in the House of Commons.[2] In practice, the federal Conservatives were far from anxious to defend the constitutional order they had so recently constructed.

In the House of Commons in Ottawa, the struggle for the rights of the Catholics of New Brunswick was led by John Costigan, an Irish Catholic from Saint John. On May 20, 1872, Costigan proposed a motion in the House to request that the governor general of Canada disavow the provincial school law in New Brunswick. Faced with a potential political disaster that would split the party, the Macdonald government saved face by supporting instead a motion offered by Charles Carroll Colby, an anglophone member from Quebec. The motion, which passed, merely expressed the regret of the House that the recent schools act in New Brunswick had not brought satisfaction to a part of the people of the province. It expressed the hope that at its next session the legislature of New Brunswick would modify the act so as to remove the cause of this discontent.[3]

The weak-kneed posture of the Quebec Conservatives in the House of Commons proved highly costly to the party in the 1872 federal election. The defence of the school rights of Catholics in New Brunswick became a hot issue in the electoral campaign in Quebec. While the Conservatives held on to power, they lost seven seats in the province. Shockingly, Cartier, an architect of Confederation with Macdonald, lost his own riding of Montreal East.

The election also brought a new group of French Canadian nationalists to Parliament, including Honoré Mercier, then thirty-three years old. He won a seat in Rouville, under the banner of the Parti National. (In the mid 1880s, Mercier became premier of Quebec when he led the Parti National to victory in a provincial election powered by the outrage French Canadians felt against the hanging of Louis Riel in 1885.) In the new parliamentary session John Costigan returned to the attack in the House of Commons, this time proposing a motion that would strike down the tax arrangements set up to finance education in New Brunswick. Mercier rose in the House, coming to the aid of Costigan's motion. In a stirring address, he called on the fifty French Canadians in Parliament to come to the aid of those being persecuted in New Brunswick, to whom they were linked through ties of religion and blood. His appeal was especially effective because, for reasons of parliamentary tactics, the largely Protestant Liberals of Ontario were prepared to vote for the Costigan motion.[4]

Prime Minister John A. Macdonald warned the House against the dangers of interfering with the constitutional authority of the province of New Brunswick in the area of education. Macdonald threw Hector Langevin, the minister of public works, his new right-hand man from Quebec following the defeat of Cartier, into the fray. In this debate, however, the deck was stacked against the prime minister. Only four French-Canadian members voted with Macdonald, and when the votes of the remaining French Canadians, other Catholics and Ontario Liberals were totalled, the motion was adopted by a vote of ninety-eight to sixty-three. Macdonald had suffered a humiliating political defeat, though not on an issue having to do with the policies of his government in the arena of federal affairs.

In the aftermath, the prime minister showed that he retained the tactical skill for which he was legendary. Three days after the vote in the Commons, Macdonald told the House that he had handed the matter over to the governor general, and that he regarded the tax measures embodied in new laws in New Brunswick in 1873—the subject of the Costigan motion—as mere amendments to the school law of 1871, which had been ruled intra vires, or within provincial jurisdiction. He further announced that the government was putting up five thousand dollars to have the matter decided by the Judicial Committee of the Privy Council in London, at that time the highest court of appeal for Canadian questions. The result of Macdonald's manoeuvre was that the Costigan motion had no practical effect on events in New Brunswick.

Not long after, as a consequence of the so-called Pacific Scandal, which implicated the prime minister in a sordid affair with American railway moguls, the Conservatives resigned from office and the Liberals, under Alexander Mackenzie, formed a government. In 1874, Canadians, who were still angered by the scandal, elected Mackenzie's Liberals with a majority government. Once in power, though, the Liberals showed themselves to be as unwilling to come to the side of the Catholic minority in New Brunswick as the Conservatives had been.

In July 1874, the Privy Council in London agreed with Macdonald and ruled that the Common Schools Act was intra vires, within the realm of provincial authority, and that, therefore, the taxing arrangements set up to support the act should not be struck down. The ruling was the same as one made the year before by the New Brunswick Supreme Court, which had found against a resident of Kent Country, New Brunswick, who had refused to pay the tax and had challenged its legality.[5] The consequence of failure to find a solution in either the federal Parliament or in the courts was that the issue would be fought out in New Brunswick.

At the heart of the issue for New Brunswick Catholics was what they saw as "double taxation" and the consequences for them if they tried to resist by refusing to pay the tax. In 1858, prior to Confederation, New Brunswick had applied a voluntary tax, which was paid only by those parents who were sending their children to state-supported schools. The Common School Act and subsequent tax measures made the payment of the tax obligatory for all, whether their children attended public schools or attended private Catholic schools. In addition, the new law stipulated that, where necessary, local school districts could collect a further sum from each local elector for the support of schools. This regulation raised the political stakes, because anyone who refused to pay this tax would forfeit the right to vote and would not be allowed to hold public posts, included the position of school trustee. Since a very large number of Catholics were inclined to refuse to pay the tax as their only means of protest, this meant that joining the protest movement against the tax would result in the removal of the right to participate in public affairs.

As tension grew in the province, despite the potential consequences, in Catholic districts the payment of the tax dropped appreciably. In Gloucester County, for instance, where 1,433 students had attended 37 schools before the 1871 law went into effect, two years later only 479 students were attending 13 schools. Sharp declines in attendance were also recorded in Kent and Victoria counties, where there were large Acadian populations.[6] Priests and bishops and the Church as a whole campaigned strongly against the law. To strike back at the resistance, the authorities took aim at the Church. In September 1873, a Saint John priest, M. Michaud, was arrested and jailed for failing to pay the tax.

The conflict reached its tragic climax in January 1875 in Caraquet. What made this town a potential tinderbox in the conflict was the fact that, along with an overwhelmingly francophone population, Caraquet had a Protestant anglophone minority that included relatively affluent business people. Only 79 anglophones lived in the town out of a total population of 3,111.[7] Since the anglophones had paid the tax, they were eligible to seek public office, while the francophones who had refused were not. This meant that the school board in a town that was almost completely opposed to the Common School Act could end up in the hands of a minority that supported it.

The result was a social explosion, and a tragic incident that would stamp the struggle indelibly into the collective memory of Acadians. On January 4, 1875, a meeting convened by Robert Young, a local anglophone, and attended only by anglophones, drew up a petition, signed by nineteen people, making the case to provincial authorities that a meeting held the previous November to select a school board was invalid. The argument put it that the decisions arising from the meeting had been made by persons who had failed to pay the tax. The January meeting set up a second school board for the town, made up of three Protestants. Those in attendance then selected a teacher for the town's school, a woman who a year later married one of those elected by the meeting to serve on the school board. In effect, the anglophone minority was staging a *coup d'état* to take over the local school board in support of policies that were strongly rejected by the vast majority of the population.

The members of the school board chosen at the January 4 meeting announced that a public meeting would be held on January 14, open to all ratepayers in the town. That meeting would take decisions to fix the local school tax.[8] At the appointed time and place, a large number of francophone townspeople turned out, despite the fact that, under the law, they were not permitted to vote since they had refused to pay the tax. The school board members, chosen by the anglophones, selected Philip Duval, a Methodist originally from Jersey in the Channel Islands, to preside over the meeting. The francophone majority pronounced themselves against this choice of chairman, but since those running the meeting did not recognize their right to vote, Duval took the chair and declared the session open for business.

Then three men in attendance leapt to their feet, headed for the front of the hall, removed Duval from his chair and propelled him toward the door. Another local man seized the papers of James

Blackhall, one of the anglophones purporting to be a school board member, and showed him the door. Blackhall, a Presbyterian of Scottish origin and a local businessman, was one of the anglophones who was most adamantly opposed to the francophone rejection of the school law.[9]

Those who remained in the hall after the expulsion of Duval and Blackhall expressed their determination to prevent the group that had been elected on January 4 from taking any further steps to gain control of the local school system.

The next morning, January 15, some of those present at the explosive meeting the previous night set out for the local school. When they got there, they found the door locked. Hoping to convene a meeting of Catholics there, they proceeded to the nearby house of James Blackhall and demanded that he turn over the key to the school. He refused, but most of the group stayed in his house. The few who left proceeded to a local store where they purchased a gallon of rum. Armed with the rum, they returned to Blackhall's residence, where there were now about fifty men on the premises. Emboldened by their large numbers and the effects of the rum, the ringleaders of the group demanded that Blackhall sign a letter of resignation in which he would undertake to refrain from participation in future school board affairs.

Things turned ugly when windows were broken and the stove in the house was overturned, creating the danger of a fire. Under intense pressure, Blackhall signed the paper, as did a second member of the so-called school board who feared that a hostile visit to his house could be next.[10]

Having succeeded in intimidating anglophone opponents, the rebellious group went to the store and house of Robert Young, one of the chief targets of their wrath, but Young happened to be in Fredericton at the time. There they purchased more rum and made menacing comments to a store employee who had paid the school tax. Finally they dispersed and went to their homes.[11]

Robert Young's wife, no doubt terrified by what had transpired, sent a telegram, warning her husband that those who had come to their premises were under the influence of drink and that they had threatened Young's life should he return. Her incendiary telegram ended with the claim that the rebels had threatened to pay visits to the towns' merchants and to burn their records of accounts owing. Young, who was on his way home, received a copy of the telegram in the vicinity of the town of Sackville.[12]

From Sackville, Young did not proceed directly home. Instead, he stopped off at the home of a friend in Chatham, New Brunswick, en route. He did not finally reach Caraquet until January 22. By then, much of the anglophone press in the province had published alarmist articles with headlines that read: "The Caraquet Mob," "The Anti-School Law Crusade Country" and "Mob Violence in Caraquet."[12]

The English press in the province, with the exception of Saint John's Catholic *Morning Freeman*, portrayed the francophone population of Caraquet and northern New Brunswick in ways that fitted in with long-held prejudices and stereotypes. Anglophones in the province were inclined to see francophones as lawless, drunken and riotous. It was common for the press to depict Acadians as ignorant, priest-ridden and easily manipulated by agitators—all of which threatened the maintenance of public order.[14]

In this already tense situation, those who had participated in the events of January 15 decided once again to confront Robert Young. On Monday morning, January 25, about one hundred men set out for Young's house with the goal of setting things straight. Along with a few well-armed friends, Young barricaded himself in his house, and when what was described in the English press as a "drunken mob" arrived at his door, he did not open it. This confrontation ended peacefully enough, with those outside Young's house leaving and dispersing without having had a chance to confront him.[15]

The balance of forces in Caraquet was transformed abruptly in the middle of the following night when Sheriff Robert B. Vail arrived from Bathurst at 3:00 a.m., accompanied by six constables. They had with them the names of those who were alleged to have participated in the riot of January 15 and possessed warrants for their arrest. Later that morning the sheriff and his constables were joined by two other constables. Then the arrests began, with an anglophone police force arresting francophones. Before leaving Bathurst for Caraquet, Sheriff Vail sent a telegram to William Kelly, at whose home Robert Young had spent the night on his way home, in the neighbouring county of Northumberland. Vail asked Kelly for reinforcements. At dawn on January 27, twenty men from the region of Miramichi arrived in Caraquet and joined the sheriff and his constables.[16]

Under the law, constables could not be called into Gloucester County, and therefore Caraquet, without the formal request of three justices of the peace from Gloucester. In this highly unusual situation, such a formal request was not made. Were the outsiders constables, a special force that had been properly sworn in, or were they vigilantes? Whatever the legalities, the armed men were determined to bring the troublemakers to justice. The sheriff and his men set up their headquarters in the Hotel Sewell.[17] The sheriff received a tip that some of the men they were searching for were holed up in a nearby house, the home of André Albert. Indeed, some of those on the run from the police were in the home of Albert, selected no doubt because it provided such a good view of the Hotel Sewell and of the comings and goings of the constables.

Sheriff Vail ordered his assistant, Stephen Gable, to take some men to check out the Albert home. With twenty men, and with James Blackhall to serve as an interpreter, Gable arrived at André Albert's front door. While Blackhall questioned Albert about whether one of the suspects was in the house, Gable and several armed men penetrated the building, leaving the rest of the force outside to watch for any attempted escape out of the windows. In the kitchen, the armed men encountered two women and, fearing that one of the women might throw boiling water at them, they threatened them with their rifles.

Suddenly, one of the constables, Robert Ramsay, heard a noise emanating from the floor above. Aiming at the opening to the attic, he fired his gun. Several constables tried to force their way into the attic but they were repulsed by the men hiding there. Then the occupants of the attic fired two shots. In the midst of this furious melee, John Gifford, a twenty-two-year-old from Newcastle, managed to push his head and shoulders into the attic. A shot rang out and Gifford fell dead.[18] Later investigation revealed that before he was himself hit, he had discharged a single shot from his .22 calibre Smith and Wesson pistol.

Several other constables had also fired. In the confusion and the smoke from the firing of guns, two of the men hidden in the attic leapt down into the kitchen. One succeeded in getting away, while the other was captured. Several constables climbed into the attic and found two other men, one of them wounded. Then they spied a third man in the corner, Louis Mailloux, who had been struck in the head by a bullet and who was lying in a pool of his own blood.

After those who had been arrested were taken away and deposited in the house of Robert Young, which had been used for the past day as a prison, the constables allowed Mailloux, who was still breathing, to be brought down from the attic. By this time, Mailloux had been bleeding for close to an hour, and shortly thereafter he expired.

The two deaths in Caraquet created a sensation in the province, as did the judicial proceedings that followed. As news of the shootings spread, a New Brunswick senator and two justices of the peace called on the militia to send troops to Caraquet to deal with a potential riot. From Newcastle on January 28, two officers and forty-one artillerymen armed with two nine-pounder cannons left for Bathurst, arriving there the following day. Similarly, from Chatham four officers and forty-six men from the 73rd Infantry Battalion set out for Bathurst, also arriving on January 29.[19]

Anglo-Protestant New Brunswick saw in the events the tragic death of a young man who was committed to upholding the law. The province's English-speaking majority welcomed the subsequent show of muscle as a way to deter rioters and their leaders, who had been refusing to bow to the rule of law since the passage of the school law in 1871. On February 2, 1875, a thousand people turned out for the burial of John Gifford in Newcastle. The local newspaper eulogized him as a hero who had died to safeguard the country's institutions and predicted that his memory would be cherished in the centuries to come.[20]

Following a coroner's inquest, the twenty-four men arrested by Sheriff Vail and his constables were charged with having participated in a riot, and nine of them were also charged with the murder of John Gifford. The accused were to wait eight months before their trial got underway. Meanwhile, the other death, that of Louis Mailloux, was treated very differently. The coroner's inquest concluded that he had been shot by someone unknown and that he had met his death in an incident that had occurred while the forces of law and order were seeking to arrest the rioters who were hiding in the house. No charge was brought in the Mailloux case.[21]

In September 1875, a grand jury was called into session in Bathurst to rule on whether there was sufficient evidence to proceed with criminal cases in the matter of the riot and the murder of John Gifford. The accused rioters and murderers would be tried individually. What lent the procedure greater drama and weight was that appearing for the Crown in the proceedings was none other than George E. King, the procurer general and the premier of New Brunswick, the leader whose government had passed the inflammatory school law four years earlier.[22] The role of the premier at the trial gave the affair a political character. Anglo-Protestant New Brunswick was putting Catholic New Brunswick on trial. In many ways, the proceedings prefigured the trial of Louis Riel in Regina in 1885.

The judge in the case, John C. Allen, was descended from a prominent New Brunswick Loyalist family. During the trial, over which he presided in Bathurst in the autumn of 1875, he was named chief justice of the Supreme Court of New Brunswick. In his charge to the jury, in a trial conducted in English with translation provided for the defendants, all of whom were francophones, Judge Allen put the case in terms that were highly prejudicial to the defence. He stated that it was his duty to explain to the jurors that if the persons who were in the attic were there with the goal of resisting officers in carrying out their duty, and if their goal was to prevent the capture of Joseph Chiasson, one of the defendants, then they were each as guilty of the murder of Gifford as the one who actually fired the fatal shot.[23]

His charge to the grand jury in the second case, which concerned the riots on January 15 and 25, 1875, was equally one-sided. He told the members of the grand jury that when the rioters assembled outside the house of James Blackhall they sang "La Marseillaise," which he said had the goal of exciting nationalist prejudices. He made his views very plain on the subject of the school law that was under attack in Caraquet. He explained that when a law was passed, those who were discontented with it had no choice but to submit to it.[24]

Two days after arguments began, the grand jury ruled that a sufficient case had been made against the nine accused of the murder for a trial to be held. The following day, the same grand jury ruled that the cases should proceed against the accused in the matter of the riot of January 15. However, the grand jury rejected the accusations for rioting and illegal assembly arising out of the January 25 gathering at the residence of Robert Young.[25]

At first, it had been hoped that the lead defence advocate in the two cases would be Adolphe Chapleau, the eminent Quebec lawyer who had defended Ambroise Lépine, a close associate of Louis Riel's during the period of the provisional government at Fort Garry in 1869–70. Chapleau had defended Lépine against the charge of murder, a charge brought in the aftermath of the execution of an Ontarian by the name of Thomas Scott at the hands of the provisional government. In the end, those handling legal strategy decided that the defendants would be better off not having a prominent Québécois as lead attorney, since this could alienate New Brunswick's anglophone majority. In the event, the lead role in the defence was taken by S. R. Thompson, an eminent Saint John lawyer of Irish descent.

With the work of the grand jury completed, the cases went before the trial juries. The riot charge was heard first, and over a two-week period the court heard from twenty-two witnesses for the Crown and eleven witnesses for the defence. The jury brought in a guilty verdict against those charged with having participated in the riot. The judge announced that sentences would be handed down at the next meeting of the court in July 1876. Those convicted remained behind bars, since bail for them had been set at $1,200, a very high sum for the era.

Next came the murder trial. Having won a guilty verdict on the matter of the riot, the Crown was able to use that finding to argue that the riot of January 15 was the root cause of the violent events of January 27. With a jury selected, the murder trial began on November 8, 1875. The Crown, calling thirty witnesses, set out to prove that the fugitives who were hiding in André Albert's attic on the fateful day were engaged in a deliberate effort to resist the forces of law and order. The defence pinned its case on proving that it was the constables who opened fire first in the encounter. The testimony of Robert Ramsay, one of the constables, proved embarrassing for the Crown when he declared that he had fired first for the purpose of intimidating the men in the attic. All the other constables contradicted Ramsay on this crucial point.

At the end of the trial, the jurors deliberated for five hours before bringing in a verdict of guilty against Joseph Chiasson, one of the accused. Eight others remained on trial facing the same charge. At this point, the Crown proposed a deal, that the other eight would plead guilty to the lesser charge of involuntary homicide. In addition, their culpability in the matter of the riot would be subsumed in their guilty plea. Feeling that they had no real choice, the defence attorneys accepted the deal. Charges against the two youngest of the eight—one aged sixteen, the other eighteen—were dropped. Meanwhile, Joseph Chiasson, who had been convicted, was to remain in prison, awaiting sentence, which, in a deal made by the judge, the Crown and the defence, was to be handed down by the Superior Court of New Brunswick.[26]

The end of the trials did not conclude the affair, which still had more strange twists to come. Throughout the criminal trials, defence attorney S. R. Thompson made frequent objections to the proceedings, and he objected to the way in which the Crown had associated the question of the riot of January 15, 1875, with the events of January 27, 1875, the day of the killings. These objections served as the basis for his appeal to a higher court. Mention has been made of the fact that in the autumn of 1875 Judge Allen was named chief justice of the Supreme Court of New Brunswick. This put him in the decidedly odd position of having to review the cases he had himself judged at a lower level.

In the winter of 1876, the provincial Supreme Court reviewed the cases, and in the absence of S. R. Thompson, the side of the defendants was taken by another lawyer, Kennedy Burns. In its review of the case concerning the riot, the review court upheld the guilty verdict of the lower court. The review of the murder case resulted in the conviction against Joseph Chiasson being dropped, because of the way the trial had linked the riot of January 15 with the killing of John Gifford on January 27. The court further found that the trial had not established that those in the attic along with Chiasson had been there for the purpose of resisting arrest rather than because they feared being attacked by the sheriff's constables. In shelving the Chiasson verdict, the court also dropped the involuntary homicide verdicts against the other six defendants. The court further decided that it would impose no sentence against the rioters because of the amount of time that had passed since the event during which they had been behind bars. When the court's decisions were announced in June 1876, the people of Caraquet rejoiced. For the town, the terrible trauma of the past eighteen months had come to an end.[27]

In 1875, while the Caraquet affair and its legal aftermath held the attention of the province, a deal was reached between the government and the province's Roman Catholics that made the school law less onerous in its application. In August of that year, in response to proposals put to it by leaders of the Catholic community, the provincial government agreed that, in districts with two or more primary schools, students could attend a school other than the one in the district where they lived. In practice, this allowed for the formation of schools that would be largely Protestant or largely Catholic in composition. In schools with a preponderance of French-speaking students, French could be used as the language of instruction. In these schools, some French textbooks were added to the roster of available texts, although most texts were bilingual, with sections in both French and English.[28] It was further agreed that a person who had obtained a teaching certificate from a Catholic order would be allowed to teach without having to attend a teacher's training school in New Brunswick. Books offensive to the Catholic minority could be submitted to the school board so that material of an objectionable kind would not be used in classrooms. After the formal school day had ended, a period of religious education was to be allowed in the school for those who wished to attend.[29]

The Louis Mailloux affair and the struggle for Acadian schools blunted the drive of the New Brunswick anglophone majority to impose its ways on the francophone minority. But it did not halt it. Nearly ninety years more would pass before the Acadians won educational and linguistic rights that would have been unimaginable during the tense days of the 1870s.

—

CHAPTER 8

THE CAJUN ODYSSEY

"This is our Cajun land, right, podna?" I said. "We make the rules, we've got our own flag."

—Dave Robicheaux, in James Lee Burke's
novel *Black Cherry Blues*

WHILE A NEW ACADIE was being created in the Maritimes, another homeland, in the distant and exotic setting of Louisiana, was established by exiled Acadians. Joseph Broussard, the legendary Beausoleil, who was born in Port Royal and died in Louisiana, provides a direct link between old Acadie and the Cajun community in Louisiana. He remains a heroic figure to Acadians, but his memory is cherished even more by the Cajuns, among whom his fame is second only to that of the fictional Evangeline.

Largest of the components of the Acadian Diaspora is the Cajun community in Louisiana, with a population today in the range of 800,000 people, close to 20 percent of the state's total population of 4.4 million. Those who were to become the Cajuns reached their new homeland following lengthy and harrowing journeys.

During the decades when Acadians were establishing themselves in Louisiana, their new home was anything but tranquil and secure. Sovereignty over Louisiana was first held by France, and then transferred to Spain in 1762 (in the secret Treaty of Fontainebleau that did not become public for many months). The following year, under the Treaty of Paris, which ended the Seven Years' War and ratified the cession of Canada to Britain, the British also acquired France's Louisiana territory east of the Mississippi and north of the Île of Orleans (where New Orleans is located). In addition, Britain gained from Spain its territories of East and West Florida. The British built a fort at Baton Rouge (the present-day state capital of Louisiana), which they named New Richmond. In 1779, during the American Revolutionary War, with Britain already at war with France and the nascent United States, war also broke out between Britain and Spain. The Spaniards succeeded in capturing Baton Rouge and regained control of West Florida. In 1800, with Europe torn asunder by the wars in the aftermath of the French Revolution and the rise of Napoleon, Spain handed the Louisiana territory west of the Mississippi back to France under another secret agreement, the Treaty of San Ildefonso.

Control was not actually established by France until November 1803, but then, in a transfer of great historic importance, the United States purchased the immense Louisiana territory for $15 million. The territory, out of which thirteen states or parts of states were to be carved, transformed the United States from a country on the eastern seaboard of America to a continental power. In 1810, the Americans who resided in Spain's West Florida territory took power there and declared their new fiefdom a republic. Later, the region was to become a part of the state of Louisiana (statehood was achieved in 1812, with Louisiana admitted to the Union as the fifteenth state). In present-day Louisiana, the West Florida territory is known as the Florida Parishes.

The Acadian refugees were not heading into an unpopulated wilderness when they reached Louisiana. From the early eighteenth century, New Orleans, with its pivotal position near the mouth of the Mississippi River, was already the rising metropolis of the colony. In addition to native peoples, the colony was home to French and Spanish populations, as well as slaves from the Caribbean islands and West Africa. The history of the Acadians in Louisiana was to be intertwined with that of the Creoles. Today, the word Creole generally refers to people of colour or mixed race. When the Acadians landed in Louisiana, though, and for a very long time after that, the word Creole, of Portuguese derivation, referred to anyone born in America whose ancestors were from elsewhere. That meant that a Creole could be French, Spanish or English.

Among the French Creoles in Louisiana there was a slave-owning upper class whose members dominated the territories in which the Acadians established themselves. The Creoles looked down on the Acadian newcomers as poverty-stricken interlopers. For the Acadians who made their way to the prairie north and west of the present-day city of Lafayette and became ranchers, friction with the big Creole cattle-owners was unavoidable. The Creoles were used to allowing their large herds to roam across the open prairie. As the Acadians established their own much smaller herds, their cattle were often mixed up with the herds of the Creoles and conflict ensued. The new Acadian ranchers wanted fences around their properties to keep their herds separate. The Creole ranchers resisted this idea at first because they wanted what they had previously enjoyed, the run of the whole prairie for their cattle. The Cajuns ultimately won this fight, and, over the long term, intermarriage between Cajuns and Creoles drew many of the Creoles into the emerging Cajun community.

From the old Acadie to the new, the migrants brought their language, culture and ideas about architecture. Houses in the style of those built in their settlements along the Bay of Fundy rose in south Louisiana. And the newcomers found ways to make a living, despite the fact that they had arrived with nothing but their willingness to work. Within a few years, the Acadians were raising livestock and had discovered that with sugar cane and sweet potatoes they could grow crops for cash, much needed for the building of their new settlements.

Over the course of their two centuries in Louisiana, the Cajuns diverged culturally from the Acadians in Canada as they had to cope with the pressures and societal changes that confronted them. During the first decades of the nineteenth century, the Cajuns made a remarkable adaptation to their new environment. They began by building houses very much on the model of the houses they had built in old Acadie before the expulsion. But living in a subtropical land instead of a cold temperate climate, changes to these structures were quickly made. In their new environment, the émigrés encountered vast stands of cypress trees along the bayous of south Louisiana. And on the open prairie, while there was not the stone that was readily to hand in Nova Scotia, there was clay. Utilizing these materials, the newcomers built what came to be called the Cajun Cottage. The cypress wood was straight-grained, relatively free of knots and could be sawed and split into planks and used to build the frame of the house. The houses built in Louisiana were raised a couple of feet off the ground and sat on cypress logs. This innovation was needed in a land where floods were common. And by raising the houses, a cooling breeze was allowed to flow beneath the dwelling.

While in Nova Scotia the builders had filled in the walls with stone, in their new location they employed a mixture of clay and Spanish moss. On the outside, to protect the walls from the ubiquitous torrential rains, a sheathing of overlapping cypress planks was put in place. Double doors, constructed of solid boards held together by dovetailed battens, were mounted on the front and rear of the houses. To save space in the mostly small-sized dwellings, the doors swung outwards. On the two side walls, one or two window spaces were created. No glass was used; instead the window coverings were constructed of wood in a manner similar to the doors. These shutters swung outwards. The doors and window shutters were mounted on wooden or iron strap-hinges. Either inside the frame of the house or outside and against it, a chimney and a fireplace, made of sticks, clay and moss, was constructed, to be used both for cooking and to provide heat when needed. The roof on the Cajun Cottage was high and was overlain with hand-hewn cypress shingles. The space inside the roof allowed room for storage or for a sleeping area, and this space was accessed by a steep, ladder-type stairway. Outside the front door, the dwellings featured a front porch, which added to the living space. Across the front of the porch four square posts gave support to the overhanging roof.

These houses, constructed in the early period without the use of nails, were not painted. Over time, they turned a natural grey. With the exception of the small pieces of iron used to mount the doors and windows, the materials used in the construction of the houses were immediately to hand. Based on the model of these first simple structures, more elaborate and larger dwellings were constructed as the Cajuns became more affluent and could afford to purchase imported materials.[1]

In addition to the Creoles, the Cajuns came in contact with both the slave population in their new homeland and a large and important community of free persons of colour, who made up the largest number of free blacks in the United States. Free persons of colour were often former slaves who had been paid for work on Sundays and who had saved up money to purchase their own freedom. Many of them also bought the freedom of their relatives. Some of the free persons of colour became slave owners themselves.

As for Louisiana's very large slave population, some of these had been forcibly imported from West Africa and some from the Caribbean islands. In the aftermath of the revolution in Haiti at the beginning of the nineteenth century, thousands of French-speaking Creoles fled to Louisiana from the island, bringing their slaves with them. A large proportion of Louisiana's slaves were French-speaking.

During the first years of Acadian settlement in Louisiana, the language of the majority of the non-slave population in the colony was French. That changed in the decades following the Louisiana Purchase as Anglo-Americans flooded into this new territory of the United States. In 1803, among Louisiana's non-slave population, French-speakers outnumbered English-speakers by a decisive seven to one margin. When Louisiana became a U.S. state in 1812, even though nearly ten thousand French-speaking refugees had arrived from Haiti in 1809, the ratio of francophone to anglophone non-slave Louisiana residents had fallen to three to one.

It was during the pre–Civil War decades that Cajuns, now living in an American state, came in contact with Anglo-Americans in very large numbers for the first time. The Anglo-American migration into the state was driven by Texans seeking new prairie lands and by migrants who needed new lands on which to grow cotton, because of the soil depletion of cotton fields in the Old South. By 1860, on the eve of the war, the enormous influx of Anglo-Americans into the state had wrought a demographic revolution, so that 70 percent of the free residents of the state were English-speakers. Despite the transformation in the state as a whole, in 1870 Acadians were still more numerous than Anglo-Americans in nine of Louisiana's fifteen Acadian parishes.[2]

Upon their arrival in Louisiana, the Acadians brought with them the frontier egalitarianism that was the legacy of their former homeland. That spirit was one reason why they had found French society so intractably alien to them. In old Acadie there had been no slavery, so the "peculiar institution," as it came to be known in America, was not a part of their experience. Slavery was, however, very much a part of the Louisiana to which they had emigrated. The upper-class Creoles, who saw themselves as the social betters of the Acadians, relied on slave labour to sustain their high standard of living and their love of leisure. While the first generation of Acadians never became much interested in acquiring slaves, those born in Louisiana soon became slaveholders where circumstances permitted or where additional labour was highly useful. This was the case for those living along the Mississippi, who faced the enormous toil of clearing dense forest cover from their properties. By the turn of the nineteenth century, it had become commonplace for many Acadians in Louisiana to own slaves, an experience that both altered their egalitarian outlook and brought them into contact with a slave population that made a significant impact on the culinary and cultural habits of the Cajuns.

By and large, the Cajuns prospered in the pre–Civil War decades. And the widely varied experiences of Cajuns—as ranchers, cotton growers or fishermen—promoted social class differences within their ranks. A slave-owning upper class emerged, made up of those Cajuns who became members of the planter aristocracy. Class differentiation among the Cajuns was heavily influenced by where they lived. Only a minority of the whole Cajun population owned slaves in the early 1800s, but by 1810 a majority of Cajuns living along the Mississippi River and the Bayou Teche, where cotton production for export was the dominant way to make a living, did own slaves.[3]

Not only did slave ownership negate the frontier egalitarianism that had characterized the whole of Cajun society, it injected a previously alien materialism into Cajun life. In old Acadie, and in the early days of Cajun settlements in Louisiana, the goal of life was to achieve a modicum of personal comfort, but no more. Capitalist accumulation and the drive to acquire great wealth were essentially unknown. But the ownership of slaves, the potential for exporting large quantities of cotton and the social example of the wealthy Creoles transformed the point of view of many Cajuns. Drawn into the market economy and slave ownership, many Cajuns abandoned the outlook that had prevailed in a more self-sufficient economy and society.

The rise of a slave-owning elite among the Cajuns also meant that Cajun society lost its former cohesiveness. The great durability and solidarity of Acadian communities was the essential attribute that had allowed this small people to persevere in the face of the loss of their settlements, exile and the establishment of a new homeland in south Louisiana. Acadian solidarity had been the bane of the English rulers of Nova Scotia in the decades leading up to *le Grand Dérangement* and had provoked incomprehension among those in France who had come up against exiled Acadians.

As the Cajuns became rooted in south Louisiana, and as they adapted to the roles they played, that solidarity began to dissolve. Cajuns found themselves on opposite sides of political and social questions. And depending on their own circumstances, they developed different outlooks on life. Wealthy Cajuns first saw upper-class Creoles as their role models, and later they looked to the growing Anglo-American community in the region for their social norms. Still later, a large number of elite Cajuns abandoned Cajun culture and values. During the dark decades in the mid twentieth century, when the Louisiana school system did all it could, meting out healthy doses of punishment, to eradicate the use of French by students in classrooms and in schoolyards, wealthy Cajuns often supported the policy of anglicization. Having rejected their own culture, they adopted the idea that its suppression would be an enlightened step toward progress.

By the eve of the Civil War, which broke out in 1861, Cajuns could be found playing leading roles in opposing political camps. This was in sharp contrast to the behaviour of the Acadians during their early years in south Louisiana, when they had displayed a marked tendency to be reticent about involving themselves in the political process. Their experience of representative government had been a far from happy one prior to *le Grand Dérangement* of 1755. In old Acadie, they had elected delegates who dealt with the British governors, but these delegates had shown themselves to be impotent when the community was threatened with expulsion and the destruction of their settlements. In the late eighteenth century, when they lived under Spanish rule in Louisiana, Acadians had, on occasion, elected *sindics*, representatives whose job was to oversee local public works projects. During their early years in Louisiana, Acadians found that when their interests clashed with those of the wealthy Creoles they did not fare well. Similarly, during the brief period of French rule and in the first phase of American control, which began in late 1803, the Acadians saw little point in participating in politics.

When American rule was first established in Louisiana, under the administration of William Charles Cole Claiborne, the Americans wanted to curry support for the regime from French-speaking elements of the population. In 1805, Claiborne appointed five Acadians as justices of the peace, and ten were made officers in the militia. The same year, three Acadians were elected to the first territorial legislature of Louisiana. This promising beginning, however, ended abruptly when Claiborne's administration brought English common law into the jurisdiction. Acadians were displeased as well by what they saw as Claiborne's excessive use of the executive veto. This displeasure was punctuated when Joseph Landry, one of the Acadian members of the legislature, resigned in protest.

Louisiana statehood in 1812 did little to prod the Acadians into participation in politics. It was a long time before most Acadians in Louisiana identified with the American Dream, and even when they eventually did, American values and ambitions were perceived through their own cultural lens. Only one Acadian representative was elected to the first state constitutional convention. That convention, which drew up the rules under which state politics would operate, was dominated by the large planter interests. The resulting state constitution was highly conservative, with substantial property requirements established for office-seekers. To win the office of representative, a male adult in Louisiana had to own five hundred dollars' worth of property; the office of senator was restricted to those owning at least one thousand dollars' worth of property; and the property requirement for governors was set at five thousand dollars. The vote itself was restricted to those who owned at least some property. The consequence was that Acadian males along the Mississippi River and the bayous Teche and Lafourche, where they generally owned property, kept the vote. However, landless Acadians in the south-west, in the lower Lafourche and in Terrebonne Parish, were mostly disenfranchised. Wealthy and mostly slave-owning Acadians in the river parishes were able to participate in the political process. But for the most part, poorer Acadians participated hardly at all.

In the 1820s, the new democracy of Andrew Jackson's populist campaigns for the presidency in 1824 and 1828 did strike a chord in Acadian communities. Poor, prairie-dwelling Acadians took up the cause of the man who was a hero for his victory over the British in the Battle of New Orleans at the end of the War of 1812, a battle in which several hundred Acadians had fought on the American side.

From the late 1820s on, politics in south Louisiana was divided between the conservative Whigs and the populist Democrats. Acadians were drawn into these two camps depending on their geographical location and on their socio-economic status. In the river parishes, the wealthier slave-owning Acadians rallied to the Whig side, while the prairie-dwelling Acadians were drawn to the Democrats and Jacksonian Democracy. Acadians at the bottom of the wealth scale were almost exclusively on the side of the Democrats, but many of them were denied the vote under the 1812 constitutional rules.

The most prominent Acadian politician to emerge in the pre–Civil War era in south Louisiana was Alexandre Mouton, himself a third-generation Louisiana Acadian. Born near Lafayette in 1804, Mouton was a slave-owning planter. A man with prominent ears, a thin face and a hawk-like nose, Mouton had the appearance of a natural aristocratic, born to be a leader. As a young man, he was clean-shaven. In his later years, he retained a full head of grey hair and sported a carefully coiffed grey beard, and he wore glasses that made him appear rather owlish. He was first elected to the Louisiana legislature and then to the U.S. House of Representatives. From 1837 to 1842, Mouton was a U.S. senator, serving under the banner of Jacksonian Democracy. Returning to state politics in 1842, he became the voice of reform in Louisiana. He denounced the constitution of 1812, with its limited franchise. Mouton advocated the elimination of property qualifications for voters, and he championed the cause of direct election of state officials. He took aim at the quasi-aristocratic planter domination of state politics. His target was Governor Isaac Johnson, one of the drafters of the state constitution of 1812.

Mouton's campaign for constitutional change won him the support of a wide constituency across the state, including most Acadians, poor whites in the northern regions of Louisiana and the poor of New Orleans. With these groups as his base, Mouton won the governor's office, the first Democrat to do so. At first, his attempts to convene a constitutional convention to revise the rules of politics in Louisiana were blocked by conservative Whig legislators. But in 1843, the state's legislative elections put new, reform-minded legislators in place, and an enabling act was passed by the state legislature in 1844 to convene a constitutional convention the following year. After a round of political manoeuvring in which Mouton was centrally involved, the constitutional convention took the crucial step of extending the franchise to all white males over twenty-one years of age.

The proposals of the constitutional convention were ratified by a large majority of voters in a state-wide referendum in 1845. The endorsement of extended democratic rights was especially strong in Acadian parishes, where 76 percent of those voting approved the new constitution. In Ascension, Lafourche and Lafayette parishes, where Acadians made up a majority of the white population, the constitutional changes were approved by more than 85 percent of those voting. Meanwhile, in Terrebonne Parish, where the voting regulations of the 1812 constitution disenfranchised most Acadian males, the proposed changes were turned down by a six-to-four tally.[4]

Mouton, who was easily the most influential Acadian politician in Louisiana in the pre–Civil War era, chose to retire from public life following the approval of the state's new constitution. Although he left the governor's mansion and did not seek any other office during the following decade, Mouton remained a highly influential voice in south Louisiana politics. He had been the champion of universal white manhood suffrage and he was also a strong voice on behalf of Southern rights. This record and these views gave him continued currency, and he drew large crowds to rallies he addressed in Acadian parishes.

The combined effects of the 1845 constitution, with its wider franchise, and the populism of Andrew Jackson and Alexandre Mouton transformed the Acadians of south Louisiana into a solid bastion of the Democratic Party. During his time in office, Mouton was an early advocate of public education in Louisiana, but also a supporter of cheap government and lower taxes, which he wished to achieve by selling off state assets. Mouton personified the contradictions in the Acadian outlook on politics and society during this crucial period. He fought for a wider democracy, but only for whites, and when the time came to make a choice in the great American struggle, he chose the side of the South and the defence of its "peculiar institution." While the Acadians had begun their odyssey in Louisiana with an egalitarian outlook, this had been modified by their experience with slave ownership.

There is little doubt that Acadians, both those who owned slaves and those who did not, shared the general belief of white

Southerners that blacks were inherently inferior to whites and that slavery was defensible, or, as paternalists would have it, the best possible arrangement for black people. While in the 1840s Acadians in south Louisiana were caught up in the cause of populism and an expanded democracy, in the succeeding decade, as national politics focused ever more on the issues of slavery and the rights of the South, the Acadian leadership staunchly took the Southern side. In part, this was a consequence of the very logic of slavery, a system in which human chattels could be kept in their place only through intimidation and force.

The ultimate fear of Southern whites throughout the era of slavery was of slave revolts, of which there were a number. Slave uprisings, such as that led by Nat Turner in Virginia in 1831, were put down with great savagery. Fear and paranoia spread across the South in response to the Virginia rising, and in south Louisiana, as in other places, new and repressive rules were established to prevent slaves from assembling or interacting with free persons. Indeed, in 1840 a failed slave uprising did occur in the Lafayette area.[5] Huge plantations, with their very large black populations, only exacerbated the nervousness. Whites in these vicinities, and this came to include Acadians, lived in fear of the potential consequences.

Anxiety about slave uprisings was strongest, of course, in the areas where the plantations were located. On the prairie, where there were fewer slaves, Acadian ranchers had concerns of their own. Cattle rustling became a serious problem for them in the late 1850s. Large herds of cattle, not subject to much surveillance, were easy prey for lawbreakers. In response to this threat, in the absence of police protection, Acadian ranchers turned to their own devices, setting up vigilante groups that roamed the prairie at night, on the lookout for outlaws. A major sponsor and supporter of the vigilante movement was none other than Alexandre Mouton, the former Louisiana governor. Rough justice was dispensed to those believed to be rustlers, who, once caught, were banished from the territory, flogged or even executed. Punishments were meted out on the spot, on orders from the vigilante groups' judicial councils.

A consequence of vigilante justice—practised throughout much of the South and Midwest of the United States during this period— was that those who tasted the lash of the vigilantes set up their own armed bands to fight back. In south Louisiana, armed anti-vigilante bands sprang up in south-western St. Landry Parish. The result, in September 1859, was armed conflict on the prairie. The struggle came to a head at what was dubbed the Battle of Bayou Queue de Tortue. The battle was triggered when a force of several hundred vigilantes, equipped with a homemade brass cannon, invaded an area of anti-vigilante strength. Riding at the head of the vigilante column was Jean-Jacques Alfred Alexandre Mouton, son of the former governor. Born into this privileged family in the town of Opelousas in 1829, Mouton was a swashbuckling, heroic figure with a dark beard and piercing eyes. He had graduated from the U.S. Military Academy at West Point, a member of the class of 1850. Having briefly served in the United States Army, Mouton had then gone to work as a civil engineer with a railroad firm. He also operated a sugar plantation in Lafayette Parish. Later, he was to become a legendary figure in the Louisiana Confederate army.

Mouton's vigilante army set up its battle position in front of its adversaries, about two hundred of whom were holed up in and around the fortified home of a man by the name of Émilien Lagrange. When the vigilante brigade opened fire, many of the anti-vigilantes fled or surrendered straightaway. The feeble resistance, however, did not save the losing side from terrible retribution. A number of the anti-vigilantes were beaten to death and others were shot while trying to escape to the open prairie. In addition, about eighty captives were taken by the victorious vigilantes to Lafayette Parish, where they were summarily lynched.

The bloodbath in the aftermath of the battle was sufficiently notorious that it forced a response from the state government. Under pressure from anti-vigilante forces and sympathizers, the governor threatened to send in the state militia to deal with the vigilantes, a threat that forced the vigilantes' committees to wind up their activities. The attempt by the authorities in Baton Rouge to

put a stop to the vigilantes enjoyed no more than a temporary success, however. Within a few months of the Battle of Bayou Queue
de Tortue, the vigilantes were back in operation. On the prairie, they
had the support of most Acadians, not least because the godfather
who oversaw them and provided political cover for them was the
highly respected Alexandre Mouton.

The rise of vigilante movements in south-western Louisiana in
the late antebellum period occurred for the same reasons that vigilante movements appeared in many other regions of the United
States during the same period. Such movements formed where
property owners felt threatened by people who were seen as lawless
outsiders or thieves attacking the sanctity of property. In the case of
Louisiana, the ability of the authorities to deal with cattle rustling
and other forms of theft was inadequate. The consequence was the
emergence of a characteristically conservative movement of local
property owners, involving local elites, who were determined to deal
with the problem directly. The best known cases of vigilantism in
American history were the powerful vigilante committees that were
established in San Francisco in 1851 and 1856. There is evidence that
south Louisiana vigilante groups were inspired by, and organiza-
tionally modelled on, those in San Francisco. About four thousand
men were members of the various vigilante groups in south
Louisiana, making it the second-largest such movement in nine-
teenth-century America.[6]

The vigilante movement in south-western Louisiana, as was the
case elsewhere in the United States, was motivated by raw issues of
social class and race. The vigilante bands, led by the well-to-do and
their followers, meted out their brand of justice, not only to those
they believed to be guilty of theft but also to social undesirables.
Their victims were often newcomers, small property owners and
the landless, and in many cases they were free people of colour or
those of mixed race. A study of the vigilante movement revealed
that of the first twenty-two victims of south-western Louisiana vigilantes, twelve were either European immigrants or the offspring of
immigrants. The very first person to be picked on by the vigilantes

was a man named August Gudbeer, who was the son of German (likely Alsatian) immigrants. In the eyes of the vigilantes, Gudbeer was a petty thief, but what really seems to have provoked their ire was that he was a social outsider. He was sexually involved with a woman whose father was black and whose mother was white. For the vigilantes, the ultimate nightmare was sex between black males and white females. The vigilante committee that "tried" and "convicted" Gudbeer was strongly influenced by who the man was and how he lived, rather than by his supposed petty crimes.[7]

Noteworthy in the operations of the vigilante committees was that they set themselves up as self-appointed bodies that took state functions into their own hands, challenging the monopoly of the means of force claimed by the state. Their self-created judicial councils were clearly just private actors taking over state functions. The "law" they dispensed was not the law of the land but their own privately concocted law. Characteristically, the judicial council of a vigilante committee met in secret to consider the case of a suspect. If they found the person guilty, they determined a punishment, which could be expulsion from the area, a lashing or execution by hanging. With the decision made, members of the vigilante band then rode out during the night to the house of the accused, roused him from his bed and meted out the sentence.

In one particularly notorious case, vigilantes from Anse-la-Butte, drawing recruits from the neighbourhood for their cause, launched a raid on the premises of the mixed-race Coco family, made up of one black man and two white sisters. While the vigilantes alleged that the members of this household were guilty of petty theft, selling stolen goods and prostitution, it was the suggestion of mixed-race polygamy that seems to have been their main objection. On top of that, there was the suggestion that the household was located on land coveted by others. Fearing for their lives, the members of the Coco family fled to another parish.[8]

During the pre–Civil War decades, most Acadians in south Louisiana adhered to a highly localized, even parochial view of politics, not taking much interest in the great national debates of the era. But they followed their leaders and thus were drawn into the larger national struggle on the side of the South and of slavery. In 1861, when the crisis over whether to leave or stay in the American Union was at hand, Alexandre Mouton chaired the convention that presided over the secession of Louisiana from the United States. Mouton had been involved in the breakup of the Democratic Party the previous year, when he and his supporters backed Vice President John C. Breckinridge of Kentucky for president. Breckenridge, with his pro-slavery position, won the support of every cotton state, along with North Carolina, Delaware and Maryland, in the election of 1860, the election that brought Abraham Lincoln to the White House. For a few weeks, Louisiana was on its own after seceding from the Union. Then it joined with the other Deep South states in forming the initial seven-state Confederacy, with its capital in Montgomery, Alabama. When the states of the Upper South, including Virginia, seceded to join the Confederacy, the capital was transferred to Richmond.

The war brought dramatic and negative changes to south Louisiana and the Acadians. Occupying a crucial geographical position in the Confederacy, Louisiana was an important battleground during the war. First, New Orleans was blockaded by the federal navy, which shut down its operations as a great port exporting cotton and sugar to Europe. Then in April 1862, U.S. naval forces, under the command of the famed David G. Farragut, landed troops and seized control of the city, the largest in the Confederacy. This gave the Union control of the mouth of the Mississippi River. The following year, with the Union victory at Vicksburg, federal forces gained control over the whole of the Mississippi River, thereby effectively cutting the Confederacy in half. Federal control over New Orleans did not mean the loss of the state for the Confederates. While federal forces moved upriver and seized the capital at Baton Rouge, the secessionists held the bulk of the state. They moved their capital to Opelousas, not far north of Lafayette, a town located in the heart of Acadian south Louisiana.

While many Cajuns did fight for the secessionist cause, and three of their number, including Alfred Mouton, achieved the rank of brigadier general, many other Cajuns sought to avoid military service. Cajuns were sharply divided in their attitudes to the war, with class interests at the heart of the divide. Wealthy Cajun planters and large farmers, who were major slave owners, strongly supported the Southern cause, as devoted to the defence of slavery as were the members of the Creole planter aristocracy and wealthy Anglo-American slave owners. On the other hand, Acadian small farmers and ranchers had little at stake in the South's fight.[9]

What brought the war home with a vengeance to many Acadians was the Confederacy's decision to conscript all able-bodied men between the ages of eighteen and thirty-five. Conscription was enforced very unevenly, with many men being let off because of their political connections and many others hiding out in the woods, swamps or on the farms of their families. Confederate units were sent out across the prairies of south Louisiana in search of draft dodgers, who were rounded up and forced into local regiments. Desertion from these units was very common, and men who deserted were often rounded up again, although in some cases they were charged with desertion and executed. In the latter days of the Civil War, Acadian soldiers were lampooned in newspapers both in the North and the South as unwilling conscripts who had to be chained to a tree to keep them from running away.

At the top levels of Acadian society, though, enthusiasm for the Southern cause was heartfelt. During the war, Alexandre Mouton's mansion near Lafayette was occupied by federal troops, his sugar mill was destroyed and his slaves were set free. As Union forces moved across south Louisiana, the destruction of the productive capacity of the whole region was enormous. By the end of the war, most of the mills located on plantations were in ruins.

Colonel Alfred Mouton, commanding the 18th Louisiana Infantry Regiment, whose companies were formed mostly of Acadian recruits, saw action at the Battle of Shiloh, Tennessee, in April 1862, where he was wounded. After his recovery, Mouton returned to the

Confederate cause with the rank of brigadier general and saw action in Louisiana in the Lafourche, Teche and Red River campaigns. On April 8, 1864, General Mouton was one of the commanders of a Confederate operation against the Union army at Mansfield, Louisiana. Late in the war, and coming after federal campaigns that had wreaked havoc in the state, the battle was a desperate bid to reverse the fortunes of war, at least in Louisiana.

The action at Mansfield was fought in a wooded area. One account that survives was written by Confederate Captain S. A. Poché, commander of Company B of the 18th Louisiana Regiment, Mouton's own regiment. According to Poché, the Confederates were readying themselves to repel a Union attack on the morning of the battle. Out of the pine woods behind the Confederate line, General Mouton rode up and shouted: "Captain, those are Yankees!" The general then ordered the captain to open fire. On the captain's order, eight-six muskets sounded and about thirty federal soldiers were cut down. Captain Poché's account continued: "General Mouton hurrahed and said the Eighteenth was the first to draw blood."[10]

On the afternoon of that long day of battle, General Mouton led a charge against fleeing federal soldiers. He swept past thirty-five enemy soldiers, who dropped their weapons in apparent surrender. Mouton raised his hand to signal to his own men not to fire on the federals who had thrown down their arms. At that second, five of the enemy soldiers picked up their weapons, aimed at the general and brought him down with five shots to his breast. Mouton fell from his saddle, instantly killed. Confederate soldiers who saw this act of cowardice gunned down the thirty-five Union soldiers. A captain in Mouton's regiment cradled the dead general in his arms, pulled out a silk handkerchief and soaked it with the general's blood. To this day, the blood-stained handkerchief is a treasured relic among the captain's descendants.

The battle in which General Mouton played his heroic part was the largest Confederate victory west of the Mississippi. Mouton, originally buried on the field of battle, was reinterred after the end of the war in the cemetery at St. John's Cathedral in Lafayette.

Heroism and the myths it engendered could not save the Cajuns from what was to come in the aftermath of the war. Post-war Cajun society was markedly different from its dynamic pre-war counterpart. Before the war, most Cajuns were improving their lot, even if, for those at the bottom, the improvements were slight. For wealthy planters and for prairie ranchers, the pre-war decades were a golden age that could only be imagined in the terrible times to come. For Louisiana, as for much of the rest of the South, the post-war era was one of economic depression. In the case of south Louisiana agriculture, the bad times endured right through the Great Depression of the 1930s, only lifting significantly at the end of the Second World War. Most of the Cajuns who had made it into the planter aristocracy were ruined, not only by the destruction wrought by the war, which tore up plants, roads, railroads and bridges, but by the freeing of the slaves, who represented the bulk of their capital. For those who had been less well-to-do, markets and access to markets disappeared. Thousands of Cajun farmers were forced into subsistence agriculture. In the hungry years that followed the war, all they could hope for was to keep their families fed. Several times in the immediate post-war period many Cajun families were actually on the brink of starvation. During the decades following the Civil War, many if not most Cajuns lived in poverty on the margins of American society.

In the general economic misery of the Reconstruction era, a tiny class of wealthy, educated Cajuns occupied the top rung of the social ladder. Most Cajuns, however, were members of a large and expanding underclass composed of landless sharecroppers. Between the few rich and the many poor Cajuns, there was only a small and declining middle class made up of urban professionals and yeoman farmers.[11] It was during these terrible post-war decades that the Cajuns of south Louisiana came to be seen in the United States in a largely negative light, as a lazy, ill-educated, swamp-dwelling people who won their meagre living in a forbidding landscape that was crawling with alligators.

The transformation wrought by the Civil War in south Louisiana can be captured more prosaically. In 1860, on the eve of the war, Acadian real estate holdings in wealthy Ascension Parish, a stronghold of the planters, had a median value of $10,330.98. Ten years later, after the war, the median value of these holdings had plunged to $1,024.78. While the dollar values are virtually meaningless in today's terms, what we can comprehend is that median values sank by 90 percent. In other planter-dominated parishes, Iberville, St. James and West Baton Rouge, the real estate holdings of Acadians dropped in median value respectively by 70 percent, 63 percent and 86 percent.[12] In the prairie parishes, while the reductions were not, on average, as steep, they were nonetheless severe. In Calcasieu, Lafayette, St. Landry, St. Martin, St. Mary and Vermilion, the decline in the median value of Acadian property holdings was respectively as follows: 49 percent; 19 percent; 42 percent; 80 percent; 82 percent; and 55 percent.[13] Property value declines of these magnitudes were not mere abstractions. They had ruinous effects. When a landowner's property value plunged, his ability to borrow money to purchase agricultural machinery or to restore a mill (much needed after the war) was drastically reduced. His ability to hire labour was similarly thwarted. The consequence of such loss of wealth was to push people from their former position in the market economy, where they could produce crops for sale and purchase goods in return, to the margins of society. That was the fate that lay in store for most late-nineteenth-century Cajuns.

One consequence of the marginal position of the Acadians was low school attendance and high rates of illiteracy. In 1870, school attendance rates in Acadian parishes ranged from a low of 3 percent in Cameron Parish to a high of 37 percent in Terrebonne Parish. Illiteracy in Acadian parishes was as high as 43 percent in Calcasieu Parish and 44 percent in St. Landry Parish.[14]

The end of the war brought with it a return to the civil disturbances and violence that had ruptured south Louisiana in the immediate pre-war period. Indeed, the civil disturbances that roiled the peace had their origins during the war itself. Not only was

Louisiana torn during the conflict by both the Union and Confederate armies commandeering supplies during their campaigns, it was the scene, as well, of violent struggles within the society. Confederate efforts to draft men into the army were resisted by armed bands of men who came to be known as Jayhawkers. In Cajun regions, the Jayhawkers grew to the status of a formidable force that could actually take on units of the Confederate army and prevail against them.

The Jayhawkers rose as the Confederacy fell. In the latter months of 1863, after the Confederates had lost the crucial battles of Gettysburg and Vicksburg, violent resistance to Confederate efforts to keep conscripts in the army erupted in south Louisiana, especially among poor Creoles. In 1862, a large number of Creoles were drafted by the Confederates, and when the Union army pushed through the bayous where they lived in the spring of 1863, many of them deserted and returned to their homes. In the summer of 1863, deserters congregated in the area west of Opelousas to resist campaigns by the Confederates to force them back into their units. The leader of the Jayhawkers was Ozémé Carrière, who managed to take what began as a rabble and to knit them into a force with military capability.

Carrière, who was raised in Bois Mallet, was born in 1831, a few months after his father died. When he was a teenager, Carrière joined a group of local bandits whose stock in trade was to rob livestock and valuables from their neighbours. While they moved about over a wide swath of south Louisiana, their favourite haunt was on the prairies in Acadie Parish and in the western reaches of St. Landry Parish. By the late 1850s, Carrière had become a seasoned outlaw and was solidly ensconced as leader of his criminal band. The violent outrages committed by the Carrière gang, which included the murder of people who resisted while being robbed, provoked vigilantes to go after them when law enforcement officials proved unable to do the job. Vigilantes managed to capture Carrière's older brother, Hilaire, along with several other gang members. While these men were hanged, the vigilantes were unable to catch Ozémé Carrière, whose band of followers now included a number of women.

The outbreak of the Civil War gave Carrière the chance to turn himself into more than a mere thug and killer who had attracted camp followers. He became a guerilla fighter, mobilizing those in the region who did not want to be conscripted to fight for the cause of the South. Now a Jayhawker, Carrière drew large numbers to his banner as a rebel against the rebels. In 1864, the Confederates decided to conscript Creoles of colour from south Louisiana to serve as forced labourers in the north of the state. Carrière drew these victims of the South's desperate fight, as well as whites who were resisting the draft, into his ranks. Prior to the war, Carrière had lived with the sister of a prominent free man of colour, Martin Guillory. At the height of the band's career, Guillory served as Carrière's chief lieutenant.[15]

Carrière, who was not particular about his politics, was happy to welcome Union deserters as well as those fleeing the banner of the "Stars and Bars" into his ranks. When Union General Nathaniel Banks, who commanded the federal army in south Louisiana, sent his chief of staff to try to recruit Carrière to the Union cause, offering him an army commission, the long-time outlaw said no. He had no interest in fighting for either side in the war.

The success of Carrière's irregular army created logistical problems. It became more and more difficult to find food and supplies to keep the band intact. To do this, Carrière raided Confederate army camps where weapons, horses and food could be acquired. Confederate units were ordered to shoot Carrière on sight, but the Jayhawker leader was able to stay out of view for long periods because of the support he enjoyed in the countryside among Creoles of colour and among whites whose family members were on the run from the Confederate army.

From late 1863 to early 1865, Carrière's force managed to control much of the south-western Louisiana prairie. While the gang was eager to find supplies where it could, it was careful to leave untouched the agricultural caches that were hidden by Creoles of

Robert Monckton, the British commander who captured Fort Beauséjour and oversaw the first phase of the deportation of the Acadians.

Lieutenant Colonel John Winslow, the commander of the New England regiment, organized the detention and expulsion of the Acadians of Grand Pré.

Charles Lawrence, the Acting Governor of Nova Scotia, triggered the deportation of the Acadians.

Massachusetts Governor William Shirley. Massachusetts provided men and ships to carry out the deportation.

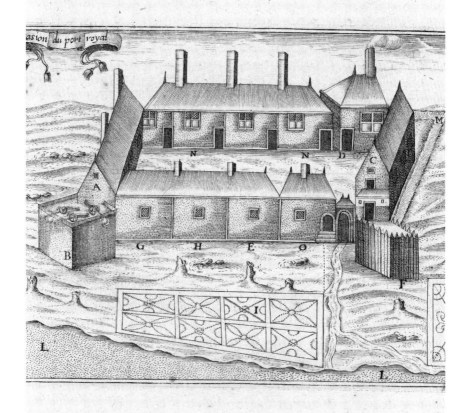

as ion du port royal

A Logemens des artifans.	F Paliffade de pieux.	rebaftir, & y logea le fieur
B Plate forme où eftoit le	G Le four.	Boulay quand le fieur du
canon.	H La cuifine.	Port s'en reuint en France.
C Le magafin.	O Petite maifonnette où	P La porte de l'abitation.
D Logemét du fieur de Pont-	l'on retiroit les vtanfiles de	Q Le cemetiere.
graué & Champlain.	nos barques; que de puis le	R La riuiere.
E La forge.	fieur de Poitrincourt fit	

N ij

Samuel de Champlain's drawing of the Habitation in Port Royal.

ABOVE:
Among the earliest images of Acadian women.

LEFT:
Painting of the Reading of the Order of Expulsion of the Acadians in the church at Grand Pré, September 1755.

A youthful Louis Robichaud, shortly after being sworn in as the first Acadian to be elected premier of New Brunswick.

Richard Hatfield, the eccentric anglophone who identified with the Acadian cause.

Antonine Maillet, the Acadian writer who won France's coveted Prix Goncourt.

Herménégilde Chiasson, the artist and author who was appointed Lieutenant Governor of New Brunswick in 2003.

ROBERT ESTALL/CORBIS

SANDY PRICE

ABOVE:

La Rochelle, the French Atlantic port from which many of the migrants to Acadie departed.

RIGHT:

Acadian church in Grande-Digue, New Brunswick.

Statue of Evangeline,
Grand Pré,
Nova Scotia.

Evangeline Statue,
St. Martinville,
Louisiana.

Under the Evangeline
Tree, where myth has
it that Evangeline was
reunited with her lover.
St. Martinville,
Louisiana.

Symbols of Acadie on
lawns near Shediac,
New Brunswick.

colour. That way, Carrière's army did what it could to avoid alienating its base of support.[16]

Confederate authorities were alarmed, not only by the depredations of the Carrière band, but also by the fact that its leader was coming to be seen by many as a hero. Captain H. C. Morell, who was the Confederate recruiting officer at Opelousas, wrote that "Carrière is daily becoming more and more popular with the masses, and that [popularity] every day serves to increase his gang. These men [Carrière and his lieutenants] are making the ignorant and deluded suppose that they are their champions, that the object they follow . . . is to bring the war to a close, and tell them if they could only make everybody join them the war would soon be brought to a close."[17]

In the spring of 1864, the Confederates decided they had to deal with Carrière and his band of Jayhawkers. Major General Richard Taylor issued a proclamation in May 1864 ordering Confederate forces to shoot Jayhawkers on sight. He dispatched the 4th Louisiana Cavalry, under the command of Colonel Louis Bush, to eliminate Carrière's force. Lieutenant Colonel Louis Amédée Bringier, Bush's executive officer, was the man who took on the campaign against Carrière, making the fight a personal crusade. Bringier had previously shown that he was up to the job when, in an earlier campaign, his men had executed more than a hundred Jayhawkers.[18]

The Confederate hunt for the Jayhawkers was aided, not a little, by a rampage during which Carrière's band burned down houses, stole horses and murdered men who resisted their attacks. In the wake of these atrocities, the band lost popular support, which sharply reduced the number of people prepared to aid them. Ironically, the death throes of the Confederacy also brought down Carrière's once proud force. By the spring of 1865, following the surrender of Robert E. Lee at Appomattox, the Confederates ceased their efforts to conscript men in south Louisiana. It had been the Confederate draft that had raised Carrière from his career as thug to that of guerilla leader. Once conscription was gone, the Jayhawker army disintegrated, with its men flooding back to their homes. In May 1865, with only fifty men remaining under his command, Carrière was ambushed and killed by Confederate soldiers.[19]

The termination of the war and of the Jayhawkers did not signal the end of violence in south Louisiana. The forces that had once formed the backbone of Confederate strength in the region, the local elites, now organized themselves into new vigilante movements. In the post-war years, the targets of the new vigilantes were not only the men who had been Jayhawkers, with whom they had a score to settle, but new groups as well. The people most threatening to the vigilantes now were black. The great fact of post-war southern society was the presence in it of several million former slaves. Now that they were freedmen, the former slaves constituted large minorities of the population in many regions, and in other areas they formed potent majorities. In the parts of south Louisiana where the planters had had their power, blacks outnumbered Acadians and other whites by a wide margin. In the river parishes, blacks, including both former slaves and those who had been free, constituted 66.2 percent of the total population. In these areas, they outnumbered Acadians by more than ten to one. In the Lafourche Basin, blacks made up 47.67 percent of the population, outnumbering Acadians by nearly three to one. In the prairie parishes where ranching predominated, blacks made up between 16 and 21 percent of the population.[20]

If blacks were allowed to become voters in mass numbers and to occupy public positions, as appeared possible during the radical phase of Reconstruction, the political landscape of the South and of south Louisiana, in particular, would be transformed. For the former slaves, the political party to which they were wedded was the Republican Party, the party of Lincoln that had emancipated them. For that reason, the new vigilantes who waged war in south Louisiana against the freedmen also targeted activists in the Republican Party. In 1866, the year after the Civil War ended, the Ku Klux Klan was organized in Pulaski, Tennessee, by white supremacists who were determined to suppress the freedmen, rob them of their potential political power and "sustain the Southern way of life." The Klan, which was anti-Catholic as well as anti-black, could not become a major force in south Louisiana, with its large Acadian population, but it was to become a formidable power in the state's Protestant north.

Playing the same role in south Louisiana, other organizations, which included Cajuns in their ranks, sprang into existence. Most prominent were the Knights of the White Camelia, an organization whose membership included many of those who had made up the vigilante committees of the late antebellum period. Similar to the Klan, the Knights operated as a secret society, with elaborate rituals, ceremonies, signs and passwords. And the central purpose was the same—to terrorize blacks and keep them submissive.[21]

CHAPTER 9

—

EVANGELINE

Where is the thatch-roofed village, the home of Acadian farmers—
Men whose lives glided on like rivers that water the woodlands,
Darkened by shadows of earth, but reflecting an image of heaven?
Waste are those pleasant farms, and the farmers forever departed!
Scattered like dust and leaves, when the mighty blasts of October
Seize them, and whirl them aloft, and sprinkle them far o'er the ocean.
Naught but tradition remains of the beautiful village of Grand-Pré.
Ye who believe in affection that hopes, and endures, and is patient,
Ye who believe in the beauty and strength of woman's devotion,
List to the mournful tradition still sung by the pines of the forest;
List to a Tale of Love in Acadie, home of the happy.
  —HENRY WADSWORTH LONGFELLOW, *Evangeline*

IT DEFIES IMAGINATION that a national legend central to a people's identity and resurrection could be written by a poet from another land and in another tongue. But that has been the remarkable, if unintended, consequence of the poem *Evangeline*, written by New Englander Henry Wadsworth Longfellow in the middle of the nineteenth century. The epic recounts the tragic, and fictitious, tale of two Acadian lovers who are among those expelled from Grand Pré in the deportation of 1755. During the first five months following its initial publication in Boston in October 1847, five editions of one thousand copies each were sold. In the century following its appearance, *Evangeline* was published in at least 270 editions, and was translated 130 times.¹ The epic has inspired films, stage plays, operas and the marketing of perfumes, clothing and other products. Indeed, the first Canadian film ever made was titled *Evangeline*. On the occasion of its premiere at the Empire Theatre on Jacob Street in Halifax, it played to a standing-room-only crowd. The film played in many Canadian communities and was shown in New York. While several still shots have survived from the production, *Evangeline* itself has disappeared, despite efforts to reclaim it.²

Henry Wadsworth Longfellow was the most popular American poet of the nineteenth century, perhaps the most popular ever. He wrote narrative poetry that was melodic, accessible and morally uplifting, if sometimes a little starchy, that made him famous the world over. Queen Victoria was effusively positive when she granted him an audience. The only American poet commemorated with a bust in the Poets' Corner in Westminster Abbey, his home (from 1837 to 1882) in Cambridge, Massachusetts, is a National Historic Site.

Longfellow appeared at a moment in the history of the United States when there was a powerful hunger for native themes, for the epic treatment of American historical tales, and a desire for a literature that portrayed individuals and the natural setting in a distinctly American style. He was a New Englander in the age of New England's literary greatness, and he walked among giants such as Ralph Waldo Emerson and Nathaniel Hawthorne. Indeed, it was Hawthorne who first drew Longfellow's attention to the plight of young Acadian lovers as a setting for a literary work.

The son of a prominent lawyer in Portland, Maine, Longfellow was born in 1807. He was drawn to words, writing and poetry from a very early age. Although his father was not pleased about his son's dream of being a poet and hoped he would come to his senses and pursue a career in law, Henry gained admission to Bowdoin College, in Brunswick, Maine, at the age of fourteen. Upon graduation, the college offered the eighteen-year-old Longfellow a professorship in the newly created modern languages department. Although Henry accepted the appointment, the college decided that for him to be ready for the post he would need to travel in Europe and to study languages there.

Upon his return to America, having greatly enjoyed his European travels, Longfellow took up his post at Bowdoin. Feeling that the college was not giving him the full scope to make use of what he had learned in Europe, however, he accepted an offer to teach at Harvard University in Cambridge, Massachusetts. Once again, he set out for Europe to further develop his knowledge of languages, travelling with his bride, Mary Storer Potter, whom he had married in 1831. Sadly, on her travels with Longfellow in Europe she suffered a miscarriage, fell ill and died in Rotterdam.

Back in Cambridge, Longfellow took up his teaching responsibilities at Harvard. In 1854, he was so well established as a poet that he resigned his Harvard post to devote himself full time to his writing. His second marriage ended in tragedy in the summer of 1861, when his wife died in a fire in their house. Longfellow, who had tried valiantly to put out the flames, was scarred on his face from the burns he received, and afterwards he grew the beard that was to become his trademark. Devastated by the loss of his wife, Longfellow was aided in his recovery by undertaking the translation into English of Dante's *The Divine Comedy*, with its epic portrayal of enduring love. Longfellow died on March 22, 1882, at the age of seventy-five, leaving behind a prodigious output of poetry.

It was in 1844 that Longfellow heard an account of the expulsion of the Acadians from a Maine clergyman, H. L. Conolly, who came to a dinner party at the poet's home as the guest of Nathaniel Hawthorne. Conolly had heard the tale from a French-Canadian woman, whose identity is not known. Longfellow was convinced that Hawthorne, who also heard the story at the dinner party, would want to use it as a vehicle for a work of his own. The poet even pressed his novelist friend to swear that he would stay his hand until his own poem was completed.

In the aftermath of the enormous success of the poem, Longfellow explained that he had relied on two crucial sources in conceiving his work. His first source, which gave him a picture of the simple, almost idyllic life of the Acadians before the deportation, came from the work of the Abbé Guillaume Thomas Raynal, an historian and philosopher in France who wrote in the late eighteenth century. For the details of the deportation, the poet relied on an 1829 book by the famous Nova Scotia writer Thomas Chandler Haliburton with the curious title *Historical and Statistical Account of Nova Scotia*. Born in Windsor, Nova Scotia, a town not far from Grand Pré, Haliburton is best known today for his humorous writing and the creation of Sam Slick, the fictitious American who fast-talked and outwitted the gullible Nova Scotians he encountered. Raynal and Haliburton, who were both sympathetic to the Acadians, helped reinforce Longfellow's own inclination toward the Acadian story.

There has been much speculation that Longfellow was influenced in his telling of the story by the journal of John Winslow. This seminal document, written by the commander of the British forces at Grand Pré in 1755, is held at the Massachusetts Historical Society, a body Longfellow joined in 1857, a decade after the poem was published. Although he may have read the manuscript at an earlier date, there is no conclusive evidence of this.[3]

Longfellow's poem is written in unrhymed hexameters, a style he drew from epics of classical Greek and Latin poetry, a mode that had not been used much by English-language poets. Not only did this give the poem a heroic cast, it also set the events and the characters firmly in the past. Longfellow's haunting tale derives its power from the fact that it operates so successfully on a number of levels. First there is the tragic story itself. Longfellow depicts Evangeline and Gabriel as young people growing up in a peaceful, abundant Arcadia. The Acadie in which they live is a place outside of history, guided by the seasons and the rhythm of life. It is a place of dreams, where people are virtuous and beautiful and where passion can lead to lifelong happiness. The poet depicts Grand Pré thus:

Columns of pale blue smoke, like clouds of incense ascending,
Rose from a hundred hearths, the homes of peace and contentment.
Thus dwelt together in love these simple Acadian farmers—
Dwelt in the love of God and of man. Alike were they free from
Fear, that reigns with the tyrant, and envy, the vice of republics.
Neither locks had they to their doors, nor bars to their windows;
But their dwellings were open as day and the hearts of the owners;
There the richest was poor, and the poorest lived in abundance.

This is an earthly Eden, or, at the very least, a working utopia. From the vantage point of industrializing New England a century after the expulsion, Longfellow saw Acadie existing in a lost golden age. French-Canadian historians, such as Lionel Groulx, writing long after the Conquest, shared a similar vision of the society of New France. The idea of the lost golden age has captivated many cultures. For the Italians and the Greeks, it is found in ancient Rome and Athens. Americans think back to the days of the settlement of the advancing frontier across the continent. A golden age is a space in the imagination that has little to do with historical truth. Instead, it is a space where the values and way of life that are associated with the vanished past can be contemplated. It has often been the case that those who contemplate a golden age of the past make use of it to advance their own agendas for the present and the future. If Longfellow can be said to have had an agenda in his epic, consciously or unconsciously, his was an American agenda. He juxtaposed an innocent society on the American continent with the British redcoats who came to despoil it.

The characters in Longfellow's epic are Acadian, but they are elemental and universal, and a connection is easily made by them to people of other cultures. The poem's potency does not derive so much from the compelling traits of its characters as it does from the unalterably terrible circumstances in which they find themselves. This is a source of the poem's utility as the basis for a national myth. The characters, although caught in their own poignant drama, stand in as representatives of their whole people.

For his chief character, Longfellow passed over the name Celestine, a name that was used by Acadians, and chose instead Evangeline, a name concocted by him that was unknown to the Acadians prior to the publication of his poem. The young woman, Evangeline Bellefontaine, daughter of Benedict, the wealthiest farmer in Grand Pré, is a vessel of beauty and spirituality, of loving devotion and a strong sense of duty:

> Fair was she to behold, that maiden of seventeen summers.
> Black were her eyes as the berry that grows on the thorn by
>   the way-side,
> Black, yet how softly they gleamed beneath the brown shade of
>   her tresses!

Evangeline is seen carrying flagons of home-brewed ale at harvest time to those who are reaping the crop. On Sunday mornings, she is pictured attending church, and "after confession, / Homeward serenely she walked with God's benediction upon her." Not surprisingly, Evangeline stirs the hearts of the young men of the community, but she has eyes for one of them only, Gabriel Lajeunesse, the son of Basil the blacksmith. Basil and Benedict are friends and "their children from earliest childhood / Grew up together as brother and sister."

The childhood of the two passes swiftly and Gabriel grows to become a "valiant youth" as Evangeline becomes a young lass "with the heart and hopes of a woman."

One evening Basil arrives at the home of Evangeline and her father to be welcomed by his friend Benedict. He has brought alarming news: for the past four days English warships outfitted with cannon have ridden at anchor in the mouth of the basin, not far from Grand Pré. Adding to the alarm, he informs Benedict, "'all are commanded / On the morrow to meet in the church, where His Majesty's mandate / Will be proclaimed as law in the land.'" Many of the people in the village fear the evil intentions of the English.

To this, Evangeline's father replies: "'Perhaps some friendlier purpose / Brings these ships to our shores. Perhaps the harvests in England / By the untimely rains or untimelier heat have been blighted, / And from our bursting barns they would feed their cattle and children.'" The blacksmith, who is much more wary, believes his friend is being too optimistic: "'Louisbourg is not forgotten, nor Beau Sejour, nor Port Royal.'"

But Benedict remains cheerful and urges his friend to think not of the English ships, but of the marriage of Evangeline and Gabriel, which is to take place in two days. In preparation for the wedding, the lads of the village have built a house and a barn for the young couple, and they have "'Filled the barn with hay, and the house with food for a twelvemonth.'"

The next day, the ancient notary arrives to put his seal on the wedding contract. He writes "with a steady hand the date and the age of the parties, / Naming the dower of the bride in flocks of sheep and in cattle." Having completed his task, the notary affixes his seal to the document and Benedict throws down on the table three times "the old man's fee in solid pieces of silver." And so the happy day ends with the young couple's future set and with only the marriage vows still to be taken.

The following morning, on the day when the men of the village are to meet in the church to learn His Majesty's orders, the time is passed in festive preparation for the wedding, with people in the village calling at the home of Benedict and being served ale by the bride-to-be.

At noon, the men gather inside the church, with the women waiting outside in the churchyard. Into this scene of anxious people the soldiers march, accompanied by the beat of their drummers. In the church, the commander (in a close paraphrase of the words spoken by John Winslow and recorded in his diary) announces the decision to deport the people of Grand Pré. As the commander finishes his address, the sultry air is shattered by a sudden and violent storm and hailstones rain down on the herds in the fields and damage the roofs and the windows of the farmers' houses.

With no hope of escape for the men in the church, Basil, the blacksmith, rises to his feet and shouts: "'Down with the tyrants of England! We never have sworn them allegiance! / Death to these foreign soldiers, who seize on our homes and our harvests!'" For his outburst, he is attacked and beaten by a soldier who throws him to the pavement. Into this scene of strife, the village priest enters, to address the people. He urges his flock not to forget "'all lessons of love and forgiveness'" and to repeat the prayer "'O Father, forgive them!'" Heeding his rebuke, the people in the church repeat the prayer.

Outside the church, the women and children wander in deep distress from house to house. But in this scene of misery, all hope has not been lost. When Evangeline returns to the empty house of her father that night, she is at first confronted with the emptiness of each room "haunted with phantoms of terror." But then her mood becomes more hopeful as she contemplates God's firmament:

> In the dead of the night she heard the whispering rain fall
> Loud on the withered leaves of the sycamore-tree by the window.
> Keenly the lightning flashed; and the voice of the echoing thunder
> Told her that God was in heaven, and governed the world he created!
> Then she remembered the tale she had heard of the justice of heaven;
> Soothed was her troubled soul, and she peacefully slumbered
>   till morning.

In relating the tale of Evangeline, the poet examines the question of how to account for the presence of evil in God's world. Why is it that terrible things can befall the innocent and the good? For Evangeline and Gabriel, that is the question that will wrack the whole of their lives.

On the fifth day of their captivity, the doors of the church open and the soldiers march the farmers down to the shore, where the ships await them. Evangeline remains resolute as the sad procession approaches:

> And she beheld the face of Gabriel pale with emotion.
> Tears then filled her eyes, and, eagerly running to meet him,
> Clasped she his hands, and laid her head on his shoulder
>   and whispered—
> "Gabriel! be of good cheer! For if we love one another,
> Nothing, in truth, can harm us, whatever mischances may happen!"

But the words are scarcely spoken when Evangeline sees her father, who has been shockingly transformed. "Gone was the glow from his cheek, and the fire from his eye." Evangeline makes her way to the shore with her father, to see Gabriel and his father, Basil, herded on to separate ships. With the first of the deportees on board, the day brings with it even deeper tragedy. Still with her ailing father, Evangeline watches as "columns of shining smoke uprose" as the houses of Grand Pré are put to the torch. Overwhelmed by the horror, her father slumps to the ground and dies. When the ships sail out of the harbour, they leave "behind them the dead on the shore, and the village in ruins."

Thus ends the first part of Longfellow's epic. The second part begins with years having "passed since the burning of Grand-Pré." On the vessels that bore them, "a nation, with all its household goods" has gone into exile, an "exile without end, and without an example in story."

Scattered were they, like flakes of snow when the wind from
   the northeast
Strikes aslant through the fogs that darken the Banks of
Newfoundland.
Friendless, homeless, hopeless, they wandered from city to city,
From the cold lakes of the North to sultry Southern savannas.

In this endless desolation, we find Evangeline among the exiles:

. . . a maiden who waited and wandered,
Lowly and meek in spirit, and patiently suffering all things.
Fair was she and young; but, alas! before her extended,
Dreary and vast and silent, the desert of life.

"Urged by a restless longing, the hunger and thirst of the spirit," she has begun her search to find Gabriel. As she travels, she comes upon people who have seen him with his father in some far-off place. She hears that he has gone to the prairies, where he and his father have become famous hunters and trappers. Later she hears that he has been seen in the lowlands of Louisiana. Many urge her to give up her dream of finding Gabriel:

"Here is Baptiste Leblanc, the notary's son, who has loved thee
Many a tedious year; come, give him thy hand and be happy!"

But these entreaties fall on deaf ears, and Evangeline follows the dictates of her heart and continues the search. Together with other exiles, Evangeline's journey takes her through the heart of America, through the Ohio country and then on a boat, "rowed by Acadian boatmen" down the Mississippi. Travelling south, to a territory where she has heard rumours of Gabriel, Evangeline has been borne to a landscape that is completely different from her native soil. As she dreams of finding her lover, and has visions of him being near, Evangeline is led by the poet through the magnificence of the American continent, with all its vast promise. Hard though his story is, Longfellow is finding solace in the New World and the hopes that it inspires in those who have been wounded by the struggles of the Old World, the kind of struggle that drove the Acadians out of their homes.

At last, Evangeline's journey through the southern landscape brings her face to face with Basil, Gabriel's father, who tells her that his son has left him just that morning, still restless in his own endless search for Evangeline. The father explains that Gabriel has "'moody and restless grown, and tried and troubled, his spirit / Could no longer endure the calm of this quiet existence. / Thinking ever of thee, uncertain and sorrowful ever.'"

Evangeline learns that her lover has departed for the distant Ozark Mountains, where he will hunt for "'furs in the forests, on rivers trapping the beaver.'"

Basil, the blacksmith, has made a go of it in the new land. The exiles travelling with Evangeline are much "marveled to see the wealth of the ci-devant blacksmith."

Thus they ascended the steps, and, crossing the airy veranda,
Entered the hall of the house, where already the supper of Basil
Waited his late return; and they rested and feasted together.

Longfellow is relating the familiar American saga of the poor, the wretched and the dispossessed who have come to the new land and have made good. Contrast the fate of Evangeline's father, who dies tragically in the light of the flames that consume Grand Pré, with that of the wary Basil, who finds wealth and success in America.

Evangeline, while mindful of the beauty and abundance of the new land, has not given up her life's quest. Outside in the evening:

"O Gabriel! O my beloved!
Art thou so near unto me, and yet I cannot behold thee?
Art thou so near unto me, and yet thy voice does not reach me?
Ah! how often thy feet have trod this path to the prairie!
Ah! how often thine eyes have looked on the woodlands around me!
Ah! how often beneath this oak, returning from labour,
Thou hast lain down to rest, and to dream of me in thy slumbers.
When shall these eyes behold, these arms be folded about thee?"

As Gabriel pursues his wandering life as a hunter and a trapper, travelling to the Oregon country and then back to the Great Lakes in what is now Michigan, Evangeline follows his trail. Seasons pass and years glide by but she does not find him.

Fair was she and young, when in hope began the long journey;
Faded was she and old, when in disappointment it ended.

Finally giving up on ever finding him, while never forgetting him, Evangeline becomes a Sister of Charity in Philadelphia and devotes her life to serving the sick and the poor. During a smallpox epidemic in the city, Evangeline recognizes one of the sufferers as her Gabriel.

"Gabriel! O my beloved!" and died away into silence.
Then he beheld, in a dream, once more the home of his childhood;
Green Acadian meadows, with sylvan rivers among them,
Village, and mountain, and woodlands; and, walking under their
    shadow,
As in the days of her youth, Evangeline rose in his vision.
Tears came into his eyes; and as slowly he lifted his eyelids,
Vanished the vision away, but Evangeline knelt by his bedside.

He dies in her arms, and she does not long outlive him.

Side by side, in their nameless graves, the lovers are sleeping.
Under the humble walls of the little Catholic churchyard,
In the heart of the city, they lie, unknown and unnoticed."
. . .
Still stands the forest primeval; but under the shade of its branches
Dwells another race, with other customs and language.
Only along the shore of the mournful and misty Atlantic
Linger a few Acadian peasants, whose fathers from exile
Wandered back to their native land to die in its bosom.
In the fisherman's cot the wheel and the loom are still busy;
Maidens still wear their Norman caps and their kirtles of homespun;
And by the evening fire repeat Evangeline's story.

So powerful is Longfellow's epic that many Acadians have believed it to be fact. More than once Acadians have set out to find Evangeline's remains so they can be returned to her homeland. Controversy has been rekindled a number of times about whether Longfellow's epic is based on a true story. In part, this can be put down to the simple fact that families were separated during the deportation and that the broad outlines of the story of Evangeline must have mirrored the actual stories of some Acadian families. In Louisiana, the Evangeline story was reworked to place it in a Cajun setting. In 1888, the Louisiana Creole writer Madame Sidonie de la Houssaye published her novel *Pouponne et Balthazar*. In this version,

Evangeline and Gabriel have been recast as upper-class Creoles who look down on their Acadian neighbours. In 1907, Felix Voorhies, a playwright from St. Martinville, Louisiana, published an English-language work titled *Acadian Reminiscences: The True Story of the Acadians*. His tale was meant to correct what he regarded as the annoying features of the tale penned by de la Houssaye. In Voorhies's treatment, Evangeline and Gabriel have been renamed Emmeline Labiche and Louis Arceneaux, both common surnames in Cajun Louisiana. While Voorhies set out to write a work of fiction, his tale, like that of Longfellow, was so powerful that it came to be seen by many as telling a real story. And, of course, the subtitle of his work reinforced this view. Even some Louisiana scholars concluded that the tale described actual people and events.

Twice in the 1920s Hollywood films told the Evangeline story. In the second of the films, released in 1929, Dolores del Rio starred as Evangeline. She went so far as to donate money so that a statue of Evangeline, to resemble the star, could be created and mounted in Louisiana. In 1930, the statue was placed in St. Martinville next to the St. Martin de Tours Catholic Church. The spot chosen for the statue was said to be on the gravesite of Emmeline Labiche, in the minds of many the "real" Evangeline. St. Martinville's fame as the place where the two star-crossed lovers were reunited under a great oak tree has made the town a tourist attraction. And while tourists continue to visit the place to see the statue and the tree, they are in fact seeing the third tree that has been designated as the great oak in the fable. Although the Voorhies publication has made many conclude that the Evangeline story is a true one, the reasonable conclusion is that Longfellow's tale was a work of fiction, as have been the works based on it. Whether the setting for the stories was Nova Scotia or Louisiana, it was the power of the epics that drew people to conclude that they were based on fact.

Within a couple of decades of the original publication, *Evangeline*, the poem and the character, were strongly embraced by the Acadians. For daughters in Acadian and Cajun families, the name Evangeline became a fashionable choice. Once the poem had been translated into French, it quickly became popular reading for the general public and was made a part of the curriculum of Acadian schools. Leading members of the Church, who played a crucial role in the Acadian renaissance of the period, endorsed the poem, not only for its utility as a vehicle of Acadian nationalism, but also because of the life of selfless piety that it promulgated. *Le Moniteur Acadien*, the first Acadian newspaper, which was launched in Shediac, New Brunswick, in 1867, published a serialized version of the poem for its readers in French translation.[4]

Longfellow wrote *Evangeline* as an American idyll. In it, the evil figures are the British redcoats who separate and expel Evangeline and Gabriel. Gabriel travels all over America and ends up being transformed by the experience into the kind of person who is to be found in the new America, someone who has left his European past behind him. The poem sings the praises of America. It is a nationalist American work. There is no hint of the role played in the expulsion by New Englanders, who provided many of the soldiers as well as the ships in which the deportees were moved. The vast irony is that Longfellow's work was transformed into something it was not intended to be. It became a keystone in the archway of the new Acadie. Instead of bolstering American nationalism, it helped give birth to Acadian nationalism.

Longfellow portrayed Acadian women as pure, as sufferers and as helpmates. His picture of womanhood was painted from his own idealized vision of New England women in the mid nineteenth century. While the Evangeline myth has been satirized by contemporary playwrights in Acadie, most notably by Herménégilde Chiasson, its potency can be seen on public occasions. On the fourhundredth anniversary of the first Acadian settlement, the celebratory concert in New Brunswick just opposite Île St. Croix featured a song about Evangeline and Gabriel. While Acadian elites are ready to poke fun at the myth, because they believe it relegates Acadians to a folkloric tradition, Evangeline remains the most compelling symbol of *le Grand Dérangement*. The Evangeline myth is crucial to the Acadian Diaspora. Its utility for the project of building a modern French-speaking society in New Brunswick is another matter, a matter around which controversy swirls. Be that as it may, the tale of Evangeline remains as powerful in the memory of Acadians as ever.

One effect of Longfellow's poem, which was also a highly effective political tract, was that it provoked defensive responses from British North Americans, and later Canadians, in the mid nineteenth century and for decades after that. A few years after the publication of the poem, the government of Nova Scotia decided to publish all the official papers that existed concerning the forcible expulsion of the Acadians. Their motive, at the time, was to provide a record that would explain why the removal of a people was deemed necessary. Over the course of the past hundred and fifty years, as the world has come to understand ethnic cleansing, the record published by the Nova Scotia government has effectively turned from a defence to an indictment, a crucial source that illustrates how the acting governor, Charles Lawrence, and his associates planned and executed the deportation.

On the eve of the First World War, a highly impressive effort to record the history of Canada was undertaken by one hundred historians, under the direction of Adam Shortt and Arthur G. Doughty, two leading Canadian historians of the day. The result was the publication of *Canada and Its Provinces*, a twenty-three-volume history of Canada. Overwhelmingly, the massive history presents the Anglo-Canadian view of the time of the development of Canada. The passages of the history that deal with the expulsion of the Acadians, written by Archibald MacMechan, amount to an apologia on behalf of Charles Lawrence and his co-conspirators:

> The situation was highly critical and the English governors met it, not as all-powerful tyrants, but as men who in the midst of danger take obvious precautions for their safety. . . .
>
> He [Governor Lawrence] soon proved his value to the colony as a soldier in the field and as an energetic administrator in civil affairs. In person he was a giant, six feet two inches in height; in character he was

a typical soldier, frank in manner, fearless of opposition, devoted to duty and the interests of his country as he understood them. . . .

In deciding to remove the French population from the province Lawrence and his council felt that they were obliged to act swiftly in a crisis. . . .

Before passing judgment on the men who conceived and executed this removal of an entire population, it should be remembered that they acted as did Louis XIV in expelling the Huguenots from France and the United States in expelling the Tories. All were precautionary measures dictated by the need of national self-preservation; and they were regarded by those who took them as imperative in a dangerous crisis. Lawrence acted like a commander of a fort expecting a siege, who levels trees and houses outside the walls in order to afford the enemy no shelter and to give the garrison a clear field of fire.[5]

In 1924, in a similarly defensive vein, the chairman of the board of governors of the University of Toronto, the Reverend Dr. H. J. Cody, attempted, without success, to have Longfellow's poem banished from school curriculums in Canada. He was offended by the poem because, in his view, it created "a wrong impression of British justice, chivalry and administration."[6] Dr. Cody's negative response to the poem's sympathetic view of the plight of the Acadians, while far from typical, was not the sole expression of this point of view. The author of a tourist brochure for Kentville, Nova Scotia, a town not far from Grand Pré, bluntly reminded American visitors to the region that their own ancestors had participated in the deportation. "We cannot overlook the fact," wrote this observer, "that a vast amount of sympathy has been misplaced and wasted on the Acadians."[7]

If the backlash against the poem was comparatively mild, the favourable responses were overwhelming. In English Canada, poets who were inspired by Longfellow's epic and by the plight of the Acadians produced their own work. In 1894, Bliss Carman wrote "Low Tide at Grand Pré," and six years later Charles G. D. Roberts wrote "The Salt Flats," poems dealing with the themes of lost love and of the lost past.[8]

Not only was Longfellow's epic widely studied in schools in the United States and Canada in the late nineteenth and early twentieth centuries, the tale of Evangeline drew a considerable number of tourists to the Annapolis Valley, mostly from the big cities of the United States. Railway companies featured the wistful figure of Evangeline in their advertisements. For travellers who longed to find a simple, pastoral setting where the values of loyalty and devotion prevailed, Evangeline's Nova Scotia was a powerful magnet. The tragic tale of the young woman who lost her lover has remained a drawing card for tourists ever since.

Longfellow's epic played a role in drawing the Acadians and the Cajuns of Louisiana together. It was a bond shared between them. In the mid 1930s and in later decades, pilgrimages to Grand Pré from Louisiana were undertaken, and these featured young women dressed in the garb of Evangeline. Not only did Evangelines travel north from Louisiana to Nova Scotia, they also travelled south, in their regalia, from Quebec and Acadie to St. Martinville, Louisiana, to the site of the famed "Evangeline Oak." In 1910, A. T. Bourque wrote a song titled "Evangeline," a song that has been sung ever since by Acadians. Visitors to the Grand-Pré National Historic Site, from Quebec and France, who are the descendants of those deported, have on occasion sung Bourque's song during their pilgrimages.[9]

If Longfellow's poem has been a windfall for Nova Scotia tourism, it has also been a boon to the cause of Acadian nation-building. But while Acadians have embraced the epic, there has also been an effort to grapple with the image it has created of Acadians, in particular Acadian women, as passive victims. Antonine Maillet, the most celebrated of contemporary Acadian writers, who has herself been criticized by younger writers such as Herménégilde Chiasson, has portrayed Acadian women in a different light. In her play *Évangéline deusse*, she creates an Evangeline who is a twentieth-century Acadian woman who lives in exile in Montreal and who spends her time in a park with a Jew and a Breton, two other exiles. In *La Sagouine*, an Acadian charwoman, speaking the Acadian

French of her region of New Brunswick, speaks to the audience in a feisty manner, holding nothing back in her cutting commentaries on her troubles and those of her people. In her novel *Pélagie-la-Charrette*, Maillet tells the story of Pélagie, an Acadian woman who has lived in Georgia in exile and who leads a group of Acadians back to the land from which they were deported. In these portrayals, strong Acadian women, speaking in their own distinct language, have replaced Longfellow's model of Victorian piety.

Underlying the responses of Maillet and other writers is the large question of the utility of myths in the creation and sustaining of a culture. Longfellow's epic appeared in the mid nineteenth century, at a time when Acadians had re-established their communities but had taken few steps to create institutions and symbols that would tie them together. That was to come in the age of the Acadian renaissance in the last decades of the nineteenth century. Through the leadership of crucial figures in the Church and elite politicians, Acadians became connected to one another as members of a national community. For this generation of leaders, the story of Evangeline was ideal. Her story not only informed the wider world of the plight of the Acadians, it provided contemporary Acadians with an example of piety and devotion, qualities much cherished by a religious elite that saw the people of Acadie as the members of their flock. It also provided an image of womanhood that embodied religious teachings. Evangeline was faithful to her family, her Church and her betrothed. And she carried this faith unswervingly through all the days of her life, despite her bitter disappointment at never becoming a wife and a mother. At the 1890 Acadian National Convention, held at Church Point, Nova Scotia, Valentin Landry explained why he had chosen the name *L'Évangéline* for the newspaper he had founded three years earlier: "We needed a messenger who could go into the Acadian homes of Nova Scotia, to speak with the accents of our forefathers, and I thought that none could do the job better that the poetic and historic Evangeline."[10]

For later generations of Acadians, however, the Evangeline myth gradually grew into a hindrance while it continued to be a useful source of national pride. What was portrayed in the poem, as with any historical epic, had little to do with contemporary life and problems. By the 1960s and 1970s, when young Acadians were stirring to the new themes of a modern secular society, the tale of Evangeline stood in the way of their advance and self-expression. While Evangeline was never to be dethroned, she would have to be content to share her throne with the works of Acadian artists for a new age.

PART III

MODERN ACADIE

—

CHAPTER 10

LOUIS ROBICHAUD
AND THE
GREAT TRANSFORMATION
OF THE 1960S

A MAN OF SLIGHT STATURE with a large, round face that made him look perennially jovial, youthful and even comic, Louis J. Robichaud, who died in January 2005, remains the saint of Acadian politics. When people look back on his decade as premier of New Brunswick, from 1960 to 1970, they compare him to Martin Luther King, Jr., Mahatma Gandhi and Nelson Mandela. He is seen as a man who led his people from poverty and marginalization to a better world.

So enormous was the impact of Louis Robichaud on the lives of Acadians, and on the shape of New Brunswick society as a whole, that it is appropriate to speak in terms of "Before Robichaud" and "After Robichaud."

In the decades before the 1960s—Before Robichaud—New Brunswick Acadians lived in the shadows of society, economically and politically. To be sure, Acadians had their institutions, in particular their colleges, which operated under the umbrella of the Church. The legacy of the late-nineteenth-century Acadian renaissance had awakened the idea of the Acadians as a people. In a series of conferences, the Acadian leadership, closely linked to the Church, had created the crucial symbols—the Acadian flag and national anthem—as well as establishing August 15, Ascension Day, as the Acadian national day. Not to be ignored in this was the vast importance of the tale of Evangeline. Longfellow's poem, and all the works that were spawned by it, gave the Acadians a standing in the world and made their tragic history accessible to people in many countries.

While these gains for Acadians as a people were crucial for the future, they fell far short of transforming the lives of most Acadians. The large majority of Acadians lived on the margins of the modern Canada that was taking shape. Living in the poorest regions of New Brunswick, they mostly worked in the fishery and in the forest products industry or toiled to make a living farming land that was often substandard. Over the decades, a very large number of Acadians were driven out of these traditional occupations, often to migrate to find work in the New England states, or to make new lives for themselves in south-eastern New Brunswick in the greater Moncton area. In Moncton in the latter decades of the nineteenth century, indeed right down to the 1960s, the Acadians were second-class residents. They worked in menial jobs, never coming close to the elite levels where decisions were made.

A man who remembers the years Before Robichaud is Dr. Phil LeBlanc. In a conversation one afternoon in his summerhouse in Pointe du Chêne, New Brunswick, a few blocks from the sea, he painted a picture of what Acadian society was like in the decades before the great changes of the 1960s. He was born into a poor family in Moncton's French-speaking east end in the mid 1920s. French was the language spoken in the home and the neighbourhood, and it was French that was mixed with very little English. Dr. LeBlanc did not speak any English until his family moved to Saint John when he was eleven.

LeBlanc's father worked for many years in the Canadian National Railway shops in Moncton; in those days, CNR was the city's most important employer. Out behind their house, located near the Petitcodiac River, the family had coops where they raised chickens for their own consumption. It was common then for families to raise chickens or grow vegetables in their backyards. "Those were the days," he joked, "when the poor ate lobster and the rich ate balogna." The LeBlanc family was poor, as were most of the Acadians in town. Very few people had cars in Moncton in those days, and that certainly included the LeBlancs. Nor did they have a radio, although young Phil did have a set of earplugs with wires he could attach to a pipe to let him hear music on a local radio station. The kids in the family and in the neighbourhood did not have skates. The LeBlancs had two bikes to share among seven children. He and his brother, who became a priest, served at mass every morning in the nearby church. Thinking back on his childhood, Dr. LeBlanc has no sense of having been deprived. "We had good food, warm clothes and a decent place to live," he says. And the kids had fun.

As a child, Dr. LeBlanc was bullied by English-speaking children when he encountered them. He remembers being beaten up by English kids on numerous occasions. He doesn't know where the dislike came from. In his own community he does not remember being taught to hate the English, he says. But he remarks, uncharacteristically for him, that the English kids were "shits" to French kids like him.

Because of the emphasis his father placed on education, Phil LeBlanc was able to attend the Collège St. Joseph at Memramcook. At St. Joseph, a boys-only school, where tuition and room and board cost only a couple of hundred dollars a year, dormitories housed sixty or seventy students. The discipline was strict. One huge priest patrolled the study room in the evenings. When he saw a boy slacking off or acting up, he would come up behind him, kick his chair and lift the unfortunate victim into the air.

The boys at St. Joseph's were roused at six in the morning to attend chapel. They saw girls only when they were outside the college in large groups and they passed the nearby women's college. The young women were required to turn their backs toward them as they passed. Sometimes, at night, Phil and his friends would sneak out of the college to follow the seniors to watch them meet up with girls.

When he graduated in 1947, Phil LeBlanc had no idea what to do next. He knew he didn't want to be a priest and he didn't want to be a lawyer. He heard friends talking about becoming doctors and he decided that could be the direction for him to take. With a little luck and a lot of determination, and almost no money, he set out for the University of Ottawa, where he earned his medical degree. After a five-year stint in the Royal Canadian Air Force, Dr. LeBlanc worked in Vancouver and Detroit before he settled with his wife in Guelph, Ontario. They now spend nearly half the year in Pointe du Chêne, just outside of Shediac.

The life Dr. LeBlanc remembers is typical of the recollections of many Acadians who grew up in Moncton before the 1960s. But that was before Louis Robichaud arrived on the scene.

Robichaud was descended from a family that is believed to have emigrated from France to Port Royal around 1660. In the 1730s, the family moved to a more remote settlement on the St. John River. During the period of the deportation, the Robichauds moved to L'Islet on the St. Lawrence River. Following the Treaty of Paris in 1763, the family tried returning to the St. John River, but finding their home a charred ruin, they resettled on the Petitcodiac River. It was Pierre Robichaud, born in 1778, who moved to Kent County, where members of the family have lived ever since.[1]

Kent County, where Robichaud was born, has in some ways been a microcosm of New Brunswick. Historically dependent on ship-building and forest products, as well as fishing and some subsistence farming, the county has experienced economic problems as a consequence of the decline of these traditional economic pillars. The county is predominantly Acadian, with a large minority of residents who are English-speaking Irish and Anglo-Canadians of Loyalist stock.[2]

Young Louis's fascination with politics was passed on to him by his father, who was an active Liberal organizer in the region. Even as a child, he often sat at his father's feet during those Depression days in the 1930s, taking in everything that was said at political meetings in the family home. Although he didn't reveal this secret to anyone at the time, from an early age he had conceived the idea of becoming premier of New Brunswick. When Allison Dysart led the Liberals to an overwhelming electoral majority of forty-three out of forty-five seats in the provincial legislature in 1935, the twelve-year-old Robichaud, without letting his parents know, borrowed a friend's bicycle and rode to a neighbouring town to see the new premier speak.[3]

In 1940, Robichaud was sent by the family to attend the Collège
Sacre-Coeur in the northern New Brunswick town of Bathurst,
where he received a classical education including French, English,
Latin, Greek, rhetoric, history and philosophy. At this time, the
Robichaud family dream was that young Louis would become a
priest who would devote himself to teaching, but by 1943 Robichaud
had concluded that the priesthood was not for him. His avid interest in politics and the realization that a life of chastity did not appeal
closed off a path that had often been taken by members of Acadie's
educated elite, of which he was now becoming a member.[4] Like other
young men during the Second World War, Robichaud had to make
up his mind whether to volunteer to fight in Europe against the
Fascists. While he considered this a just war for the cause of democracy, he decided that he lacked the military spirit and that he would
seek out a role as a leader to improve civil society.[5]

The next stage in his education placed Louis Robichaud in close
contact with the thinkers and the ideas that were to transform
Quebec in the Quiet Revolution of the 1960s. In the spring of 1947,
he decided to enrol in the School of Social Sciences at Laval
University in Quebec City. The school's dean, Father Georges-
Henri Lévesque, a Dominican priest, was a powerful source of the
critical thinking that was to challenge the authoritarian regime of
Premier Maurice Duplessis in Quebec. Father Lévesque espoused a
doctrine of social action and social justice that rejected the corpo-
ratism of the Duplessis government. In the late 1940s, academics
and activists such as Pierre Trudeau took up the doctrine of social
action when they aligned themselves with workers in the great
strikes of the era. So dangerous was the teaching of Father Lévesque
in the eyes of Duplessis that the Quebec premier threatened to
withdraw funding from Laval University if the priest was not
removed from his post.[6] Lévesque stood his ground. During his
career he did no less than train many of the key figures who would
transform both Quebec and New Brunswick during the 1960s.

For Louis Robichaud, the social and intellectual ferment of these
years in Quebec broadened his liberalism, taking it beyond devotion

to Wilfrid Laurier and Allison Dysart, the twin idols of his youth. Half a century after his years in Quebec, Robichaud looked back on the ideas and political approach of Georges-Henri Lévesque as crucial to his own later political course.[7] In Quebec City, Robichaud rubbed shoulders not only with the architects of the changes to come in Quebec, but also with a number of figures who were to play a role in the transformation of New Brunswick. These included: Adelard Savoie, Robichaud's future brother-in-law, who later became a member of the New Brunswick legislature and rector of the Université de Moncton; Gilbert Finn, Robichaud's friend who was to direct Assomption Vie, the Acadian insurance firm; Leon Richard, the future surgeon and leader of the Société Nationale des Acadiens; and Bernard Jean, Robichaud's future minister of justice.[8]

Louis Robichaud's days at Laval were followed by a period in which he worked for a law firm while taking his law degree in English through correspondence courses from the University of New Brunswick. In February 1952, the young lawyer mounted a wooden sign, which he himself had made, on the outside wall of his office, announcing to the people of the coastal town of Richibuctou that there was a new lawyer in town.[9] Not far from his boyhood home in Saint-Antoine, Richibuctou, a solidly Acadian and Liberal town, proved to be an ideal launch pad for his law career, and for his rapid political ascent. By the time he opened his law office, Robichaud had met and married Adelard Savoie's sister Lorraine, who had been teaching school in Bathurst.

Always a man in a hurry, Louis Robichaud chose to launch his political career the same year he hung out his shingle in Richibuctou. In August 1952, only a month before the province was propelled into a general election campaign, Robichaud was chosen as one of three Liberal candidates to seek seats in Kent County. The premier of the day was John B. McNair, who had succeeded Allison Dysart as Liberal leader and premier in 1940. After twelve years in office, the McNair government was up against Hugh John Flemming, leader of the Conservative Party and son of a former provincial premier. The campaign of 1952 became a Conservative crusade against the long-ruling Liberals. Flemming assaulted the McNair government for its taxation policies and for its links to construction industry scandals. The result was a solid majority government for the Conservatives, with the Liberals reduced to sixteen out of forty-nine seats in the legislature.[10] One of those seats, though, was captured by young Louis Robichaud, who was soon able to use the Liberal debacle as the opportunity for his own political advancement. In the autumn of 1952, Robichaud had three strikes against him as he took his seat in the legislature in Fredericton. He was only twenty-six, he was a Roman Catholic, and he was an Acadian. While the first disadvantage would diminish with each passing day, the other two were serious obstacles to a man who was determined to be premier. No Acadian had ever won that office in a general election in New Brunswick.

Many a twenty-six-year-old would have paused at this point, having achieved so much, before aiming at still higher goals. But Louis Robichaud was never that kind of man. While he was not very vocal in the legislature at first, he began to take a leading role among Liberals in making free-time political broadcasts in French and English on behalf of the party. He even ran for the interim leadership of the party when Dysart stepped down, and came within one vote of winning that post within the Liberal caucus in the legislature. In 1956, when Conservative Premier Hugh John Flemming called the next election, the Liberals, led by Austin Taylor, a sixty-three-year-old former minister of agriculture, lost one seat, ending up with only fifteen. During Robichaud's first four years in the legislature, the Liberals had failed to make a dent in the Conservative hold on the province.

This time, the Liberal defeat opened the way for the young Acadian politician to make the move that allowed him to ascend to power four years later. In the spring of 1958, the Liberal Party called a leadership convention so it would be ready to fight the next provincial election. Without a moment's hesitation, Robichaud threw his hat in the ring. Given his lack of real resources, he had to organize and publicize his own crusade, whose centrepiece consisted of his visits to every corner of the province to line up key Liberal riding organizers." Robichaud, at the age of thirty-three, arrived at Fredericton in October 1958 for the leadership convention, having made himself known to Liberals across New Brunswick. But he had one more hurdle to surmount. The other candidates in the race did not have any support to stop a Robichaud victory, and this motivated a group of party elders to come together on the eve of the leadership vote to try to find a candidate who could block his advance. They came up with a man named Wesley Stewart, a former Liberal member of Parliament, who had previously been the mayor of Grand-Sault.

If Robichaud felt challenged by the last-minute display of opposition, he showed no sign of it when he delivered his address to the delegates in Fredericton, passionately and without a slip. The vote at the convention for the leadership of the party went to three ballots, with Robichaud first and Stewart second on all three. Robichaud's lead widened on each ballot until he was over the top on the last one, with 517 votes out of 836 to Stewart's 304.

With his ascension to the position of party leader, the road ahead for Louis Robichaud involved two sharply divergent possibilities. One was that the young Acadian would end up as a one-term leader who would be ground up by the powerful Conservative machine of Hugh John Flemming in the next election. The other was that he would change the mould of New Brunswick politics by winning office on a program that would forever change the province. The first possibility seemed much more plausible than the second in the days following Robichaud's convention victory.

Assaulting the heights of an opposition party was far from the same thing as winning the population over to the Liberal cause. Again he set out on the road in his ancient DeSoto automobile. This time his goal was to win over opinion leaders in every community. His tactic was to visit a community's priest or Protestant clergyman. A favourable or at least a neutral impression in these quarters could only help. In the eighteen months following the leadership convention, Robichaud logged about 80,000 kilometres in his car. Not a main street in the province had not been host to his DeSoto by the time he was done.[13]

In the sitting of the legislature that came immediately after the Liberal convention, Robichaud decided on a bold act of political theatre. In New Brunswick, unlike many other jurisdictions, questions in the legislature to members of the Cabinet could not be put orally. Instead, they had to be presented in writing, which gave the government plenty of time to prepare its responses and also robbed the Opposition of the drama of face-to-face confrontations that could be reported by the press.

Robichaud rose in the legislature and asked the premier a rather routine question: how many unemployed people were there in New Brunswick? Angrily, the premier charged the Liberal leader with violating the conventions of the legislature for the cheap purpose of making an impression on the spectators in the gallery. To this, Robichaud shot back that under the Legislative Assembly's Rule 40, oral questions could be asked on routine matters. Then came a long and acrimonious debate about what constituted a routine question, at the end of which the speaker of the assembly ruled in favour of Robichaud. Following the ruling, a government minister stood up to say that there were thirty-five thousand unemployed people in the province. The young leader had faced down the veteran premier and had won a dramatic victory.[14]

In the spring of 1959, Robichaud decided he needed a kind of political expertise that his energy alone could not provide. On a visit to Ottawa, he visited federal Liberal leader Lester Pearson, who was then leader of the official Opposition. He asked Pearson to provide him with the services of Ned Belliveau, a man of Acadian origin who had left New Brunswick years before to work for *The Toronto Star*, and later for Pearson's Liberals. Pearson agreed to send Belliveau to Fredericton, but Robichaud had another request. Ned Belliveau's services would cost Robichaud ten thousand dollars, and the New Brunswick Liberals didn't have the money. Pearson found the money and Belliveau packed his bags and drove to his native province.[15] For Belliveau, this was to be the beginning of an eighteen-year-long association with Liberal politics in New Brunswick.[16]

Ned Belliveau's return to New Brunswick turned out to be an affair for life. Following his years of service to Robichaud, Belliveau stayed in a clapboard house he owned on the sea at Shediac Cape, north of the town of Shediac. (Belliveau's house is next door to the house of my wife's family, where I have spent a part of my summers for more than twenty-five years. For twenty of those summers, before his death in 1999, I passed many pleasant hours with Ned Belliveau, who regaled me with his encyclopaedic knowledge of New Brunswick politics.) He was about the same height as Robichaud, but he was a wiry, thin man with a longish face and a prominent nose. Belliveau loved political wars. He could recite every political battle in which he had been engaged with a relish that made it seem as though they had taken place yesterday. His was not a forgiving nature. If someone said kind things to him about Dalton Camp, the long-time Conservative strategist and renowned newspaper columnist, Belliveau would act offended. Their wars were long in the past by then, but it made no difference.

It was apparent to Belliveau, as it was to Robichaud, that to win the upcoming provincial election the Liberals would have to make major gains in anglophone regions of the province while holding on to their strong Acadian base. Shortly after Robichaud became Liberal leader, Belliveau spent an afternoon with him near Richibuctou and came away favourably impressed with his sharpness. It was when he saw the young Liberal leader speak to an anglophone audience in Maugerville, near Fredericton, though, that Belliveau concluded that the Acadian politician could be a winner throughout the province. He was impressed that Robichaud won such a warm hearing from a crowd in the very heart of anglophone Loyalist New Brunswick.[17]

Belliveau calculated shrewdly that there were anglophone regions of the province where resentments had built against the Conservative government. In those days, there were still multiple-seat ridings in New Brunswick, where three members were elected in one constituency. Robichaud's own riding was one. Belliveau figured that with quite small swings of the vote, the Liberals could win multiple new seats. He also anticipated that it could be in regions of the province where there were very few francophones that the Liberals would make gains against the Flemming government. In such regions, the antagonisms over language and government jobs that created resentment against Acadians among nearby anglophones did not exist.[18]

Notwithstanding the preparations that Robichaud and his team made, when the Flemming government gave all the signs in the spring of 1960 that a provincial election was about to be called, keen observers of New Brunswick politics were mostly convinced that the Conservatives would hold on to their majority. The government did not have about it the smell of *fin de régime*, and while it could be criticized for the kinds of things one would expect after eight years in power, no large scandal stood out. The premier, a master of the old school of patrician politics in New Brunswick, remained respected, even popular. The idea that he could be toppled by an untried young Acadian seemed at best a long shot.

But beneath the surface calm of New Brunswick, currents of change were flowing, currents that were to become plainly evident once the election campaign was underway. While some of the factors that were leading to change were unique to the province, much broader forces were at work across the country, indeed throughout the industrialized world. The onset of the 1960s marked more than a change of decade. It also heralded the beginning of a societal transformation that was to be revolutionary in scope.

In Quebec, two Union Nationale premiers had died in quick succession, and the province was about to head into a provincial election that would usher in the Quiet Revolution and an epoch of crisis for Canadian federalism that has not yet ended. During the quarter century when Maurice Duplessis's Union Nationale had dominated Quebec politics, it had seemed that the province was locked in a permanent ice age. An authoritarian government and a Church-centred society in which traditional nationalism held sway appeared to be the permanent order of things. But the intellectual, political and trade union stirrings that Louis Robichaud had witnessed during his years in Quebec City had matured to the point where they might overturn the old order. Remarkably, the historic victory of the Quebec Liberals under the leadership of Jean Lesage occurred only two weeks before Louis Robichaud and his Liberals swept out the old order in New Brunswick.

Outside francophone Canada, change was also in the air. In Saskatchewan, Tommy Douglas led his social democratic Co-operative Commonwealth Federation (CCF) government back to power armed with a program that was to transform first his own province and then all of Canada. Having been premier of the prairie province since 1944, Douglas made a universal, tax-supported medicare system the issue of the election campaign, pledging that if the CCF were re-elected, he would regard this as a mandate to introduce medicare. Two years later, the CCF, under the leadership of Woodrow Lloyd, introduced Canada's first medicare plan. Douglas had by then left provincial politics to become federal leader of the newly founded New Democratic Party. Following a fierce three-week strike by Saskatchewan doctors against medicare, the new system of health care went into effect. A few years later, Lester Pearson's federal Liberals picked up the idea of medicare and introduced it as a federal program, a move that was to alter the meaning of Canadian citizenship.

In 1960, the youthful John F. Kennedy was challenging Americans to move away from the safe harbour of the Eisenhower years. A youth culture of a kind never experienced before was developing across the western world. Young people chose their own music, their own dress styles, their own culture in a revolt against established ways. This cultural change fused with political revolt and by the late 1960s unleashed political movements that came close to toppling governments. The civil rights campaign in the United States, the outbreak of Quebec nationalism, the worldwide movement against the Vietnam War and the rejection of the established order were to culminate in 1968 with the strike of 10 million people in France that very nearly overturned the regime of President Charles de Gaulle. That same year, the revolutionary tide was felt in West Germany, Italy, the United States and Canada.

One change that was transforming culture and politics as the decade opened was television. The new medium was only beginning to make its power felt in 1960, the year not coincidentally of the famous Kennedy-Nixon television debates, the first such encounters in American politics. In New Brunswick, the importance of television was barely understood in the arena of provincial politics. Understandably, Hugh John Flemming, the sixty-one-year-old Conservative premier, had no idea what television could do. Interestingly, Robichaud's Liberals, including their communications expert Ned Belliveau, were only slightly more in tune with the new medium at the beginning of the campaign.

When Flemming called the New Brunswick election for June 27, the plan of the provincial Liberals was to barnstorm the province, putting young Louis Robichaud on platforms with local Liberal candidates. In this way, the new leader could reveal his energy and charisma to the people of the province. While this style of campaigning was much more imaginative than the old Liberal approach, which had the leader remaining in Fredericton and putting his message out to newspaper reporters and over the radio, it still failed to take account of how television could change the image of parties and leaders. Ned Belliveau's main communications idea, and it was a good one, was to telegraph the speeches of Louis Robichaud to the Canadian Press, so that his message would be reported to the people under the imprimatur of the respected CP label.

But television's power, much to everyone's astonishment, played an important role in the New Brunswick election campaign. That year, there were only two television studios in the province—one in Saint John, the other in Moncton—for politicians wishing to reach the populace on the black-and-white signals of the day. In addition, there was one more television station, in the Gaspé region of Quebec, whose broadcast area included many Acadian communities in northern New Brunswick. Robichaud travelled to the

Quebec studio to beam his message to its New Brunswick viewers. He also stopped in at the studios in Saint John and Moncton whenever possible to do interviews.[19]

Right from the start, Robichaud had a deft touch with the new medium. Many politicians of the day were uncomfortable in front of the camera. They tended to project their voices as though they were speaking in front of a large crowd. Robichaud understood from day one that television was an intimate tool, that through it he was speaking to people in their homes. His more natural, soft-spoken approach on television made him a winner in its use, and the impact showed up immediately. Ned Belliveau, who had not been counting on television as a major factor in the campaign, saw midway through that it could be just that. One night, the contrast between Robichaud and Flemming was shown to maximum advantage for the young leader when the Liberals purchased half an hour of television time immediately following a broadcast by Flemming.[20] While the premier looked ill at ease and older than his sixty-one years, Robichaud appeared comfortable and in control as he answered questions from several so-called "voters," who were in fact Liberal militants. Following the broadcast, the effect was immediate. When Robichaud and Belliveau stopped at a restaurant outside Saint John, they were met with enthusiasm from other diners who had seen the show.[21]

On election day, most of the press corps went to Woodstock, the premier's home town, to wait for the results, and to report, as they expected, a third consecutive victory for Hugh John Flemming. Robichaud, with Belliveau and another advisor, were stationed in the leader's house in Richibuctou. As the results came in that evening, from the start the Liberals led. They finished by overturning the government, winning thirty-one seats to twenty-one for the Conservatives. To the astonishment of many, not least in his own party, the young Acadian had won a solid majority government. As the first Acadian ever to lead his party to an electoral victory in New Brunswick, Robichaud had now to reassure the province that he would govern for all New Brunswickers, while setting out to meet the hopes of his fellow Acadians for a better deal.

On the morning after his electoral triumph, Louis Robichaud went out for a walk by himself to gather his thoughts. He had spent the night in a river cabin that he had built a few kilometres from his house. On his way back home, the local milkman, out making his deliveries, spotted the premier-elect and gave him a ride. Later in the morning, a figure of great importance in the province literally dropped out of the sky to visit Robichaud. Unannounced, the seaplane of K. C. Irving, the business mogul who dominated New Brunswick business, landed at the new premier's fishing wharf. En route to Quebec on a business trip, Irving climbed onto the wharf to spend a few minutes alone with Louis Robichaud. Irving, who was used to getting his own way in New Brunswick, in politics as well as in business, was well disposed to the young Liberal leader. He had contributed handsomely to the Liberal electoral cause in 1960, having decided that he had seen enough of Flemming. No ideologue, years before he had grown weary of Liberal Premier John B. McNair and had helped fund a Conservative victory.[22]

Robichaud's victory demonstrated, as no event ever had, that Acadians could gain power through the electoral process. Until then, Acadians had been a minority people with only a limited ability to prod the state to act on their behalf. On average, Acadians were poorer than other people in the province, their schools were underfunded and their health care facilities were second-rate.

As a people without a defined homeland and without control of a state, the Acadians had had to find ways to defend and advance their interests that were decidedly unorthodox. One way had been through the creation of a shadowy organization called La Patente or the Order of Jacques Cartier. Actually, the Order of Jacques Cartier was not first established in Acadie, but rather in Ontario, the initial goal being to assist French-speaking people to find employment in the federal civil service. Chapters of the order were set up by Acadians in New Brunswick in 1934. Membership and the activities of La Patente were to remain secret, according to the organization's rules. During initiation ceremonies, new members even wore masks.

La Patente brought together elite Acadians for secret meetings to work out an agenda to be pursued with governments, business and other decision-makers. Before he became leader of the provincial Liberals, Louis Robichaud had been involved with La Patente, but as soon as he won the leadership, Robichaud resigned from the board of governors of the organization.[23] As premier, he had to make it clear that his job was to govern the whole province, and that he could not act as a lobbyist on behalf of a secretive Acadian organization. (La Patente ceased to function in New Brunswick in 1964.)

Many years after he left power, Robichaud reflected on the attitude of some leading Acadians, members of La Patente, to his accession to the highest office in the province. For these people, he mused, the victory of an Acadian leader was a one-time thing, a political fluke that would never be repeated. Therefore, it was their view that Robichaud had to use his control of the state apparatus to deliver justice to the Acadians, justice that had been denied far too long. As they saw it, the young Acadian premier should use this term in office as though there would never be another.

Nothing could have been farther from the thoughts of the new premier. Robichaud planned to bring about change gradually, at a pace that would be acceptable to the anglophone majority in the province. His first task, as for all incoming premiers, was to construct a Cabinet that would reflect the regions and the linguistic makeup of the province. His twelve-member Cabinet included six francophones and six anglophones. While he gave the important health portfolio to an Acadian, Georges Dumont, he handed the critical education post to an anglophone, Henry Irwin. The new premier believed that the most important reforms would have to be made in the area of education, but he decided that an anglophone should be the one to deliver those reforms, on which the future of Acadian society would so largely depend.

Before he came to grips with educational reform, Robichaud made a first stab at changing the province's antique liquor laws, which had last been updated in 1927. The way the existing law was applied made it easy for the well-to-do to have access to liquor in clubs and hotels, but poor and rural-dwellers of New Brunswick who bought alcohol from bootleggers were subject to the full force of the law, which could involve fines or even a jail sentence. During the days of Prohibition in the United States in the 1920s and early 1930s, the Acadian coast of New Brunswick had been a key part of the route for the shipment of booze from the French islands of St. Pierre and Miquelon to Maine, and on from there to the speakeasies of New York and Chicago. For a year and a half, the debate about alcohol pitted religious leaders against the new government. When legislation came, it was a modest step toward allowing the people of the province to purchase alcohol from government stores and to order a drink in a licensed restaurant.

And there was the question of the province's straitened fiscal position. To carry out the ambitious reform program Robichaud envisioned, New Brunswick would need more tax room and additional tax transfers from Ottawa. A key theme of the 1960s, not only in New Brunswick but across Canada, was the need for provincial governments to acquire much greater revenues to meet their mounting responsibilities in education, health care and highway construction. Especially in the wake of the victory of Jean Lesage in Quebec, federal-provincial fiscal showdowns were the order of the day. Robichaud could add weight to Quebec's drive for additional tax room and revenue, but Quebec had its own autonomist agenda that, by definition, made alliances with other provinces problematic.

As the fights about alcohol and fiscal reform were underway, the government prepared for the step that arguably, more than any other, would transform the life of Acadians of New Brunswick: the establishment of the Université de Moncton. Robichaud had always believed that for young Acadians to have the chance to thrive in their own province they had to have a French-language university to attend. Powerful vested interests stood in the way. The English-language University of New Brunswick, located in Fredericton, was established in 1785, a year after the creation of New Brunswick itself. The administration of UNB and the anglophone elite of the province saw this venerable institution as embodying the traditions of New Brunswick dating all the way back to the arrival of the Loyalists. In his own case, Robichaud had had to take correspondence courses in law in English from UNB to become a lawyer. Establishing a French-language university would be no easy task. Not only would the government have to contend with the established university, it would also have to deal with the three francophone classical colleges in New Brunswick—in Memramcook, Edmundston and Bathurst—institutions tied to the Church that were already providing a post-secondary education.

To move forward on this tricky and crucial issue, the premier turned to John Deutsch, a highly respected political scientist who was a professor emeritus at Queen's University in Kingston, Ontario. Deutsch agreed to head up a commission of inquiry on whether to establish an Acadian university in New Brunswick. The response of the UNB administration and of the province's anglophone elite was flatly negative to the proposal. To maintain its monopoly as the province's established university, suggestions were made that UNB could offer some courses in French. The Deutsch Commission handed down its report in June 1962, a report that called for the establishment of an Acadian university separate from UNB to which the existing classical colleges could affiliate. Robichaud was lucky that the commission, with its eminent chairman, had come down on the issue the way he had hoped it would.

The report and the sentiments of Louis Robichaud made it appear to opponents that the battle over the idea of a French university was over. Opposition switched to focus on the question of whether there should also be a French Normal School in the province for the training of francophone teachers. A highly scurrilous accusation was made by some in the province's anglophone community that to create a separate Acadian Normal School would be to follow in the footsteps of whites in the American South who were fighting fiercely at the time to preserve their segregated schools against the admission of blacks. The comparison, of course, ignored the fundamental reality that anglophone New Brunswick had always dominated the province, keeping the Acadians in a marginalized position.

Fifteen months before the end of his four-year term, sensing that his government was still popular and that the opposition Conservatives had not yet become a real threat, Louis Robichaud called a snap election, using suggestions of scandal surrounding a construction project in northern New Brunswick as his excuse. The election left the great reforms the premier planned still incomplete, but the premier's hunch that he could win an early election was proved correct when his party was re-elected on April 22, 1963, with a gain of one seat in the legislature.[24]

The second Robichaud mandate brought to fruition the premier's agenda for the promotion of social equality, which by definition ensured greater equality between anglophones and Acadians. When Robichaud came to power, education, health care and roads in New Brunswick were financed by counties. This meant that the wealthiest counties had the best hospitals, schools and highways while the poorest ones were left wanting. For the Acadian counties in the north, this system of public finance was disastrous, engendering as it did a vicious circle. Poor services contributed to a weak economy and a weak economy condemned these counties to poor services. In realizing his bold agenda, Robichaud was forced into a bitter conflict with K. C. Irving, the business mogul who had helped fund the Liberal campaign in 1960. The combat between the premier and the great industrialist was, to some extent, a clash of personalities, but much more it was a product of the changing relationship between government and business in the 1960s.

Robichaud and Irving both grew up in small towns in Kent County, Robichaud in St. Antoine de Kent and Irving in nearby Bouctouche. Irving shared much in common with the future premier. Both were men with a common touch, who could cope with events in the real world. Irving, from a Scottish background, was raised in the harsh precepts of Presbyterianism. While they were divided by a great gap in age, the young premier and the aging mogul had strong personalities and were both determined to proceed with their agendas. By the time Robichaud came to office in 1960, one-seventh of New Brunswick's workforce was employed by an Irving-owned enterprise. Irving's empire in forest products, petroleum, service stations, communications media and other sectors gave him power in his province on a scale unequalled by any single entrepreneur in any other province.

Irving regarded New Brunswick as his fiefdom. As far as he was concerned, it was his job and that of other entrepreneurs to keep the economy of the province running. Government should not interfere with his corporate strategy. In the 1960s, however, in many parts of the industrialized world, including Canada, the political current ran strongly in favour of governments acting to ensure greater equality among citizens. In those days, governments were held responsible for keeping the economy growing and providing jobs for the population. Strengthening social programs, improving educational systems and providing wider accessibility to higher education were regarded as priorities in a number of provinces. Significantly, when the government that launched Canada's first medicare program, the CCF government of Saskatchewan, was defeated in an election in 1964, Louis Robichaud was quick to recruit some of the best administrative brains from the defeated regime.

To do his job as a political reformer, the New Brunswick premier was almost certain to run afoul of K. C. Irving. Feeling that it was his responsibility to bring jobs and development to various regions of the province, on several occasions Robichaud encouraged ventures that would promote competition with an Irving enterprise or facility. Sometimes the mogul got the better of the premier and sometimes it was the other way round in these conflicts, which grew increasingly bitter. On one occasion during Robichaud's first mandate, Irving met the premier and a rival corporate executive in the premier's office to wrangle over timber rights in the province. On this occasion, Irving dropped his usual cool and even chivalrous manner and behaved in a "rough and angry" way, as Robichaud later recalled the meeting. In this fight, it was Irving's rival who got his way, something the New Brunswick baron would not forget.[25]

During Robichaud's second mandate, Irving became an implacable foe. Tension between the premier and the tycoon rose dramatically in February 1964 with the publication of a massive report on the delivery of public services in New Brunswick, a report that exposed the enormous inequalities that existed from region to region. Ed Byrne, a lawyer from Bathurst who had served as mayor of the city, chaired the Royal Commission on Finance and Municipal Taxation in New Brunswick. Byrne's experience as mayor of a city in the province's poor north-east made him an ideal person to head up an investigation of the disparities that lay at the very heart of New Brunswick life, and that, among other things, left most Acadians on the margin.

The Byrne Report, based on two years of work, detailed disparities that existed from county to county in the province in the level of public services that were provided. Relatively rich places such as the city of Saint John, for example, enjoyed well-funded services. On the other hand, in the poor Acadian Peninsula in the province's north-east, services were subpar. The inequities revealed were stark indeed. In five hundred villages in the province, education was provided in one-room schoolhouses and stopped at grade eight. More than half the population of New Brunswick did not have access to secondary education. Thousands of pupils in the province's schools were being taught by teachers who did not have a teaching diploma. These teachers were in the classrooms on the strength of local licences, issued by county councils, the majority of whose members did not themselves have schooling beyond grade eight. For young people living in these deprived communities, only those in families with the means to send them elsewhere could get schooling beyond the primary level.[26] In Kent County, from which Robichaud hailed, the average annual salary in 1961 was $1,853, a sum two times lower than that in Saint John. While Saint John was able at the time to spend $300 a year per person on education, the Acadian county of Gloucester in the north-east could spend only $144 per person per year.[27]

The report served as the basis for Louis Robichaud's Program of Equal Opportunity, a sweeping set of reforms to equalize the provision of education, health, justice and social services across New Brunswick. To achieve these goals, the Byrne Report proposed a complete overhaul of taxation, the funding of programs and the delivery of services in the province. The report called upon the province to take charge of the administration of education, health care, justice and social services and to eliminate the role played by the counties in the delivery of these services. The county councils, which the report concluded had neither the means nor the know-how to run these programs properly, would simply be eliminated. Along with the abolition of county councils, the Byrne Report proposed the elimination of a variety of local taxes levied in the counties to fund programs. The report proposed that increased provincial funding be achieved by raising New Brunswick's sales tax from 3 to 5 percent. In addition, it advised that the property tax be made uniform across the province and that the many tax exemptions offered by individual counties to enterprises located within their boundaries be eliminated. This latter proposal, which struck at the corporate practice of shopping from county to country and deciding to locate where the best tax deal could be had, threatened to be very costly for K. C. Irving, who oversaw the province's most extensive private empire.

For Robichaud, whose basic goal was to achieve equality among the regions of the province as well as between anglophones and Acadians, the Byrne Report was no less than a weapon he could wield to his advantage. Determined though he was from the start to push ahead with the full reform proposed in the report, the premier decided to wait until the government was fully ready before taking action. As time passed, with the government not showing its hand, popular unrest began to build, particularly in the Acadian north-east of the province. Demanding better services and relief from a raft of local taxes, protest organizers threatened to bring a cavalcade of eight hundred vehicles from their region to the provincial capital to demand the full implementation of the Byrne Report. While the premier's office succeeded in convincing the organizers to call off this public protest, Robichaud agreed to meet the spokesmen of the protesters at a regular meeting of his Cabinet. The premier's message to those seeking reform was to be patient. He assured them that action would come in the 1965 autumn session of the legislature.

To prepare for action on the report, Robichaud set up a committee of five Cabinet ministers, including himself, to oversee implementation. The bureaucracy was mobilized. In train was the preparation of changes to more than one hundred pieces of provincial legislation. Members of the Cabinet committee and the top bureaucrats often worked seven days a week and long into the night to prepare the way for the great reforms to come.

As anticipation of the reforms grew, an issue that threatened Robichaud was concern among leading Acadians about how the educational system was to be reorganized. The Byrne Report had called for a single provincial educational system to administer both English and French schools, while there was a demand among Acadians for two systems of education, one English and one French, to be administered separately. For his own part, at the time of the report, Robichaud did not favour two separate systems. He did not believe this was the best way to meet the needs of the Acadians. In any case, the cleavage within the province in response to the Byrne Report tended to be along rural-urban lines, rather than along French-English lines. Rural anglophone counties, like their Acadian counterparts, welcomed the reforms the report proposed, while it was in the wealthier urban centres that opposition mushroomed.[28]

When action was taken in the legislature in the autumn of 1965 to advance the reforms advocated in the Byrne Report, the most potent opponent was not sitting on the Opposition benches, but rather in his corporate headquarters in Saint John. K. C. Irving benefited enormously from the patchwork quilt of taxation that prevailed in New Brunswick from county to county. With his production facilities operating in many parts of the province, counties were anxious to attract mills or plants to their turf. This led to frequent bidding wars among counties for the favour of the great entrepreneur. The medium of exchange in these wars was tax breaks. For a magnate like Irving, it was an ideal world—he was big and the counties were small. The Byrne Report threatened to end all this by establishing uniform taxation across the province. Not only would this deprive Irving of future tax breaks, it threatened the tax advantages he had already carved out for himself.

With Robichaud in the premier's office, the relationship between government and business was changing. In earlier days, including the first days of the Robichaud government, K. C. Irving could count on kid-gloves treatment from the premier's office. He could call the premier on the phone or visit him in his office and expect favourable treatment. By 1965, those days were over. In December of that year, K. C. Irving was reduced to appearing before a legislative committee that was charged with considering changes to the province's laws. What underlined how things had changed was that on the day he appeared, Louis Robichaud was out of the province. Those who witnessed the hearing described the demeanour of the businessman as one of barely controlled rage.[29]

At the hearing, an Irving lawyer made the case that a number of Irving companies faced a difficult financial situation and would be threatened with insolvency should the tax breaks they enjoyed be removed. Then Irving himself spoke, telling the members of the committee that he was deeply concerned about what he saw as a breakdown in confidence between the government and business. In tearing up deals entered into in good faith, he charged, enterprises that were fated to lose the concessions they enjoyed were being condemned to failure. To drive home his threat of possible closures, Irving claimed that his paper mill had lost $4 million in the past twenty years and that without tax concessions it would never have survived. Asking rhetorically whether anyone could believe that the economy of New Brunswick would be improved by abolishing the tax concessions for the mill, K. C. Irving warned that no sane government would proceed with the measures that were being considered. Having thrown down the gauntlet, the tycoon rose from his chair and, without a further word, walked out of the hearing.[30]

Following his spectacular departure, K. C. Irving withdrew behind the solid rampart of his New Brunswick media empire. As the owner of four of the five English-language daily newspapers in the province, in addition to being the proprietor of New Brunswick's only English television outlet, Irving was powerfully placed to fight it out with Louis Robichaud. The Irving media launched a full-fledged assault on the proposed reforms and on the premier.

To make matters worse, the province's fifth English daily, the Fredericton *Gleaner*, was owned by a swashbuckling character, Brigadier Michael Wardell, a disciple of Fleet Street media baron Lord Beaverbrook. Wardell, who wore a patch over one eye, the consequence of a hunting accident in the company of the Duke of Windsor, once had a romantic relationship with the American actress Tallulah Bankhead. When Wardell purchased the *Gleaner*, he ran it in the manner of a Loyalist organ, affecting a staunchly anglophone posture that, not surprisingly, put him at odds with Louis Robichaud. To make matters worse for the premier, Wardell hugely admired K. C. Irving—Irving would purchase the *Gleaner* in 1968—and was happy to make his newspaper a battering ram in the struggle against the government's reform plans. Reflecting the views of the publisher, the *Gleaner*'s cartoonist regularly depicted Louis Robichaud with a small moustache and swastikas emblazoned on his arm. The words "Little Hitler" were written across the top of the cartoon.[31] Wardell's newspaper was also fond of depicting Robichaud in cartoons as a latter-day Louis XIV, seated on his throne, with the inscription, "*La Province, c'est Moi!*"[32]

The personal attacks on the premier created an atmosphere of rising tension for the Robichaud family in Fredericton. The premier's wife and children received frequent threatening phone calls in their home. At school, Robichaud's four children were taunted by classmates. The small and usually quiet provincial capital became a pressure cooker. As Robichaud was the target of death threats, some analysts went so far as to compare the situation in the city to that in Dallas in the lead-up to the Kennedy assassination, which had occurred a few years earlier.[33]

The media assault on Robichaud played particularly on the fears of those English-speaking New Brunswickers who experienced a virulent reaction against the changes that were taking place in the province during the 1960s. Chedly Belkhodja, a political scientist at the Université de Moncton, has written widely on right-wing populism. Looking at this phenomenon from a North American perspective, he has written that "the liberalization of society brought about a democratization of the political space, leading to the recognition of pluralistic demands from minorities such as blacks, the Spanish-speaking community and Francophones. In reaction, a certain type of white voter began to lose patience, finding it difficult to grasp the changes taking place in society."[34]

In addition to the elite attack on Robichaud led by K. C. Irving, other figures in the business community and the English-language press, there was a populist backlash as well among radical anti-francophone elements in New Brunswick. During the same years that Robichaud was fighting for a wider space for Acadians in his province, Prime Minister Pierre Trudeau was leading the struggle for bilingualism in Canada. A number of small, English-Canadian organizations, including the Voice of Canada, the Canadian Protestant League and the Canadian Loyalist Association (CLA), hotly opposed the push for the recognition of French and English as official languages.

In New Brunswick, the CLA, which also went under the name Maritime Loyalist Association, advocated the retention of Canada's ties to Britain, including the Union Jack, "God Save the Queen" as the country's anthem and English as the nation's only official language. Strongest in the Moncton area, where Acadian influence was sharply on the rise, the CLA used invective in its campaign, as is shown in a letter sent to Robichaud's office on October 5, 1967: "The Canadian Loyalist Association wishes to congratulate you on the masterful manner in which you have deceived the people of New Brunswick and Canada by leading them to believe that New Brunswick has two official languages. Your senseless, degenerate and ruinous official language act is one of the worst evils anyone ever tried to perpetrate on the citizens of this province."[35] For his part,

Pierre Trudeau was depicted by the CLA as "Trudeau the legalizer of the sin of homosexuality; Trudeau the friend of France and Communist China." "Today, Canada is in the hands of three Frenchmen," stated the bulletin of the CLA, "Trudeau, Marchand and Pelletier (a hater of all English) and no English-speaking person of consequence is attached to the Prime Minister's staff."[36]

Though under fierce assault, Louis Robichaud had good access to Acadians through the television outlet of Radio-Canada and in the pages of the French-language newspaper *L'Évangéline*. Countering the media crusade against him in anglophone New Brunswick was much more difficult.[37] The personal war between the premier and K. C. Irving reached its climactic finale just a few weeks after Irving testified before the legislative committee on the proposed reforms. When he visited the studios of CHSJ, Irving's television station, Robichaud had a surprise encounter with the businessman. Irving challenged the premier, asking him what he thought he was doing. Robichaud replied that there was only room for one legitimate government in the province. It was the last time the two men ever exchanged words.[38]

In the winter of 1966, the campaign against Robichaud's program of reform became extremely personal. Accusations circulated that the premier was accumulating great personal wealth for himself, or that his planned changes would take money out of the pockets of the English and give it to the French. With incendiary attacks being made against Robichaud in the English-language newspapers of the province, the Conservative opposition in the legislature launched a veritable filibuster against the adoption of the proposed reforms, hoping to force the government into the use of closure, or even into calling an early general election.

To counter these attacks, the premier turned to Ned Belliveau, his former communications chief, who was now running his own communications firm in Toronto. Belliveau's advice was to fight fire with fire, to mount a propaganda campaign on behalf of the proposed reforms to offset the disinformation that was being propagated by the other side. Under Belliveau's guidance, a government information office was established. To take the fight directly to the population, key ministers, including the premier, crisscrossed New Brunswick speaking to meetings in school auditoriums to make the case for the social equality agenda. As in his earlier political campaigns, Louis Robichaud demonstrated his ability to enter a hall filled with people who were skeptical or even hostile and to win them around to his point of view.[39]

Robichaud's struggle to transform the province drew the sympathetic attention of major newspapers, both English and French, across Canada, and received attention from the national CBC. Even *The New York Times* sent a reporter to learn about the struggle in the Canadian province. The residents of Fredericton were not necessarily pleased to see journalists from afar in their streets, placing New Brunswick's way of life under a microscope.

The Robichaud government stood its ground and pushed its massive agenda—no fewer than 130 bills—through the legislature, despite the fact that the Conservatives fought tooth and nail over every bill. By the beginning of 1967, the key elements of the reforms had been passed into law, and the opposition to Robichaud shifted its focus from blocking his equality package to defeating him in a general election.

To best the charismatic, youthful premier, the Conservatives picked a showman of their own, a man by the name of Charlie Van Horne, who hailed from the northern New Brunswick town of Campbellton. Van Horne's mother was Acadian, his father Dutch. He spoke the French of the streets, and his English was that of the salesman or impresario. A man who had tried his hand at a number of things—who had been, for a time, a federal Conservative member of Parliament—Van Horne had worked for K. C. Irving assembling parcels of land in Newfoundland. Many in New Brunswick believed that Irving was behind Van Horne's decision to seek the leadership of the Conservative Party. Although no proof was ever obtained to show a definite link between Van Horne and the business baron, the rumour that Van Horne was Irving's hand-picked gun persisted. In February 1967, three months after capturing the leadership of his party, a by-election opened up in the riding where Van Horne was born, the riding he had previously represented in Ottawa. Van Horne was swept into the legislature in the by-election campaign.[40]

Having presided over the establishment of the Université de Moncton, tax reform and the transformation of the delivery of public services, the Robichaud government was plainly showing the strains that went with its seven years in power. The premier was fortunate that 1967, Canada's centennial year, was a time of optimism and celebration across the country. While the focus of the national celebration was Expo 67 in Montreal, there were plenty of opportunities everywhere in the country for political leaders to take the spotlight at the opening of arenas and other projects launched for the centennial. All was not sweetness and light, however. Indeed, the coming decades of debate about Quebec secession were foreshadowed in 1967 with René Lévesque's rupture with the Quebec Liberal Party and with French President Charles de Gaulle's famous cry of "*Vive le Québec libre*" at Montreal City Hall. But for Louis Robichaud, the celebrations created the chance for him to repair an image that had been damaged by the constant assaults on him in the anglophone newspapers as a dictator who was trying to centralize power in his own hands.

When the election was called for October 1967, Charlie Van Horne launched a furious campaign in which he sought to be all things to all people. As he toured the province in a white Cadillac, distributing his trademark white cowboy hats to voters, he promised tax cuts along with improved social services. In anglophone areas, he told people that he would not tax Peter to pay Pierre, an allusion to Robichaud's supposed plan to make the English pay for better services for the French. In francophone areas, he accused Robichaud of failing to advance the interests of Acadians, suggesting that the Conservatives under his leadership would enshrine French as an official language of the province. Adding to the circus atmosphere of Van Horne's demagogic campaign was the presence at his appearances of Don Messer and His Islanders, the highly popular Cape Breton fiddlers and dancers, whose television shows had made them famous across Canada. In the Acadian town of Shediac, close to five thousand people came out to see the Van Horne and Don Messer spectacle. Where was the money coming from to pay for the glitzy campaign? This was the nagging question that led people back to the suspicion that the shadowy figure of K. C. Irving was behind it all.[41]

Robichaud's entire campaign was devoted to making Van Horne the issue. Everywhere the premier went, he painted a portrait of the Conservative leader as a man who would say anything to anyone to win a vote, at the same time as he said directly contrary things to other people. The effort to undermine Van Horne was strongly reinforced by the national media. The *Star Weekly*, a publication of *The Toronto Star* that was inserted into some New Brunswick papers on Saturdays, published a scathing article on Charlie Van Horne and his dubious ventures in the past, creating the impression that this was a man short on character who should not be trusted. Two days before election day, October 23, 1967, *The Globe and Mail*, regarded as a pro-Conservative newspaper, published a scathing editorial attacking Van Horne and endorsing Louis Robichaud and the reforms he had wrought in New Brunswick.

The people of New Brunswick elected a Liberal majority government, giving Robichaud's party thirty-two seats, while the Conservatives won twenty-six. In this, his final electoral victory, Robichaud was heavily dependent on Acadians for his triumph. The Liberals won twenty-eight seats in the north where francophones constituted the majority. The Liberals even succeeded in winning the three seats in Restigouche, taking back the seat the Conservative leader had won in the by-election earlier in the year. Only four ridings in the anglophone south of the province voted Liberal, however. The price of his reform program and the fierce attacks against it was that Robichaud had been driven to rely more than ever on the loyalty of his Acadian electoral base.[42]

Robichaud's third victory at the head of his party took place against the backdrop of the rising question of Quebec's place in Canada. For an Acadian premier of New Brunswick and for the

Acadian people, this was a deeply difficult matter in which they were inevitably involved, however much they might wish not to be. As a small French-speaking people with no state of their own, the Acadian's had a position that differed dramatically from that of Quebec. In 1867, Confederation had placed Quebec at the heart of the new Canadian federation. Confederation, however, involved a separation as well as a union for Quebec. Through it the union of Canada East (Quebec) and Canada West (Ontario) in a single province had come to an end. The province of Quebec, with its over-whelmingly francophone population, was the state around which future debates about federalism and sovereignty would rage. The possible breakup of Canada through the secession of Quebec would place Acadians in a highly vulnerable position. They would no longer benefit, however imperfectly, from living as a minority in a country in which francophones constituted a very large percentage of the population. At the very moment when Acadians were making strides in New Brunswick to solidify their position through the establishment of the Université de Moncton, and indeed through the equality reforms that promised a much stronger educational future for Acadians, the Quebec question appeared to overshadow these gains.

There was another side to the question of Quebec nationalism. The Quiet Revolution in Quebec, the vast reforms it engendered and the rising image of Québécois as a people who could take their future into their own hands could not help but stimulate a wave of sympathy and fellow feeling among Acadians. This was particularly true for young Acadians, who were living the adventure of the 1960s, in search of answers, like young people elsewhere in North America and in Europe. And just as rising nationalism in Quebec provoked debate about bilingualism versus autonomy or separation, so too in New Brunswick did the issue of bilingualism versus autonomy find its way on to the political agenda. From the time the federal Liberals came to power in 1963, Prime Minister Lester Pearson searched for ways to accommodate Quebec. He launched the Royal Commission on Bilingualism and Biculturalism, whose purpose was to analyze the crisis that gripped the country and to seek solutions. He recruited fresh political talent from Quebec to shore up his government against the threat of Quebec nationalism. First, as justice minister in Pearson's government and later as Pearson's successor, Pierre Trudeau became Quebec's and Canada's champion of federalism. Inexorably, Acadians and their principal political leader, Louis Robichaud, were drawn into this crucial dialogue.

Immediately after his electoral victory in October 1967, the New Brunswick premier participated in a meeting of provincial premiers in Toronto that had been convened by Ontario Premier John Robarts. The challenge there was to find a formula for accommodation with the Union Nationale premier of Quebec, Daniel Johnson, a politician who stood midway between the federalists and the sovereigntists with his slogan "Equality or Independence." In 1968, René Lévesque, the popular nationalist who had been a fiery member of Jean Lesage's Cabinet in the early days of the Quiet Revolution, formed an invitation-only body, the Mouvement Souveraineté-Association (MSA), to plan the launch of a new political party. With the later creation of the Parti Québeéois, under Lévesque's leadership, the people of Quebec had a mainstream sovereigntist party to which they could turn.

During his years in power, Louis Robichaud had been slow to move on the issue of enshrining French as an official language in New Brunswick. Indeed, during the brief and tempestuous reign of Charlie Van Horne as Opposition leader, Robichaud had even voted against a Van Horne motion in the legislature to make French an official language. Robichaud's reasons for opposing the motion were tactical. He did not want to give credibility to a Van Horne effort to embarrass the government. Nonetheless, opposing the motion did not enhance the premier's standing in Acadian nationalist circles in the province.

In the Liberal government's Speech from the Throne in February 1968, there was an undertaking that New Brunswick would act so that it could play a unique role in the Canadian effort to affirm national unity in a country comprising two founding cultures.[43] The following month, Robichaud presented a motion to the legislature recognizing English and French as the official languages of the province. The motion, which did not have the force of law, merely expressed the sentiment of the government.

The effort to enshrine full linguistic rights for Acadians in New Brunswick was met with fierce opposition from anglophone traditionalists. The man who personified that opposition was the mayor of Moncton, Leonard Jones. Adamant in his refusal to recognize the French fact in New Brunswick and in his own city, in which one-third of the population was Acadian, Jones had opposed the creation of the Université de Moncton. He took the stand that not a word of French could be spoken in meetings of Moncton city council. Jones became the standard-bearer for the anglophones of New Brunswick, such as the members of the Orange Lodge, who believed in a unilingual English-speaking society, in which the Acadians would return to their quiet role of the past, doing menial jobs in places like Moncton and keeping their profile low.

Moncton was changing, however, not least because of the presence there of the new Acadian university. It was not accidental that the collision between Leonard Jones and the students of the university came to a head in 1968, the year when youth protest reached its zenith in many parts of the world, resulting in the great demonstrations in Paris and the violent suppression of youth protests by police in Chicago that overshadowed the Democratic Party's national convention. Stirred by the same passions, young Acadians decided they had had enough of second-class status in Moncton. They challenged Jones in his lair at city council, demanding their right to be heard in French. They marched through the streets of the city to demonstrate that times had changed.

In an escapade that brought matters to a head, two Québécois who were students at the Université de Moncton placed a pig's head in front of the home of Mayor Jones. When the students, Jacques Belile and Jacques Moreau, were arrested and charged with public mischief, they sought to be heard in French during their trial. Judge Henry Murphy of Moncton refused and their lawyer moved for an appeal of the decision, but Charles Hugues, the chief justice of the New Brunswick Court of Appeal, rejected the motion. The go-slow approach of the Robichaud government was now exposed in the eyes of many Acadians as ineffectual. If the page was truly to be turned and Acadians were to win their linguistic rights, a more confrontational approach would be needed, many concluded.[44]

On a Saturday night in January 1969, about a hundred students at the Université de Moncton occupied the Sciences Building on the campus. Their demand, to shocked public reaction, was that the federal government hand over $32 million to the university to close what the occupiers claimed was the gap between it and other universities and to save the institution from bankruptcy. University officials condemned the occupation as a grave misdeed. The occupiers, led by an Acadian student, Michel Blanchard, refused to communicate openly with the media and instead relied on private briefings to several journalists. All of this added to the air of crisis.[44] To counter the occupation, university and government authorities released documents to make the case that, on a per capita basis, the Université de Moncton was as well funded as other post-secondary institutions in the province, and that the university was not running a deficit and was not on the verge of bankruptcy. As it happened, at the time of the occupation Louis Robichaud was in the Congo, heading up a Canadian delegation to a meeting of La Francophonie on the subject of education. One week after it began, the occupation ended when Michel Blanchard and the other occupiers left the Sciences Building with a police escort.

The occupation was followed by a general strike of the students at the Université de Moncton, triggered by the student federation, whose leadership felt betrayed by the way the university administration had used the federation to help bring about an end to the occupation. The federation accused the university of failing to inform it that it was calling in the police to deal with the occupation.[46] The strike, which lasted only three days, was symptomatic of a new radicalism among young Acadians, many of whom were to form the

Acadian intelligentsia of the future. For these people, the approach of Louis Robichaud was doomed to failure.

Robichaud had climbed to the top of the political pyramid in New Brunswick, accomplishing what no Acadian leader had achieved before. He had harnessed a solid Acadian political base and, through the language of equality and social advancement, he had made common cause with enough of English-speaking New Brunswick for him to win and hold power for a decade. For the long term, Robichaud's reforms restructured New Brunswick society fundamentally. A fair and equitable system of public financing of infrastructure, education and social programs and the creation of the Université de Moncton opened the door for Acadians to come out of the shadows and to win a much larger space for themselves as individuals and as a people.

In a very real sense, the young people who were rejecting Robichaud's gradualist approach at the end of the 1960s were "Robichaud's children." Indeed, by that time Louis Robichaud himself had become the established figure against whom youthful Acadians, empowered by the reforms he had wrought, would rebel. Securely positioned in the new structures he had created, they went off on their own course. For some, that course would lead to a new Acadian nationalism, centred on the Parti Acadien, whose political goal was the division of New Brunswick so as to create a new Acadian province that would comprise the province's north-east, north-west and a strip of territory along the coast down to the south-east. For the new nationalists, Robichaud was yesterday's man, an expression of the bad old days when Acadians either expressed their candid views in secret in bodies like the shadowy La Patente or pursued reforms that were tailored so as not to offend the dominant anglophone community in the province.

On April 11, 1969, the New Brunswick legislature adopted a law to make New Brunswick the only officially bilingual province in Canada. Remarkably, the law was passed unanimously, a tribute to the work of the new Conservative leader who had replaced the mercurial Charlie Van Horne. Richard Hatfield, who was soon to

succeed Robichaud as premier, was able to win over the last recal-
citrant holdouts in his caucus to the historic proposition.[47]

With the passage of the bilingualism law, Robichaud's trinity of
major reforms was complete: the new system of public finance, the
creation of the Université de Moncton and official status for the
French language. In the autumn of 1970, Louis Robichaud once
again turned to the electorate, this time seeking a fourth consecutive mandate. He hoped, as in the past, that an early election call
would catch the Opposition unprepared. This time, however, it was
the Liberals who were unprepared and half-hearted. While he once
again recruited Ned Belliveau to get out the message, things went
farcically wrong when Liberal ads were not ready and the daily
newspapers ran blank spaces where the Robichaud program was
supposed to have been printed. In addition, fate took the election
campaign in a completely unexpected direction.

Three weeks before election day, on October 5, 1970, a cell of the
terrorist Front de Libération du Québec (FLQ) kidnapped James
Cross, the British trade commissioner, in Montreal. A few days
later, Quebec's labour minister, Pierre Laporte, was also kidnapped.
In response, the federal government proclaimed the War Measures
Act and sent troops to the streets of Montreal. Pierre Trudeau jus-
tified the severe steps by saying that a state of "apprehended insur-
rection" existed in Quebec. Canadians were further traumatized
when the body of Pierre Laporte was found in the trunk of a car on
the south shore of the St. Lawrence, not far from Montreal. Upon
receiving the news of the murder of Laporte, whom he knew well,
Louis Robichaud halted his campaign, returned to Fredericton and
was flown in a military aircraft to Montreal to attend the labour
minister's funeral. The New Brunswick premier declared his backing for the use of the War Measures Act, taking a position that was
very much in keeping with the views of both anglophone and
francophone Canadians at the time.

On election day, October 26, 1970, Robichaud's Liberals won
twenty-five seats and Richard Hatfield's Conservatives took thirty-
two seats, and with them the election. In Moncton, where so many

of the battles of the Robichaud era had been centred, the Liberals lost three seats, perhaps in part as a consequence of anglophone sentiment in the aftermath of the FLQ crisis. Robichaud's remarkable decade was at an end. Fortunately, for his legacy and for the Acadians of New Brunswick, Robichaud's successor was an anglophone who had no intention of turning the clock back, especially in the area of francophone rights.

On the night of his electoral defeat, Robichaud managed his loss the way he had welcomed his victories, with magnanimity. "I've never lost an election in my life," he said to advisors as the vote tally was coming in. He had not known how he would take defeat. "It's not too bad after all," he concluded.

Later that night, he drove to the CBC broadcasting centre in Moncton to appear before the cameras and to concede defeat. With his trademark grin, he announced that the new government would have his full support "in doing what is good for this province and its people."[48]

Louis Robichaud was a career Liberal Party politician. But he was much more than that. From his family, the teachings of Father Lévesque and above all the spirit of change that was blowing through the world of the 1960s, Robichaud grew with the times to become a great reformer. He was no enemy of business, but he knew that fundamental reforms that only the state could deliver were necessary if New Brunswick was to be put on a course that would benefit all of its people. Living in the poorest regions of the province, held back by second-rate education, poor health care and substandard infrastructure, the Acadians benefited from the revolution in the delivery of public services that Robichaud wrought. By providing a new fairness for all and by overturning a system that reduced many New Brunswickers to peons of K. C. Irving and big business in general, Robichaud gave Acadians the chance to compete and to climb the rungs of the social ladder. In that sense, this ebullient, diminutive man was a peaceful, democratic liberator of his people.

—

CHAPTER 11

RICHARD HATFIELD
AND THE
PARTI ACADIEN

He [Richard Hatfield] has answered la Sagouine's embarrassed question: "For the love of Christ, where do we live?" by giving back to her, and to all of us, a land called home.

—ANTONINE MAILLET[1]

IF LOUIS ROBICHAUD WAS the consummate Acadian leader who launched New Brunswick on a new and progressive course in the 1960s, Richard Hatfield was the unlikely anglophone Conservative who kept the province on that path. Robichaud's reforms were the foundation on which Acadian society was reconstructed in the decades that followed. A new Acadian professional class emerged largely as a result of the changes in the educational system and the creation of the Université de Moncton. And the transformation of the system of government in the province opened the way for the rise of an Acadian entrepreneurial class in a province where business formerly had been dominated by Anglo-Canadians.

In 1970, when Robichaud lost power to the Conservatives, there was no guarantee that the province would not revert to the ways of the past, with Robichaud's reforms essentially nullified. The provincial Conservative Party had always been the voice of business and the anglophone establishment in New Brunswick. That is why the Conservatives' choice of a highly idiosyncratic leader from a privileged family turned out to be a matter of exceptional importance for the province, but especially for its Acadians.

Richard Hatfield was the son of a prominent businessman in Hartland, New Brunswick, a town about an hour's drive north of Fredericton. Home to the world's longest covered bridge, which spans the St. John River, Hartland is an English-speaking town in the heart of the province's potato-growing country. Hatfield's father, who earned his living in the potato business and who established Canada's first potato chip plant after the Second World War,[2] was elected to parliament as a Conservative in the wartime election of 1940.

Hatfield was an unusual boy who was not given to the macho outlets of many other kids. He loved to take in the natural setting of the St. John River in long walks by himself, and he enjoyed cooking. Tall, a little diffident and lacking a strong presence on a public platform, he did not look like someone who would succeed during his career in leading his party to four consecutive majority governments. Young Hatfield attended a private secondary school for a year, apparently hated it and returned to complete high school in Hartland. He attended Acadia University in Nova Scotia's Annapolis Valley and studied law at Dalhousie University in Halifax. The practice of law was not to his taste, however, and he soon gave it up for his true love, politics. In 1961, Hatfield contested and won a by-election for the seat that was vacated in the New Brunswick legislature when former premier Hugh John Flemming resigned after losing the 1960 provincial election to Louis Robichaud's Liberals.

From day one in the legislature, Hatfield had his eyes set on becoming premier. His fellow Conservatives tended, at first, to see him as a blueblood and something of a dilettante. In 1966, when the party leadership again came open, Hatfield ran for the position but was easily defeated by the charismatic right-winger Charlie Van Horne. Following Van Horne's loss to the Liberals in the 1967 provincial election, Conservatives once again held a convention to pick a leader in 1969. While Van Horne threw his hat in the ring, despite his election defeat, the party turned to Hatfield this time. His only other opponent in the leadership race was Mathilda

Blanchard, an Acadian from Caraquet who was a trade union organizer. The mother of Michel Blanchard, the leader of the student protests at the Université de Moncton in 1968, she won only a handful of votes at the leadership convention.[3]

As leader, Hatfield took the party into the 1970 election with the message that it was time for a change. It was a tried-and-true formula for an opposition party up against a government that had been in power for a lengthy period and had alienated important groups in the province. The message worked. The election was a near thing, however. Hatfield's Conservatives won only 48 percent of the popular vote, an increase of just 1 percentage point over their 1967 tally. And Robichaud's Liberals actually won the popular vote, netting 49 percent of the votes cast, a decrease of 4 percentage points from their total in the previous election. Where it counted, though, Hatfield prevailed, with thirty-one seats to Robichaud's twenty-seven.[4]

It was far from evident when Hatfield formed his new government what kind of change he would bring to the province. But as time passed, it became clear that while the new Conservative premier did not intend to introduce large-scale reforms, he also did not plan to roll back the crucial changes Robichaud had made.

Even before he became leader of his party and then premier, there had been clues that Richard Hatfield would be sympathetic to Acadian aspirations. In 1967, when Charlie Van Horne introduced a resolution in the provincial legislature that advocated the full recognition of French as an official language in New Brunswick, Hatfield made a speech in favour of the resolution that could not easily be dismissed as an exercise in demagoguery (as Van Horne's was) by the Liberals, who opposed it. Drawing on his own difficulties in learning French the previous summer in an immersion course, Hatfield said: "Many people can get by . . . in a second language, but our native language is the one in which we express our hopes, our views, our desires and our aspirations. It is the language we use to express things which are important to us, and more than that our native language is the one that expresses our being. I came away from the school with some degree of working knowledge of the French language, but most of all, I came away with an understanding of how important a native language is to the whole person."[5]

Over time, Hatfield showed that he was willing to take political risks, to offend sections of his own party, on behalf of the Acadians and the pursuit of their rights. Even though he continued to speak French poorly himself, he came to be described by Acadians as a francophile. Throughout his years as premier, Richard Hatfield never gave up his cosmopolitan outlook and his taste for travel. He loved to go to Toronto, New York, Boston and Montreal, where he purchased stylish clothing and was often seen in fashionable night spots. He learned early on that promoting the arts was an important way to gain political approval, especially where the Acadians were concerned. On a visit to Paris as premier, Hatfield helped promote interest in Antonine Maillet's play *La Sagouine*, a work that eventually won the hearts of the French and was a milestone in the history of Acadian culture.

Even as an Opposition backbencher in the 1960s, Hatfield had cultivated contacts with Acadians. During those years he often travelled to northern New Brunswick, where he met with Acadian acquaintances, and spent long sessions with them learning about Acadian culture and aspirations. To these Acadians, Hatfield was an oddity, a Tory backbencher who did not speak fluent French but who showed a determined interest in Acadians and their problems. Before Hatfield arrived on the political scene, political analysts had assumed that the Acadians were always going to be a solid Liberal voting bloc and that there was little point trying to win them to the Conservative cause. When Louis Robichaud was elected premier in 1960, however, it became clear that the Acadians could exercise decisive political clout. Richard Hatfield learned that lesson and never forgot it.

Despite the slow advance of the Conservative Party among francophones, Hatfield never gave up the struggle to make headway where the party had barely competed in the past. This change was to be crucial for the Conservatives, who in one election in the 1940s had not even bothered to run any candidates in predominantly Acadian Gloucester County. Over the long term, it would be Bernard Lord, born in Quebec with a francophone mother and an anglophone father, who would reap where Hatfield had sown, first by winning the leadership of the New Brunswick Conservative Party and then by leading the party to power in 1999. But the Conservative Party had to cross a very wide divide from the Richard Hatfield era to that of Bernard Lord.

Shortly after he came to office in 1970, Hatfield had to deal with a crucial problem left over from the days of the Robichaud government—whether the province's school boards were to be bilingual, presiding over both English- and French-language schools, or whether there were to be separate, unilingual English and French school boards. The Acadians strongly preferred the latter solution as the only way they could gain real control over the running of their own schools. The old system included so-called bilingual schools in Acadian regions. The practice in those schools was that even if a large majority of students in a class was French-speaking, the presence of a small number of anglophones meant that classes were taught in English. In 1972, Hatfield imposed a separate-board system on the city of Moncton, home of the bitter linguistic wars of the Leonard Jones era. Two years later, the scheme of separate systems was established for the whole province. With this reorganization, while the province had a single minister of education, below the ministerial level the department was divided into two sections, one for English schools, the other for French schools.[6]

Richard Hatfield's determination to play a role in Canada's unity crisis was no mere expression of his generosity of spirit; his own province's unity was very much at stake. And just as the country faced the threat of Quebec separation, New Brunswick was confronted in the 1970s by the emergence of a political party whose goal was the creation of a separate Acadian province, the Parti Acadien.

The Parti Acadien was founded by Acadian nationalists who had become alienated because they believed the pace of change in New Brunswick was much too slow. Despite the reforms of Louis

Robichaud, they believed the truth about the province was revealed in the stiff-necked resistance of Moncton's Mayor Leonard Jones to even the slightest whiff of bilingualism in his city. If, in the very city where a French-language university had been established, the historic resistance of the anglophone community to the Acadian fact was seemingly implacable, what hope was there for the future? That the resistance to Acadian advance was deeply rooted was plain for all to see in 1974 when Jones beat the sitting Conservative MP in a Moncton riding for the party's nomination in the upcoming federal election. Although federal Conservative leader Robert Stanfield refused to allow the notorious anti-francophone to stand as a PC candidate, Jones was elected to the House of Commons as an independent.[7]

In the view of the founders of the Parti Acadien, Robichaud's decade in office had whetted the appetites of Acadians for real political power, while all they had received were a few crumbs that had been dropped from the plate of anglophone New Brunswick. The main idea of the new party, obviously influenced by the example of the Parti Québécois, was that there ought to be a separate Acadian province that would be carved out of New Brunswick. The new province that would take its place within Confederation would be made up of the predominantly French-speaking north-west and north-east and a strip of territory down the coast to the linguistically mixed south-east.

In January 1971, five professors and two civil servants set up a Committee of Seven which proposed that a political party to represent Acadians should be formed. Over the next year, the committee held public meetings, which led the following February to the election of an interim committee whose task would be to draft a constitution and to work on generating support. In May 1972, the first manifesto of the party was issued, and the following November a founding convention was held at which the Parti Acadien was launched, with Euclide Chiasson, a professor at Collège de Bathurst, chosen as president.

From the outset, the Parti Acadien opposed Maritime Union, the idea of creating a single province comprised of Nova Scotia,

New Brunswick and Prince Edward Island. An idea that Louis Robichaud had supported on occasion, Maritime Union had been advocated from time to time by political leaders from the mid nineteenth century on as a way to deliver more efficient government and as a method to increase the region's political clout. For their part, Acadians had traditionally been organized in Maritime-wide bodies, principally the Société Nationale des Acadiens. In part because federal funding for cultural minorities was delivered on a province-by-province basis in the 1970s, there was pressure on the Acadians to reorganize along provincial lines. But there was more to it than that. One-third of New Brunswick's population was Acadian, making Acadians there far more significant than in Nova Scotia and Prince Edward Island. With Maritime Union, Acadians would be reduced to 10 percent of the population of the new united province. In New Brunswick, they could wield much greater political influence, as Louis Robichaud had shown. It was natural that a new party that favoured the creation of a separate Acadian province would be hostile to having the Acadians of New Brunswick weakened politically in a Maritime Union.

A few months before the launch of the Parti Acadien, the Société des Acadienne du Nouveau-Brunswick (SANB) was established as a pressure group that would bring together the province's Acadian nationalists. Together, the Parti Acadien and the SANB were vehicles to promote the aspirations of younger Acadian nationalists who wanted to overturn the dominance of established organizations and the traditional Acadian leadership.

Not surprisingly, there was much debate about ideology in the Parti Acadien. Given the historical period, and the rise of youthful movements on the political left in the 1960s and 1970s, it was to be expected that the party would find itself somewhere on the left. Party militants debated the merits of socialism, nationalism and social reform, and argued about whether the party should enter the field of electoral politics or stick to the promotion of political education. The manifesto of the Parti Acadien favoured a utopian, agrarian socialist model for the Acadians of New Brunswick.

Opposing capitalism, the party espoused an Acadian future based on self-sufficient rural development, in which there would be a system of co-operatives for both producers and consumers. The preference for a co-operative economic model was evocative of the Coady movement in the Maritimes in the 1930s, a movement that exerted considerable influence. In terms of its membership, the new party, like other new left formations of the period, was made up mainly of intellectuals, professionals, students and workers in the public sector.

Some in the party advocated an alliance with the NDP, or even a merger with the social democrats. In 1974, when the Parti Acadien fielded thirteen candidates during the provincial election, it encouraged voters outside these constituencies to vote for the New Democrats. In the province as a whole, the new party won only 1.2 percent of the popular vote, but it obtained 7 percent of the vote in the ridings that its candidates contested. The party's electoral platform emphasized the need for duality in education with separate English- and French-language systems, proclamation of the final sections of the Official Languages Act in the province and the provision of bilingual services by municipal and provincial bodies.[8]

Over the next couple of years, the Parti Acadien decided against any link with the NDP, and in its ranks there was considerable rancour about whether the party's basic aim was socialism or the establishment of an Acadian province. Heavily influenced by similar debates within the Parti Québécois, which came to power in Quebec in 1976, at its 1977 convention the Parti Acadien adopted the position that its goal was to represent the Acadian nation and all of the social classes that made it up. This was a move away from a more militantly socialist and working-class orientation for the party.

The party was closely linked at this time with the SANB, which decided at its 1977 general meeting to organize meetings of the so-called Estates General (États Generaux), assemblies of citizens drawn from different occupational groups, to debate the political future of the Acadians of New Brunswick. (Organizing meetings of

Estates General—an idea harking back to the French Revolution—had already been undertaken in Quebec.)

Even though the Parti Acadien never became a major political force and never won a seat in the New Brunswick legislature, the party did unsettle the politics of the province, and it provoked major debates within the Acadian community about the future. During the 1978 provincial election, the party reached its zenith. While the party won only 4 percent of the votes cast in the province, in twenty-three Acadian ridings where it fielded candidates the party won 12 percent of the vote.[9] The leader of the party in 1978 was a physician from Bathurst, Jean-Pierre Lanteigne, who made the case that by having a province of their own, Acadians would truly enter Confederation as a people and would acquire the political power their marginalized status had denied them.[10]

Winning a sizable chunk of the vote in Acadian ridings, certainly enough potentially to upset the balance between the Liberals and the Conservatives in a number of cases, the Parti Acadien garnered a lot of attention from the two major parties. While the provincial Liberals in the post-Robichaud years had regarded the Parti Acadien as little more than an extremist gaggle, Hatfield and his strategists saw the upstart party as representing deeper currents that they needed to understand and respond to. By the end of the 1970s, from the Liberal standpoint, the new party posed a definite threat. Historically, the Liberal strategy had been to take the Acadian vote for granted. This had allowed the Liberals to count on winning Acadian seats without the party being forced to adopt policies that were overtly pro-Acadian. The Liberals had feared that any identification of their party with Acadian nationalism would frighten off the anglophone voters that the party needed to win power in the province. The emergence of the Parti Acadien, however, demonstrated that there was a large nationalist vote among Acadians that now had to be courted. And Richard Hatfield's Conservatives were quite prepared to court that vote.

An accountant from Edmundston, in the province's francophone north-west, Jean-Maurice Simard was both Hatfield's finance minister and his Acadian lieutenant. He hailed from an important Acadian region that has its own special flavour. The region, known as the Madawaska country, is close to Quebec and to the state of Maine. There are large numbers of Acadians on the New Brunswick side of the line and on the Maine side. On both sides of the border, people consider themselves to be inhabitants of the mythical Republic of Madawaska. While the use of the French language has declined sharply on the Maine side of the border, across the line in New Brunswick it has been maintained, indeed strengthened by the presence of a campus of the Université de Moncton, and by the fact that there are a large number of people who have moved there from Quebec. The Madawaska country is the physical meeting point between Acadians and French Canadians, and while the Acadian identity is paramount, there is a blended consciousness that makes the region different from other Acadian areas of New Brunswick. Over time, French Canadians in towns like Edmundston have come to see themselves as sharing in the more inclusive Acadian identity that has emerged in recent decades.

Simard was point man in the Conservative government, enjoying the full backing of the premier, in implementing a delicate strategy the goal of which was to win Acadian nationalist voters over to the Conservative side. Simard cultivated his image as the defender of Acadian interests within the Hatfield government and presented himself as a man who was prepared to take nationalist positions seriously. Considering that the Conservatives were in power, this gave Simard and Hatfield a huge advantage over the opposition Liberals and the fledgling Parti Acadien. Naturally, Simard had to pursue his Acadian strategy without provoking a backlash within the largely anglophone Conservative Party. In the lead-up to the 1978 provincial election, Hatfield's Conservatives added some strings to their bow to entice Acadian nationalists to join their cause. They reminded voters that they had proclaimed the final sections of the Official Languages Act. They pledged that they would found a French-language community college in the south-east and would establish a French-language agricultural institute.[11]

In the months following the party's relative electoral success in 1978, the leadership of the Parti Acadien tried to grapple with the inherent difficulties their electoral platform. The party's main claim to fame, but also its chief liability, was its advocacy of the division of New Brunswick in two to create an Acadian province. As an act of political theatre, this might be strong stuff, but if it were to be taken seriously as a proposal with which people would have to live, the viability of the idea would have to be demonstrated in a much more detailed way than it had been. In practice, the party tended to present the idea of an Acadian province as a long-term concept, while featuring more prominently its short-term goals, which were to establish French-language administrative units throughout the ministries of the government and to decentralize government powers so as to devolve them to Acadian regions.[12]

In October 1979, the Société Acadienne du Nouveau-Brunswick held a policy convention to consider the political future of the Acadians. During the convention, participants were given a questionnaire to answer on the key political questions, the idea being that the results would be representative of the way active Acadians were now thinking. The result of the exercise was a shocker. Among the 1,500 participants at the convention, 48.8 percent opted for the creation of an Acadian province, 7.1 percent said they wanted to see the establishment of an Acadian country and 32.5 percent favoured staying with New Brunswick and seeking changes beneficial to the Acadians within the province.[13]

The strongly nationalist tone of the convention stunned the New Brunswick political elite with the obvious fact that the new nationalist leadership of the Acadian population was deeply dissatisfied with the status quo. Federal bureaucrats in the Department of the Secretary of State, a key source of funding for the SANB, also showed their concern. Emissaries from Ottawa travelled to New Brunswick to try to convince those in control of the organization to distance themselves from Parti Acadien activists and to draw into their ranks more participation from the traditional Acadian elites.[14] Shaken by concerns within the

Acadian community and federal pressure tactics, the leadership of the SANB tried to back away from the political brink. In April 1980, they issued a statement that took the position that the participants at the convention had not actually adopted any specific political option, that this had not been the purpose of the convention, and that those in attendance had lacked the information on which to make an informed choice. While those in attendance had shown their preference for Acadians obtaining considerable autonomy in the management of their community affairs, the leaders of the SANB claimed that they had not opted for a separate Acadian province, which was, of course, the central aim of the Parti Acadien.[15]

Confronted with Acadian nationalism in the form of the Parti Acadien and with the palpable threat to Confederation posed by the Lévesque government in Quebec, Richard Hatfield believed that Canada had merely been granted a stay of execution in the defeat of the PQ's sovereignty-association referendum in the spring of 1980. The New Brunswick premier passionately agreed with Pierre Trudeau that the Québécois must now be shown that their "Non" vote had not been a negative vote but a vote in favour of a renewed Canada that would carve out a home for francophones within it. While New Brunswick was in theory already a province in which the French language enjoyed official status, in 1981 the Hatfield government introduced Bill 88, a piece of legislation to declare the equality of the province's two linguistic communities. The bill took a step beyond previous legislation in its affirmation of the right of linguistic communities to have their own institutions in the spheres of culture and education.[16]

The premier saw this as a gesture to Acadians in his own province, but it was also a gesture to the Québécois and to all Canadians in the aftermath of the Quebec referendum. During this same period, Hatfield was furious that Ontario's Conservative premier, William Davis, the only other premier who was allied with Trudeau in his constitutional patriation struggle, had failed to proclaim Ontario a bilingual province as a crucial gesture for national unity. On a trip to New York, Hatfield complained publicly about Davis's refusal to take this step, thus provoking the ire of the Ontario government.[17]

Armed with its new sympathy toward Acadian nationalism, the Hatfield Conservatives undertook a concerted effort to win Acadian voters over from the Liberals. The party came out in favour of further linguistic reform in the province and declared August 15 an Acadian national day in the province, without making it an official holiday. For their part, the Liberals stuck to the position, unpopular among many Acadians, that there ought to be only one holiday in New Brunswick in August, to celebrate both the traditional municipal holiday at the beginning of the month and the Acadian Fête Nationale. Election day, October 12, 1982, was a triumph for Hatfield, with wins in the Acadian regions of the province and with a gain of ten seats overall from the Liberals. On election night the Conservatives celebrated victory in thirty-nine ridings, while the Liberals ended up with eighteen and the NDP with one.[18]

The 1982 campaign was the climax of Jean-Maurice Simard's effort to win Acadians over to the Conservative Party. Simard, whose family hailed from Quebec and had been supporters of the Union Nationale, had a visceral hatred for all things Liberal, which he honed in the 1982 campaign. He had succeeded in winning over Richard Hatfield to the idea that there ought to be a separate strategy for the Conservative Party in the Acadian regions of the province, that in the francophone campaign materials should be conceived and written for an Acadian audience, rather than translated into French after being written by Camp Associates, the Toronto firm of Hatfield's close friend and collaborator Dalton Camp.[19]

Simard had a genuine sympathy for some of the ideas of the Parti Acadien, particularly the notion that Acadians should administer their own government programs, and he was often seen in the company of party insiders. He was close to Michel and Louise Blanchard, who operated a cultural co-operative bar and restaurant in Caraquet called La Grande Maison. Simard had helped secure a loan to underwrite the Blanchards' establishment. Michel Blanchard was an important figure among Acadian nationalists, having played a leading role in the student movement at the Université de Moncton in the late 1960s.[20] Some people even speculated that Simard might leave the Conservative Party to take up the leadership of the Parti Acadien.

Simard also had close contacts with René Lévesque's Parti Québécois, and remarkably he turned to the PQ for advice on how to run his electoral campaign among Acadians in 1982. To find the best possible expertise for the campaign, Simard telephoned the Quebec premier's executive assistant, Jean-Roch Boivin, to ask if he could get help. Boivin consulted René Lévesque on what was, to say the least, a highly unorthodox idea: helping a federalist government, headed by an anglophone, win re-election in New Brunswick. What established common ground for this exercise was the fact that both Simard and Lévesque hated Liberals. Not long after, Simard and his assistant, Rino Morin, flew to Quebec City, where they met with the man who had been communications director for the PQ's successful election campaign in 1981, Jean-François Cloutier. From Cloutier, Simard obtained material on how the PQ had run its campaign and an entree to a Montreal communications consultant who had helped the sovereigntist party with its election campaign, Yves Dupré.

To test-market ways of running the Conservative campaign among Acadians, Simard organized a major gathering of Acadian opinion-leaders in the town of Shippagan on the Acadian Peninsula. Held in the full glare of publicity in August 1982, Le Grand Ralliement '82 focused the spotlight on Simard and Richard Hatfield, who both addressed the rally. The event also gave Dupré the opportunity to hold behind-the-scenes interviews in the form of focus groups to find out what would work and not work with these influential Acadians.[21] The New Brunswick premier, who allowed his speech to be written for him by Simard's assistant, was highly pleased with how things turned out at the Shippagan extravaganza. A couple of weeks later, still feeling the buzz from the event,

Hatfield called the New Brunswick provincial election.

The timing of the election was good for the Conservatives in a number of ways. The Trudeau government in Ottawa had grown unpopular by 1982 and was paying the price for the harsh recession in the country at the time. The provincial Liberals were closely associated in the public mind with their federal cousins. Having recently replaced an ineffective Acadian leader, Joe Daigle, with a young anglophone, Dave Young, the Liberals were especially vulnerable in Acadian ridings. Under the circumstances, with a politically talented proponent like Simard taking care of the francophone campaign of the Conservative Party, Hatfield was able to do something similar to what would soon become the trademark of Brian Mulroney in federal politics. He was able to run in anglophone ridings as a traditional Tory, the natural representative of Loyalist New Brunswick, while also outflanking the Liberals as an Acadian nationalist in francophone ridings. Running a campaign with such a split personality led to some tense moments within the Conservative inner circle, but it was highly successful on the hustings.

The election marked the end of the Parti Acadien as a force among voters, with its share of the popular vote falling from 4 percent to 0.9 percent.[22] The nationalist party had been suffering as a consequence of internal divisions, and in the election it had managed to field only ten candidates, the minimum number needed for it to be a recognized party. The party's president for the campaign was Louise Blanchard, who was on good terms with Jean-Maurice Simard. The party's electoral strategy had been both controversial and ineffectual. Even though the Conservatives had been in power for twelve years, the Parti Acadien chose mostly to attack the opposition Liberals. The strategy paid dividends for Conservatives, who picked up most of the votes the Parti Acadien lost from the previous election. Indeed, during the campaign some Acadian activists actually worked for the Parti Acadien in one constituency and for the Conservatives in the constituency next door.[23] Though the Parti Acadien maintained its nominal existence for a time, it was a spent force, hardly even noticed, after 1982.

In an interview in Caraquet in 2005, Louise Blanchard looked back on the Parti Acadien as a vehicle that had won important gains for Acadians. When you map out a series of ambitious goals, she asserted, you don't achieve them all, but you do achieve some of them. For her, at least in retrospect, that was the point of the exercise. She pointed to Bill 88, the Hatfield government's legislation proclaiming the linguistic equality of the French and English communities of the province, as a step forward that had clearly been pushed along by the presence of the Parti Acadien. Agitation for a separate Acadian province might not have won a huge number of people to that cause, but it did force New Brunswick to come to terms with the Acadian "fact" as never before.

Following its strong association with the Parti Acadien, the SANB moved back toward a position that could be endorsed by the traditional Acadian elites, who wanted no part of a body that flirted with the idea of creating a separate Acadian province and that was favourable at times to the Parti Québécois. As it edged back toward moderation, the SANB lost the adherence of most progressive activists, but from the viewpoint of traditional Acadians it regained its respectability.[24]

In power during the 1970s and 1980s, when the issue of national unity came to a head with the rise and election to power of the Parti Québécois in 1976 and the first Quebec referendum on sovereignty, Richard Hatfield was drawn into the national constitutional fray. He believed that New Brunswick's uniqueness gave it a special role to play in the struggle to save Canada, by creating in it a space for the realization of the aspirations of francophones, both Québécois and Acadian. Hatfield felt that if bilingualism could be made to work in New Brunswick, where Acadians constituted one-third of the population, this could serve as an example to the Québécois that a bilingual country could work. In addition, Hatfield's New Brunswick was not a province that dreamed of building an empire on its own based on a treasure house of resources. The province could not be like Alberta, with its oil and natural gas, or even like Nova Scotia and Newfoundland, with their dreams of offshore energy wealth. The nature of his province, and his own nature as something of a dreamer, drew Hatfield to the side of Pierre Trudeau and the federal government in the crucial constitutional battles of the era. In the aftermath of the Quebec sovereignty referendum in the spring of 1980, when Pierre Trudeau decided to use René Lévesque's defeat to patriate the constitution along with the provision of a charter of rights, Hatfield lined up on his side. Until the last day of the struggle, Trudeau had the support of only two provincial premiers, Richard Hatfield of New Brunswick and Ontario's William Davis. The other eight premiers, including René Lévesque, were aligned in the so-called "gang of eight." Only at the very end did all the premiers, with the exception of Lévesque, come together in a deal with Trudeau that opened the way for patriation and the new charter.

The 1982 constitution bears one unmistakable imprint of Richard Hatfield. At the insistence of the New Brunswick premier, Section 133 includes the provision that New Brunswick is to be officially bilingual. In this respect, New Brunswick is unique, the only province to be so designated in the constitution.

During the years of constitutional struggle, Hatfield's peripatetic ways pulled him into the battle, sometimes as a proponent and sometimes as an observer. The New Brunswick premier, who was so often to be found outside his own province, spent a good deal of time in Montreal, trying to learn what was at the root of the drive for Quebec sovereignty and what could be done to satisfy that drive within the parameters of Canadian federalism. Given his detached, rather philosophical outlook on life, Hatfield, at times, managed to appear quite sympathetic to the Parti Québécois. While premier of New Brunswick, in a moment of zany enthusiasm in 1973, he even quietly joined the membership of the PQ.[25] In the end, though, he could not endure the thought of his beloved Montreal being lost to Canada.

When René Lévesque led the Parti Québécois to power in the historic Quebec election on November 15, 1976, English Canadians, and that included the premier of New Brunswick, received a nasty scare and a powerful wake-up call. Richard Hatfield was in Montreal on the night the votes were counted. He served on a CBC television panel of expert commentators, the only provincial premier to do so. In his shocked on-air response to what was happening, he declared: "This is terrible, we won't be able to go to Montreal any more."[26]

The New Brunswick premier threw himself wholeheartedly into the campaign for national unity in subsequent months. In 1977, he spoke to audiences on the subject in many places in New Brunswick and across Canada. He made speeches, in English and in halting French, in Montreal, Trois-Rivières and Sherbrooke. He used these speeches as an opportunity to showcase New Brunswick, with its English majority and French minority, as a model for Canada. His province, he argued, illustrated that Canadians could live together with the rights of both linguistic communities respected. A problem he faced in putting this case was that New Brunswick had not yet proclaimed all the sections of the Official Languages Act, which had been in existence for almost eight years. To meet criticism on this point, Hatfield at last proclaimed that all of the act's sections would come into effect on July 1, 1977. He also prodded fellow Maritime premiers at one of their regular meetings to provide $1 million to the Université de Moncton, so it could launch a French-language law school.[27]

Richard Hatfield had shown himself through his years as New Brunswick premier to be a genuine friend of the Acadians. Although he was born into a privileged anglophone family, Hatfield was his own person, never culturally at one with the business and political elites that dominated the Conservative Party. But if his personal qualities allowed him to break out of his party's mould and reach out to Acadians, his personal issues led to his disgrace and political demise. As an aging bachelor, Hatfield's lifestyle drew comments from observers throughout his years in office. His trips outside the province became legendary in New Brunswick, where people thought of him as the premier who enjoyed himself most when he was away.

The year 1984 should have been a proud one for New Brunswick, marking the two-hundredth anniversary of the founding of the province. It should have been a time for the premier to celebrate both the heritage of the Loyalists, who had left the Thirteen Colonies to found the new province at the end of the American Revolutionary War, and the heritage of the Acadians, who had made a new homeland for themselves in New Brunswick. In some ways the bicentennial was noteworthy for the Acadians, with the decision of the government to fly the Acadian flag permanently on all public buildings, despite a small but vociferous campaign by anglophone extremists in opposition.

Disaster struck, however, during the Queen's visit to the province. Hatfield, who loved royal visits and thought himself a master of decorum on such occasions, travelled with the Queen and Prince Philip on their plane for the short flight from Fredericton to Moncton. It appeared that all had gone well when the Queen spoke at her state dinner in Moncton of the French and English who had first fought over this land, "but their descendants learned to live here in harmony and to have a common purpose." The following day, the Queen departed for Ottawa to continue her Canadian tour. Rumours spread slowly of something untoward, until, on October 20, 1984, the Fredericton *Daily Gleaner* ran a front-page headline that read: "Senior N.B. politician under drug investigation."[28] On October 26, 1984, Hatfield was charged with drug possession. He was ordered to appear in court several weeks later. Given the controversial views that had been circulating about him for years, the charges resonated with a part of the population and came as no great shock to members of the media.

The case against the premier arose out of the rather unusual facts that were presented in evidence. On the day of the flight of the royal aircraft from Fredericton to Moncton, Hatfield had brought his suitcase to the airport, where it was then handled by several people, including the airport manager, before it ended up in the RCMP control room, where it sat for several hours. Before it was loaded onto the plane, a hand search was made of the bag by the RCMP for standard security reasons. A brown envelope was found in an outside pocket of the premier's suitcase. The envelope was opened and inside it there was a plastic bag containing what looked like marijuana. Three days later, after a lab report had confirmed that there were indeed thirty-five grams of marijuana in the envelope, RCMP Chief Superintendent Denis Ling and the officer who was in charge of the case visited Hatfield at his Fredericton home and told him that illegal drugs had been found in his suitcase and that he was a suspect.

During the trial, Hatfield's lawyer, Donald Gillis, mounted a defence based on two basic arguments. First, the suitcase had been unattended for too long for it to be established that it was the premier and not someone else who had put the envelope with the drugs in the outside pocket. Second, the person who initially tipped off the press, before a charge had been made, could have planted the drugs, seeking a sensational media explosion. Influenced by possible alternative explanations of how the marijuana could have ended up in the bag, the trial judge, Andrew Harrigan, found Richard Hatfield not guilty.[29]

Defenders of the premier who hoped that things might return to normal with the trial over were disabused when a bombshell news story was published just five days after Hatfield's acquittal. The new story claimed that two young men had met Hatfield in a Fredericton restaurant, along with two other students, and gone with the premier to his house, where they consumed alcohol, smoked marijuana and took cocaine with the premier until early the next morning. After leaving the premier's house, the story claimed, three of the young men, along with the premier, boarded a New Brunswick government aircraft and flew to Montreal. They spent the night at the Queen Elizabeth Hotel and returned to Fredericton the following day.[30]

Despite the new allegations swirling around his name, Richard Hatfield did have his eloquent defenders, most important among them Dalton Camp, who was not only the communications consultant of the premier but also a very close friend. The New Brunswick premier was a frequent guest at the cottage the Camps owned at Robertson's Point and later at the Camps' home at

Northwood, outside of Jemseg, where one of the bedrooms was known as "Richard's room." Camp defended Hatfield in a heated appearance on CBC-TV's "The Journal," in which he angrily confronted both television host Barbara Frum and a Southam News reporter.

Even though no legal charges arose out of the students' story about cocaine use at the premier's house and the trip to Montreal, for a sizable proportion of the New Brunswick public the days of giving their premier the benefit of the doubt had come to an end. Hatfield had been premier for so long, though, that he was a little like a prizefighter past his prime. He couldn't imagine doing any other job, and there was no one in his entourage who would tell him bluntly that it was time to go. Instead, Hatfield played the string out to the end. He reckoned that if he refused to discuss the scandals any further, they would recede in the public's mind over time. And as a politician who had remained in power for much longer than most, there was the hope that his Liberal opponents would figure out a way to shoot themselves in the foot, and that this would signal a change in his fortunes.

The problem, though, with having been in office for such a lengthy stretch was that people had built up resentments against the premier and his government that tended to stick. One source of resentment had been Hatfield's insistence on running a pro-Acadian government despite the fact that the political base of his party was anglophone. Under Robichaud and Hatfield, the position of Acadians in the life of the province had changed very appreciably. Schools, roads and health care in Acadian regions had improved a great deal, and among some anglophones the idea persisted that their taxes were paying for better services for the Acadians. Under Hatfield, Acadian schools and cultural centres had been established in English-speaking strongholds such as Saint John and Fredericton, the provincial capital.

A significant political backlash was evident among English-speakers against bilingualism in government services. The backlash found a natural home in the Conservative Party itself, Hatfield's political base. For the more extreme anti-Acadian voices, new parties, such as the Confederation of Regions Party, were set up to hammer home the message that the French were gaining rights at the expense of the English. One of the favourite complaints of the anglophones who resented the changes was that many government jobs were now available only to those who were bilingual, and that since most of those who could speak both languages were French, this amounted to special treatment for the Acadians. The fact that when Robichaud took office in 1960 the public service was disproportionately anglophone was conveniently ignored by those who felt this way.

—

CHAPTER 12

ACADIANS
IN A
CONSERVATIVE AGE

FOLLOWING THE SPATE OF SCANDALS that afflicted Richard Hatfield, the embattled premier's luck did not turn. The Liberals chose as their new leader a young lawyer from Chatham, Frank McKenna, a man who would not crumble over the course of an election campaign. Finally, Hatfield called the provincial election for October 1987. Even though the signs were far from favourable, he told himself that he had won in the past against the odds and could do so once more.

On the hustings, the premier spent his time reminding people of his record of achievement over the previous seventeen years. But from the beginning the people of New Brunswick behaved as though Richard Hatfield was already a part of the past. Some still respected him and showed their politeness, while others refused even to shake his hand when he came up to them in a shopping mall. On election day, Richard Hatfield received one of the most terrible drubbings ever meted out to a Canadian political leader. His governing Conservative Party won not a single seat in the fifty-seven-seat provincial legislature. During the last several years of the Hatfield regime, many Conservatives had wanted to figure out a way to rid themselves of their leader. In 1987, in a political disaster, their wish had been granted. The road back for the party would be tortuous and long.

Richard Hatfield was the last of the patrician "Red Tories" in New Brunswick politics, indeed, one of the last in Canada. He was a part of that remarkable generation of Tories that included people like his close friends Dalton Camp and Flora MacDonald, as well as Joe Clark. Red Tories had a streak of noblesse oblige in their political makeup, the belief that as members of the elite it was their job to improve the lot of the less well off. For Hatfield, that sense of using power to improve the life of the whole community was focused on the Acadians and their collective rights. During the twenty-seven-year period when Robichaud and Hatfield had been in office consecutively, government had been the main engine of reform in New Brunswick society. Government initiatives had transformed the place of the Acadians in the province, bringing them from the margins into the mainstream. Especially during the latter part of his seventeen years in the premier's office, Richard Hatfield had been a fish out of water in the wider world of North American conservatism. The political right was in transition, with the hard-edged market values of neo-conservatism coming to dominate. While Hatfield had dreamed large dreams about the fulfillment of communities, his successors in the premier's office, both Liberal and Conservative, would be devotees of small government and the creed of the market.

The first of these, Frank McKenna, was the quintessential young man in a hurry. McKenna had far more energy than Hatfield, who was always something of a dilettante, but he had little of his predecessor's romanticism. Like Robichaud, he was not born into the upper classes. His parents, of Irish stock, raised their family on a farm, on the outskirts of the little community of Apohaqui, in King's County, in the heartland of English-speaking New Brunswick. From his earliest days, Frank McKenna, who read the Horatio Alger stories of poor boys making good in America, decided that he would not be a farmer himself. As the Conservative Party disintegrated in the final years of the Hatfield government, McKenna was ideally placed to pick up the pieces. He was an anglophone leader who espoused self-reliance rather than government as the road ahead for New Brunswick—a message that was tailor-made to appeal to the very core of the Conservative Party, whose stalwarts were disgusted by the spectacle of Hatfield's personal tribulations and were alienated by what they perceived as his government's pro-Acadian stance.

McKenna focused on carving out a new economic space for New Brunswick. He was convinced that relying on handouts from Ottawa as the road to economic development for his province was a formula for failure. He concluded, in part the lesson of his own upbringing, that New Brunswick had to achieve a new self-reliance. The province had to open its doors to business, wherever that business was located, and figure out how to attract investors to set up shop. He became premier at the moment when the micro-electronic revolution was transforming the world. The new communications technology was bestowing locational advantages on unlikely places. For a province that had traditionally relied on fishing, farming and forest products to make its way in the world, the change spelled opportunity, and McKenna had the wit to see this. He set his sights on the call-centre business, which was taking off in many parts of the world. Moncton had lost the CNR yards, which for decades had been the backbone of its economy. McKenna perceived that, with its low property values, bilingual labour pool and relatively low wages, the city was an ideal place to entice call-centres to locate. The premier won kudos across North America for his success in winning a share of the business for Moncton. To back up the call-centres, McKenna's government decided to invest in wiring the province with a cutting-edge telephone system. New Brunswick became an unlikely leader in the rush to establish the infrastructure for high-speed transmission of information.

The call-centres furthered the transformation of the political economy of New Brunswick's Acadians, spurring many of them to move out of the declining north, with its traditional economic sectors, and into the burgeoning south-east. While the call-centres were a welcome source of jobs, this was nonetheless a footloose industry, heavily driven by the comparison of costs in one place against another. The question was whether Moncton could, over the long term, compete with India and other locations with large pools of skilled, low-cost labour.

McKenna's view of the economy put him much closer to the out-look of Brian Mulroney, who was in power in Ottawa, than to members of his own party. While federal Liberal leader John Turner made his opposition to Mulroney's free trade deal with the United States the fight of his life in the 1988 election campaign, McKenna parted company with his party on the issue and endorsed the free trade agreement. The small-government conservatism that Brian Mulroney was delivering to Canadians at the federal level ended up being delivered to the people of New Brunswick by a Liberal gov-ernment, that of Frank McKenna.

A strong proponent of McKenna's economic record is Donald J. Savoie, who holds the Clement-Cormier Chair in Economic Development at the Université de Moncton. Savoie makes the case that, historically, New Brunswick has been the victim of the eco-nomic policies of the federal government. In the mid nineteenth century, Savoie points out, New Brunswick enjoyed a highly devel-oped and prosperous economy for the time. With the onset of John A. Macdonald's National Policy at the end of the 1870s, however, New Brunswick became the victim of tariff and transportation policies whose major beneficiaries were Ontario and Quebec. He documents the case that subsequent federal economic policies have exacerbated the problem. The bias, he contends, is invariably one that benefits central Canada at the expense of the Atlantic region. Measures adopted to counter the negative impact of federal policies on New Brunswick, such as transfer payments, have lessened the pain somewhat, but have failed to come to terms with the essential problem, he contends.

"National economic programs have an inherent bias in favour of Ontario and Quebec," Savoie has written. "McKenna pushed and pulled all the economic levers he could, as far as he could and probably better than anyone else could, in promoting economic development in the province. His effort did have an impact. But one can only imagine the kind of impact there would have been had the federal government also pushed and pulled in the same direction. McKenna stood alone with the local telephone company in developing a call centre industry for his province, an industry now employing over 12,000 people." Did Ottawa help out? Savoie asks. Quite the contrary. The federal Department of Industry "stood on the sidelines, saying its programs were not designed for this industry. The department has never had such problems when it came to helping Ottawa's and Kanata's high-tech industry or Montreal's industrial interests."[1]

Fatefully, Frank McKenna left one major mark on the country during his years in office. Elected shortly after the Meech Lake Accord was fashioned by Brian Mulroney and Quebec Premier Robert Bourassa, and agreed to by all ten provincial premiers, McKenna made himself the first significant opponent of the accord. If Hatfield, a strong backer of Meech Lake, had pushed the accord through the New Brunswick legislature before he called the 1987 provincial election, Canadian history might have followed a different course. McKenna signalled, in advance of the provincial election of 1987, that he had some problems with the accord. Once in office, his views on the subject became a matter of vital national concern. If he opposed Meech Lake, which required unanimous provincial approval, the accord, on which so much political capital in Ottawa and Quebec City had been spent, would be blocked.

As a Trudeau-style federalist, McKenna was instinctively leery of Meech Lake as an arrangement that could undercut the strong role played in the Canadian federation by the federal government. As the premier of the province that was home to most of the country's Acadians, he had another reason for being concerned. The way Meech Lake had been fashioned, it was essentially a deal between the government of Quebec and Ottawa, and the other provinces. The accord would assign to Quebec, which was defined as a "distinct society," the constitutional role of preserving and promoting the language and culture of its French majority.

But what did that mean for the Acadians and the other francophone minorities in Canada? McKenna believed that Meech Lake left these Canadians out in the cold. He wanted the accord amended to take account of New Brunswick's unique position as the country's only officially bilingual province. He wanted Bill 88 enshrined in the accord, and he wanted the Parliament of Canada to be charged with the responsibility to preserve and promote the rights of francophones outside Quebec. As it stood under the accord as drafted, the federal government's role would be to *preserve* the rights of francophones. Acadians and other French-speaking minorities outside Quebec believed they needed a much more active role from Ottawa—that of *promoting* the rights of francophones. Without that, the equivalent of the role that Quebec was to play for its French-speaking population, they were sure they were being consigned to assimilation in the long term.

From the beginning of this crucial debate, McKenna was always anxious to negotiate. The last thing he wanted was to derail Meech Lake and to be held responsible for restarting the engines of the Quebec sovereignty movement. He was well aware that the rights Acadians had acquired would be highly vulnerable should Quebec secede from Confederation.

The effect of McKenna's opposition to Meech Lake was to open the way for Clyde Wells, when he was elected premier of Newfoundland, to take up the cause against the accord, and to present Canadians with the perspective of Pierre Trudeau, who had retired from politics in 1984, that a constitutional deal enshrining the notion of Quebec as a "distinct society" was a mistake. In the end, McKenna came on board and New Brunswick ratified Meech Lake, but by then the cat was out of the bag, and the accord expired at the end of June 1990 because ratification had not taken place in Manitoba and Newfoundland.

The consequences of the failure of Meech Lake were immediate and dire for the future of Canadian federalism. Conservative Deputy Prime Minister Lucien Bouchard resigned from the government of Brian Mulroney and bolted to the fledgling Bloc Québécois, the new sovereigntist party in federal politics. The Quebec independence movement, which had fallen on hard times during the late 1980s, was jolted back into business with a new leader and a powerful new cause. Bouchard and his allies struck political pay dirt with their charge that Canada had rejected Quebec's minimum demands for remaining in the federation.

For the Acadians, the failure of Meech Lake—and the related rise of the Bloc Québécois, demise of the federal Progressive Conservative Party and emergence of the Reform Party—made the era after 1990 one of growing political uncertainty. New Brunswick's Acadians, who had made major gains between 1960 and 1990, felt highly vulnerable because of the renewed threat of Quebec separation on the one hand and the rise on the right in English Canada of a political party that was strongly opposed to the very concept of bilingualism and that harboured within the ranks of its supporters many people who resented the francophone fact in Canada.

Vulnerability came home to the Acadians in the provincial general election of 1991 in New Brunswick. Naturally, it was highly unlikely that Frank McKenna's Liberals would repeat the historic sweep of 1987 in which they had won every seat in the provincial legislature. Analysts expected, though, that the provincial Conservatives, cleansed of the perceived sins of Richard Hatfield, would bounce back as a major political force. Instead, the political right in the province splintered in a completely unprecedented way.

The Confederation of Regions Party (COR), which had been in existence for some time, not only in New Brunswick but in Ontario and Alberta as well, became the vehicle for the resentments of a sizable portion of the anglophone population of the province. The COR channelled the resentments of people on a range of issues, which taken together could be seen as a revolt against "big government." The party's signature issue, however, was its opposition to official bilingualism. The COR wanted English to be established as the only official language in the province and advocated an English-only school system. COR adherents argued that bilingualism was highly expensive, and that vast amounts of money had been spent on the Acadian regions of the province by the McKenna government and the Conservative government of Richard Hatfield. They made the case that most Acadians spoke English. Why not have one language in the province? They claimed this would lead to greater unity, not division. With this blunt message, COR became a channel for the expression of anglophone resentment against the changing status of the province's Acadians. People who feared that French-speakers were winning government jobs, that many jobs now required an ability to function in both languages, and who opposed the creation of the Université de Moncton flocked to the new party.

Election day, September 23, 1991, revealed the extent to which New Brunswickers were prepared to move outside the political tents of the two old mainstream parties. Instead of rallying to Dennis Cochrane, the schoolteacher who had won the Conservative Party's leadership two months earlier, a tidal wave of right-wing voters chose to vote for the COR. When the votes were tallied, the Liberals ended up with forty-six seats, a handsome victory, but in second place was the COR with eight seats, ahead of the Conservatives, who won only three ridings, and the NDP, which took one. The COR now formed the official Opposition in the legislature. For Acadians who had become accustomed to the enjoyment of their rights in a bilingual province, the result was chilling. A wave of fear went through the Acadian community on election night. The gains they had made had been thrown into doubt.[2]

While the backlash was plainly evident in the results of the election of 1991, a close examination of the attitudes of New Brunswickers at the time of the previous election in 1987 showed that anti-French attitudes were already developing. While the main news out of that election had been the Liberal victory in every seat in the province, a detailed CBC poll revealed that 34 percent of respondents wanted the government to ditch its Official Languages policy. Since almost all Acadians backed the policy, this meant that roughly half of the province's anglophones opposed it.[3] Because the question was asked in the context of a poll about provincial politics with the public strongly averse to Richard Hatfield and his government, one cannot make too much of this result. It was, however, a sign of the strength of anglophone backlash in the province. For the time being at least, Hatfield's high-minded support for the rights of Acadians was being rejected by a sizable number of anglophones.

By the time Frank McKenna stepped down as premier of New Brunswick midway through his third term of office, he was credited with having set in motion an economic miracle in the province, particularly in its south-east in the greater Moncton area. He bruised a lot of knuckles along the way. He froze the incomes of public sector employees and cut public spending in critical areas, most significantly in the health care sector. Driven by the fiscal problems of his province in the early 1990s, as well as by his small-government, neo-liberal proclivities, McKenna engineered cutbacks to government spending in many areas. His closures of hospitals, in particular, led to serious social unrest in Acadian north-eastern New Brunswick. In 1995, at a key time in the struggle over abortion rights in Canada, McKenna found himself in a very personal slugging match against Dr. Henry Morgentaler, who opened a private, for-profit abortion clinic in Fredericton. The upshot was that the clinic remained open and the premier had to accept defeat.

When McKenna left politics to try his hand at business, he moved to Toronto, was appointed to a long list of corporate directorships and made more money in his first year out of the premier's office than he had during his ten years at the head of the New Brunswick government. Some of the companies that appointed Frank McKenna to their boards had recently done business in New Brunswick, and had received public money while he was premier. Some critics believed that the former premier had moved too quickly to receive rewards for his pro-business political positions from companies that would never have dreamed of asking Louis Robichaud to sit on their boards.

For a year following McKenna's resignation, Raymond Frenette served as premier and as the caretaker leader of the Liberal Party. At a convention in 1998, the Liberals chose the son of a former provincial Cabinet minister and senator, Camille Thériault, to lead them into the next general election. Thériault, a genial leader with no clear vision for the future of the province, never clicked with the New Brunswick public. With McKenna gone, the door was open for the re-emergence of the Conservative Party as a major force in

New Brunswick politics. In 1999, a scrawny young lawyer by the name of Bernard Lord, a man who looked more like an executive assistant than a premier, won an unexpected victory and led the Conservatives back to power in Fredericton.

Lord was the son of an anglophone father and a francophone mother. Ralph Lord, the father of the future premier, grew up in rural York County, not far from Fredericton. Following a five-year stint in the navy, he came back to New Brunswick, where his interests turned to aviation. From there he found employment as a bush pilot in Roberval, Quebec, on the shores of Lac-Saint-Jean, a town that was the gateway to the province's north. There, Lord learned French and met and married Marie-Émilie Morin, a schoolteacher in whose family home the young man from New Brunswick had been boarding. After a few years, Lord relocated to the Quebec City area, where he became a pilot for the government of Quebec, flying Cabinet ministers and premiers, including Jean Lesage and Daniel Johnson, Sr., around the province. Because of her husband's demanding job, which kept him away from home for long periods, Lord's wife came home to Roberval for the birth in September 1965 of Bernard, their fourth and last child. In 1972, when Ralph Lord found employment with the federal government, the family moved to Riverview, an English-speaking town across the river from Moncton.[4]

Bernard Lord spoke French at home, but he quickly learned English and soon had no difficulty switching back and forth from one language to the other. He spoke English to his New Brunswick relatives and French when he visited family in Quebec. He attended French schools, including the Université de Moncton, where he was elected president of the student federation in 1984, running on a moderate platform in which he put the provision of services ahead of student activism. When the young man who had no apparent radical edge to him was admitted to the provincial bar in 1993, he did something out of the ordinary when he refused to take an oath of allegiance to the Queen. The rules had been changed for the admission of new lawyers to the bar in New Brunswick, allowing them to decline the oath. For francophone lawyers who associated the crown with *le Grand Dérangement*, taking a pass on the oath was a way of making a political statement. For his part, Lord would not go so far as to say that his act amounted to a political statement. Instead, he shrugged it off by saying that if it was not necessary to take the oath he would not take it.[5]

When the leadership of the Conservative Party came open in 1997, Bernard Lord tested the waters, even though the idea that he could move into the leadership without ever having sat in the legislature seemed to be a long shot. With the Confederation of Regions Party in disarray, and many of its supporters edging back to the Conservatives, it was an ideal moment for a bright young candidate to make a mark in a party that had been on life support for a decade. And Lord had some very real assets. He was a francophone who spoke English without the trace of an accent. He could appeal to the party's core Anglo-New Brunswick base while being immune to any charge that he was anti–Acadian. Previous contenders for the office of premier in New Brunswick had been either anglophone or francophone and had had to reach out to the other solitude. Lord did not have this problem. He combined both streams of the provincial population in his person and took full advantage of that fact.

As the leadership race heated up, Lord's energy and his moderation appealed to an ever wider constituency within the party. Though not seen as the front-runner in the four-man race, he nevertheless came into the leadership convention with a large bloc of support and he was well placed to take votes from the two weakest candidates should the vote go to a second ballot. The convention was organized so that all members of the Conservative Party could vote, either at the convention in Fredericton, where the candidates were assembled, or at four satellite locations in Moncton, Bathurst, St. Leonard and St. Stephen. Surpassing expectations, Lord ran first on the first ballot, winning 36.5 percent of the votes. When the third- and fourth-place candidates both rallied to support him, he won the leadership on the second ballot.

The young Conservative leader found himself at the head of a party that could aspire to offer itself to the province as a government-in-waiting, for the first time since the debacle of 1987. When a by-election was called for the riding of Moncton East, Bernard Lord took the risk of entering the fray instead of waiting for a general election to be called. Even though his Liberal opponent was Charlie Bourgeois, a former NHL player from Moncton who'd grown up in the riding and was well known for his charity work, Lord scored a convincing win.

On November 24, 1998, for the first time, Lord and Camille Thériault took their places opposite each other in the New Brunswick legislature, Lord as leader of the Opposition and Thériault as premier. Instead of capitalizing on the burst of energy and good feeling coming out of the Liberal leadership convention, Thériault decided to spend a year putting his own stamp on the premier's office. It turned out to be a disastrous error.

During the months leading up to the election campaign, Bernard Lord travelled the length and breadth of the province presiding over the nomination of candidates for the upcoming election. He was faced with a sensitive and potentially risky task. In the aftermath of its collapse, stalwarts of the Confederation of Regions Party, whose stock in trade had been their opposition to bilingualism, were making their way back into the Conservative Party. The question of the hour for Lord was how to welcome these people into the broad tent of his party without stoking concerns among Acadians that a Conservative government could include a militant anti-francophone component. When he made his way around anglophone ridings in the heartland of Loyalist country, Lord stressed his father's roots in that region, presenting himself as a New Brunswicker who was determined to bring the people of the province together. In Acadian communities, on the other hand, the young Conservative leader stressed that he was a francophone who had been educated in French.

For a time, the Liberals tried to embarrass Lord by commenting on some of the former COR militants who were being welcomed into the Conservative Party, sometimes at meetings where Bernard Lord was present. The tactic went nowhere, however. The Conservative Party made it clear that it was for bilingualism, and former COR supporters, with nowhere else to go, were not making an issue of this. For their part, Acadians saw Lord as a francophone, one of their own, and were resistant to attempts to make this a wedge issue in provincial politics.

Prior to the calling of the election, Bernard Lord and the Conservatives had agreed with the Liberal government's plan to impose tolls on the new divided highway between Fredericton and Moncton. Early in the campaign, Lord sensed that the toll issue could be a winner for him. He reversed his position and promised the removal of tolls on the highway as the central pledge in his campaign. In a province where incomes are not high, issues such as fuel prices, the cost of insurance and the imposition of tolls on highways strike directly at family incomes that are already stretched to the limit. The toll issue caught fire with the general public. When Camille Thériault called the election for June 1999, the Liberals enjoyed a double-digit lead in the polls over the Tories and their new leader. Right up until June 7, election day, it seemed that the Liberals had a sufficient cushion in public support to hang onto office. Election night was a shocker, therefore. When the votes were counted, young Bernard Lord was triumphant, having led his party to its most massive win ever. The Conservatives took forty-four of fifty-five seats in the legislature, and the political right had found a new leader who might one day play a role in the rebuilding of its fortunes across Canada.

Having ducked the hot-button question of language in the run-up to the provincial election, the issue came back to haunt Lord during his first term as premier. On February 1, 2000, a City of Moncton building inspector issued an order to a man who was converting his duplex into a rooming house, informing him that his remodelling plan violated a city bylaw. Mario Charlebois, the property owner who had been served, fought back by taking the city to court, making the case that because the bylaw was worded in

English only and the inspector did not speak French, his constitutional rights had been violated. Although the trial judge dismissed the linguistic argument, agreeing that the Canadian Charter of Rights and Freedoms did not apply to municipalities, Charlebois appealed the decision to the New Brunswick Court of Appeal, where he represented himself. Because the case raised the matter of the rights of francophone minorities in municipalities, the issue had acquired importance that went far beyond the renovation of a piece of property. The Société des Acadiens et Acadiennes du Nouveau-Brunswick, the federal Official Languages Commissioner and the Association des Juristes D'expression Française du Nouveau-Brunswick, an organization that represented francophone lawyers, acquired standing to take the side of Charlebois in the case.

In its decision, issued in December 2001, the New Brunswick Court of Appeal ruled that Moncton's bylaw, written in English only, "is an outright denial of a Charter right." This meant that the bylaws of the city, and those of every other municipality issued in English only, were unconstitutional. In making the ruling, Chief Justice Joseph Daigle stayed the effect of the decision for one year to give the provincial government the opportunity to respond. He suggested that the government give thought to establishing a formula based on the population of English- and French-speakers to decide which municipalities would require bilingual bylaws.[6]

Lord's non-confrontational linguistic strategy had been aimed at holding together a political coalition that included both Acadians and former Confederation of Regions Party activists. The Court of Appeal decision in the Charlebois case threatened to blow this strategy to pieces. His government had sixty days to decide whether to appeal the decision to the Supreme Court of Canada or to draft a new language law for New Brunswick. Both choices were fraught with peril. No one could predict exactly what the Supreme Court might decide. Under the influence of one of the nine Supreme Court justices, Michel Bastarache, a New Brunswick Acadian who had co-authored the Hatfield government's language law, Bill 88, the court could end up ordering every municipality in the province to issue all of its bylaws in both languages. Such a decision would enrage those anglophones who had been at the heart of the linguistic backlash of recent years. And drafting a new language law to bring the province into conformity with the ruling of the Court of Appeal could also enflame anglophone passions.

A couple of weeks after the court decision, the interim leader of the Liberal Party, Bernard Richard, tried to kindle antagonism between the two solitudes that composed the Conservative Party. He stated that the Lord government "is very weak on languages issues," observing that the premier "has a hard time taking a stand." He claimed that what was at stake was "the very nature of New Brunswick as an officially bilingual province."[7] With ample time to decide on his course of action, Bernard Lord brooded over the options. Over dinner at a restaurant in Dieppe, he consulted with francophone supporters, who advised him to draft a new law. That way, they reasoned, the premier would be dealing with the issue as a political matter and he would be demonstrating leadership. On January 21, 2002, he announced that his government would overhaul the 1969 Official Languages Act to bring municipalities within its purview. The legislation would cover all seven New Brunswick cities, requiring them to draft their bylaws and offer services in both English and French. Towns and villages where the minority language group exceeded 20 percent of the population would be required to do the same. It would be up to the province to pay for these additional services.

Having decided on his course, the premier went to the anglophone members of his caucus who he knew would be most leery of the direction he was taking. To these members, the new act was sold not as an extension of francophone rights in the province but as a prudent step that would extend those rights only to the extent necessary for the new law to stand up to judicial scrutiny. The alternative, he implied, was that every hamlet in New Brunswick, no matter how tiny its minority population, would be required to offer services and write its bylaws in both languages. Playing on his anglophone background and his understanding of the culture of the Loyalist heartland, Lord was the ideal politician to undertake this task.

Norm Betts, a member of Lord's Cabinet, who had been runner-up to him in the Conservative leadership race, stated frankly that the premier's approach to selling his strategy "was that this bill was all about limiting rights. The Charlebois decision blew it wide open. The Charlebois decision said, taken to its extreme, that the village of Doaktown had to have bilingual services. So the approach that the premier took in addressing it was: 'The courts have said these rights are there. Are we willing to limit them?'"[8]

With all the flair of Mackenzie King in his ability to espouse both sides of a question to his own advantage, Lord explained that the new bill could indeed be seen as an expansion or a limitation of language rights, depending on a person's perspective. "In some ways, it may do both," he philosophized. "There are new things in the act that were not there before, so is it an expansion? . . . [But] some would argue those rights were in the Constitution anyway, so is it a limitation? Some would argue it defines a reasonable threshold."[9]

Under the circumstances, the Conservative legislative caucus united behind the premier on the bill. Ironically, a bill that marked a solid advance for francophone rights in the province was accepted by people who had once supported a party that was opposed to the very concept of bilingualism. No one could accuse or credit Lord with taking the lead. It had been the Court of Appeal that had forced his hand. But no one could deny that, faced with the need to act, he did so in a way that kept his government united. On June 7, 2002, the bill passed unanimously in the New Brunswick legislature, supported by the Liberals and the NDP as well as by the Tories.

Following third reading of the bill, Lord hosted a piece of political theatre in the legislature that resonated with historical significance. He invited Louis Robichaud to stand in his former place in the legislature and address the body. To do such a thing was a violation of the rules of the legislature, but no one stood on formality that day. In his emotional address, the man who had transformed the position of Acadians in New Brunswick in the 1960s said: "I was not supposed to speak today—although I've spoken from this desk many, many times in the past. I want to thank you all and I want to congratulate each and every one of you for the magnanimity that you've shown in your unanimity in passing this legislation, which is a masterpiece."[10]

Prior to the final passage of the bill, as a harbinger of Bernard Lord's success in handling the tricky question of language, the Confederation of Regions Party wound up its affairs and went out of business. On March 20, 2002, Colby Fraser, leader of the COR, whose apparatus by then amounted to no more than a computer and a few files in his home, wrote to New Brunswick's chief electoral officer asking her to cancel the registration of the party.[11]

From his first days in the premier's office, Bernard Lord received a steady stream of visitors determined to lure him into federal politics. Having taken on the challenge of reuniting a divided right in New Brunswick, Lord seemed to be the man to attempt the admittedly more daunting task of uniting the fractured segments of the federal political right. In the summer of 2002, Lord-mania was rampant among federal Progressive Conservatives, who believed that, with Joe Clark about to depart the leadership of his party, Lord could be the ideal replacement. In Alberta, at a federal PC convention, Lord was deluged with media and delegate attention. Brian Mulroney, who had become a major fan of the New Brunswick premier, enhanced the young man's status when he brought former U.S. president George Bush to the province for a fishing weekend with Lord and some big business cronies. All the party and media hype failed, however. Bernard Lord, ever cautious, and mindful that taking on the Canadian Alliance would be much more difficult than putting out the dying embers of the COR, decided against a federal run, for the time being, at least.

In May 2003, Lord called a provincial election and very nearly became a one-term premier. The issue this time was the huge increase in the cost of automobile insurance, one of those pocketbook questions that can catch on with voters in New Brunswick. In the early months of 2003, there was anger in the province, as in many other provinces, against rising auto insurance bills that were particularly directed against drivers who were seen as high-risk or drove old cars. Especially in the Acadian regions of the north, insurance rates had spiked and were cutting into the already tight budgets of poor families. With the media reporting stories of egregious cases of insurance rate increases, a committee of members of the legislature advocated an increase in the regulatory powers of the Public Utilities Board to deal with the problem.

In March, Premier Lord, ever in search of the winning compromise, tried to show that he was on top of the issue. The government was to place a cap on the level of payouts to accident victims who had received minor injuries. Such a move had been called for by the insurance industry as a way to keep insurance rates down. The government also announced that the Public Utilities Board would have to approve any increase in rates above 3 percent. That was supposed to take the edge off consumer anger. The problem was that the government's action did nothing to roll back rates that were already seen as outrageously high by much of the population. Indeed, for many people in the province, it appeared that the Lord government was anxious, above all, not to offend the powerful insurance industry.

Instead of cooling down the anger over auto insurance rates, the government's response served to fan the flames. At first, Bernard Lord did not seem to realize how serious the problem had become. When he kicked off his election campaign on May 10 with a rally at the University of New Brunswick in Fredericton, he went out of his way to point out the presence on the platform of one of his caucus members, Tony Huntjens, who was a former president of the COR. He seemed still to be fighting the war he had already won, while ignoring the one that could cost him the election. At the rally, Lord did not even mention the issue of auto insurance.

It took a while for the complacent view among Tories that New Brunswickers don't throw out governments after a single term to wear off. But Liberal leader Shawn Graham's pledge to bring in legislation to roll back auto insurance rates by 25 percent, or to consider a public auto insurance system of the kind that existed in three of the four western provinces, was winning converts. Particularly in Acadian northern New Brunswick, voters were flocking to the Liberals. By the end of the campaign, it had become clear to the premier and to the media that the race had become a nail-biter. When election night was over, however, the Conservatives had won twenty-eight seats, to twenty-six for the Liberals and one for the NDP. By a single seat, Lord held on to his majority. Whether Lord could go on to become the first premier ever to be elected prime minister of Canada would await another day. Indeed, whether his near-defeat pointed to a likely end to his career as premier after two terms remained to be seen.

—

CHAPTER 13

THE CAJUN QUEST
FOR IDENTITY

WHILE THE NEW ACADIE WAS taking shape in the Maritimes, and coming to terms with the challenges of modernity, the Cajun society of Louisiana confronted similar challenges in a very different setting, and with a quite different outcome.

For the Cajuns, the American Civil War marked a crucial transition. The stark differences between pre-war and post-war society can be seen even today. As in other parts of the South, the ghostly remains of the antebellum era are signposts of a vanished civilization. Surrounded by giant live oaks, with their enormous, drooping branches from which webs of Spanish moss hang, are the mansions of the vanished planter class. With their wide frontage, long verandahs, second-storey balconies and Greek columns, all in white, with dark roofs and French windows, the houses testify that civilizations come and go. In the river parishes of south Louisiana, the mansions stand not far from small shacks with corrugated metal roofs. From today's perspective it is as difficult to imagine the society and economy that launched the building of the mansions as it is to conceive of the wealth that supported the building of the great houses in coastal Maine, or to imagine the civilization that built the Pont du Gard in France, the magnificent portion of a lengthy aqueduct not far from Avignon that has stood for two thousand years. The spooky vegetation and the Greek columns give these Louisiana homes the appearance of spectral ruins. For novelists and painters, all this is the source of a rich mythology.

With the discovery of oil in south Louisiana in 1901, the bad times of the post–Civil War period began to ease for many Acadians. A new wind of prosperity blew across the prairie. The Louisiana oil boom drew the major oil companies and the independent wildcatters into the region in the quest for black gold. Oil and natural gas fields with names such as Anse La Butte, Coteau Frene, Evangeline and Hell Hole Bayou suddenly became familiar. While many Cajuns did not welcome the flood of Texans into south Louisiana in search of oil riches, the high wages paid in the industry attracted many others to go to work in the oilfields. Oil, first discovered on land and later beneath the waters of the Gulf of Mexico, permanently transformed the region's economy. The city of Lafayette, still a quiet agricultural town with a population of just over 19,000 as late as 1940, became an oil city with a population of over 33,000 a decade later.[1] Today, Lafayette, the city from which Louisiana's offshore oil industry is managed, has a population of over 125,000.

Not surprisingly, in Lafayette, the self-designated cultural and economic capital of Cajun Louisiana, eyes roll when outsiders depict Cajuns as swamp-dwellers who inhabit the late eighteenth century. Today's Cajuns live on a wide swath of territory, in both urban and rural settings, in south Louisiana. People often divide Louisiana in two to get a bird's-eye view of the state. The south, broadly speaking, is Catholic, with the Cajuns comprising a major segment of the population. The north is Protestant, or as Cajuns often describe it, in a good-humoured way, it is "redneck, bubba country." Huey Long, the most gifted, if unscrupulous, politician ever to take the stage in Louisiana, was fond of making speeches in the north telling audiences of his days in a Baptist Sunday school, while in Cajun country he warmly recalled his weekly outings to attend mass. Belying the common stereotypes about them, today's Cajuns are oil rig workers, farmers, ranchers, university professors, teachers and business people. They work in finance, retail, government and the arts. Their ambitions, political views and behaviours are diverse. They are very much a part of the wider American society, as evidenced by the frequency of signs on the homes of Cajuns that read "Support Our Troops" or the common sight of the Stars and Stripes on properties, or on their floats at a Mardi Gras parade.

Despite their varied pursuits and their easy fit within the wider national culture, Cajuns sustain a potent group identity. Elements of that identity include Roman Catholicism, fervent attachment to Cajun music and cuisine, strong family ties and a powerful sense of a unique, tragic and triumphant shared history. Finally, the French language is a crucial element of Cajun identity, even though the ability to communicate in French varies widely among Cajuns, from fluency to a complete inability to speak or understand the language. Several generations ago, virtually all Cajuns spoke French and many spoke little or no English, but a number of societal jolts undermined the Cajuns' use of their language. In 1944, along with compulsory schooling for children it became the policy of the Louisiana state government to discourage the use of French among young Cajuns. English was made the sole language of school instruction. Invariably, the older Cajuns speak of childhood days when they were punished for speaking French in the schoolyard. They look back on this shameful policy with considerable bitterness as the source of their own inability to read and write in French and as the reason so many young Cajuns cannot speak French. Older people find it sad that their grandchildren no longer speak the language that is still their most intimate tool of communication.

Older Cajuns, who do speak French, speak in a dialect that differs in many ways from what can be called standard international French. And they resent visitors from France or Quebec who make remarks about the way they speak the language, as though it is substandard. One aging historian, whose knowledge of Cajun history is encyclopedic, described the experience of speaking with Parisians who look down their noses and say that his is not the way French is spoken in Paris. Defiantly he listed for me the pedigree of his own ancestors, dating back centuries, and said he doubted if many Parisians could match that. He confided that when he encounters the French from France he usually tells them he doesn't speak the language so he can spare himself this kind of humiliation.

Since 1968, it has been the policy of the Louisiana government to encourage the use of French in Cajun regions of the state. Where numbers permit and where parents seek the teaching of French in schools, pupils have access to French immersion classes in grades four and five. But here again, the problem about the kind of French that is taught has become an emotional issue. Initially the teachers in immersion classes came mostly from France or Quebec. The French they spoke and taught was quite different from Cajun French, and indeed from Acadian French as well. Older people often found they could not understand their younger relatives when they proudly addressed them in the French they had learned in school. In recent years, with a far higher proportion of French teachers coming from Louisiana, a better accommodation has been reached, in which the spoken French taught is closer to the Cajun norm, while the written French adheres to a standard international model.

While the struggle for the use of the French language is far from lost in Cajun Louisiana, the situation is radically different from that in Acadian New Brunswick. In New Brunswick, the Acadian elite never stopped insisting that Acadians be educated in French. There was, to be sure, a struggle within the Catholic Church in New Brunswick for the Acadians to assert their own position vis-à-vis the Irish, who long dominated the Church in the province, but both within the Church and within the Acadian elite, determination to sustain the French language never wavered. In Louisiana, on the other hand, for much of the twentieth century, members of the Cajun elite regularly sided with the schools in the drive to impose English on Cajun children.[2]

Today the number of students taking French immersion classes in Louisiana is quite small. For instance, during the 1998–99 school year, 2,058 students were enrolled in such programs, only a shade more than .25 percent of the total student population. Furthermore, those taking French immersion were not all Cajuns. In his book *The*

Cajuns: Americanization of a People, historian Shane Bernard notes: "[O]nly about 3 percent of Cajuns born after 1980 speak French as their first language, an astounding 95 percent decline from the World War II era. Even when youths who speak the dialect as a second language are included, the probable estimate hardly approaches the critical mass of 20 percent required for linguistic survival according to sociologists who have examined language patterns among French minorities in Anglo-dominated Canada. Unless a linguistic revolution occurs, Cajun French will cease to exist as a means of everyday communication in south Louisiana."

If the use of French as a means of everyday communication in south Louisiana ceases to exist, what will become of the Cajuns as a distinctive group? In the United States, such groups as blacks and Jews, most of whom speak no other language than English, have survived with distinct cultures. Is this the sort of fate that lies in store for the Cajuns of Louisiana? Shane Bernard suggests that it is possible "for Cajuns and other ethnic groups who have partly sacrificed their cultural identity to retain a shade of their heritage through symbolic ethnicity." He draws on the work of sociologist Herbert J. Gans, who advances the notion that ethnic groups in the United States have been adopting symbolic cultures in place of their actual cultures, thereby establishing an "ethnicity of last resort." This symbolic ethnicity, according to Gans, can be seen when ethnic minorities make much of traditional holidays and festivals, consume ethnic cuisine and listen to traditional music.[4] According to this view, minorities such as the Cajuns do not live within the full range of their cultures in their daily lives, where their behaviours are much the same as those of the American mainstream. Instead, they use special occasions as the opportunity to give voice to their ethnicity.

The boisterous celebration of Mardi Gras in contemporary south Louisiana puts the Cajuns of the region on display. Mardi Gras, which falls on the Tuesday forty days (not counting Sundays) before Easter, is celebrated in one form or another in many Catholic societies. In Cajun Louisiana, the celebration goes on for many days, leading up to "Fat Tuesday," the day before the onset of Lent, with its religious requirement to live a frugal and observant life in the period prior to the sacrifice of the Saviour. Parades, concerts, radio and television broadcasts and orgiastic outings to restaurants to listen and dance to Cajun music are all aspects of the celebration. On the day before Mardi Gras—Lundi Gras as it is called—the University of Southwestern Louisiana in Lafayette closes its offices and shuts down classes for several days.

Mardi Gras is a time for people to put aside normal routines and have a good time, which makes this celebration easily accessible to people of any culture. Lafayette is the urban hub for Cajun Mardi Gras, and its nickname is Hub City, the same as that of Moncton, now the economic and even cultural hub of Acadian New Brunswick. The two cities are about the same size, with populations of about 125,000 people. By no stretch of the imagination is either city beautiful or quaint, the kind of place one usually associates with the centre of a culture. Lafayette, home to the University of Southwestern Louisiana, which offers specialized programs on the history and culture of the Cajuns, is also the milieu from which important interpreters of the Cajun "fact" have emerged.

On the Friday evening before Mardi Gras, there is a lengthy parade through the streets of Lafayette. Entering and operating the floats in the parade are social clubs that are known as Krewes. The Krewes, which often engage in charitable work, put enormous energy into planning and mounting their floats. Each Krewe chooses a king and queen for the festival, and it is regarded as a high honour to be chosen to play these roles. The participants on the floats are dressed in costumes designed to highlight the particular theme they have chosen.

The symbolism of Mardi Gras is about charity. As the Krewes pass through downtown Lafayette on their floats, they hurl bead necklaces to the crowd. To little children, who are often in costume at the side of the road, the revellers on the floats are careful to throw stuffed animals or other toys or trinkets.

The wider historical meaning of Mardi Gras is more apparent at rural celebrations than in Lafayette, where the parade, despite its particular features, could fit into almost any kind of mass celebration. In the small town of Church Point, north-west of Lafayette, the rituals that are at the heart of Cajun Mardi Gras are plainly visible. Early Sunday morning, the participants in the annual Courir (literally "to run") gather on the outskirts of Church Point. Dozens of men arrive on horseback, attired in costumes that cover their heads. The costumes are often a garish purple and green and the masks are frightening, with long, phallic noses a common feature. In addition to the strange figures on horseback, there are the floats, mounted here as in Lafayette by the participating Krewes. The floats have two useful additions that are absent in the floats in the Lafayette parade: portable toilets and barbecues.

The idea of a Courir is that the participants head out early in the day to visit farmhouses in the area. At the farmhouses—whose owners know in advance that they are coming—the revellers beg to be given food that they can use to make the gumbo that is to be concocted at the end of the day. On a Courir, those approaching the farmhouse can take two quite different tacks. They can come as supplicants, who beg by holding out the palm of their left hand and signalling with their right hand that they expect to receive a handout. But they can also come in the manner of outlaws who close in on the house threateningly, sometimes sliding down the side of the building and looking for a way to sneak inside. The high point of the ritual is reached when the farmer or a member of the family comes outside with a live chicken and releases the unfortunate fowl into the crowd. The chicken may leap into the air and race across the ground, but its fate is sealed. The men in their ghoulish costumes charge after the chicken, with those aged from ten or eleven to eighty in hot pursuit. Within a few seconds it is over. While a few men emerge with feathers, only one comes up with the chicken, which he takes proudly back to his horse or his motorized float. At the end of the day, the chicken ends up in the gumbo.

All the elements of Cajun Mardi Gras are in evidence in this horseplay. The celebration allows the normal rules of a traditional society to be suspended for a time, so that the poor and the power-less can put on airs and stand up to their social betters, so that people can demand charity and sharing, and so that young boys can overcome their fear and can bond with the men in the day's adventures. And when the Courir has returned from its ritualistic pillaging of the countryside, the community comes together to enjoy the traditional foods. In addition to the gumbo, a stew containing the ingredients that have been gathered, there will be cracklin (cooked fresh pork skins), boudin (sausages), and funnel cake (deep-fried batter), and there may be catfish doused in crawfish étouffée, alligator and even frogs' legs.

Cajun music is central to the culture and has evolved over the decades. Purists who are hoping to find an unspoiled and unchanging musical heritage that dates back two centuries and that is fighting a heroic battle against absorption into the American mainstream are looking in the wrong place. The dynamism of Cajun music is found in its capacity to retain its core vitality while borrowing from the myriad of influences of other cultures. For instance, today one cannot imagine Cajun music without the accordion, and yet the accordion, an instrument invented in Germany in the early nineteenth century, was not taken up by Cajun musicians until the late 1800s. Without Scots-Irish, black, Spanish, Anglo-American and Creole influences, today's Cajun music, enormously different from music in Acadie and Quebec, would not be what it has become.

Just east of the town of Eunice on the Louisiana prairie, at the side of the highway in a very unpromising-looking one-storey building, is the nerve centre for one of the most creative Cajun music groups. The Savoy Music Center is run by Marc Savoy, his wife Ann and their two sons. All four are highly talented musicians. Marc Savoy, who assembles accordions himself, has made it his life's work to foster the Cajun musical heritage. On Saturday mornings, the best Cajun jam session in south Louisiana takes place in the Savoy Music Center. Just drop in—there's no charge for admission—and you can take in the spectacle. If you arrive early you

might even get to sit in one of the aging chairs on which the performers themselves sit. Behind the counter are Marc and Ann, and
they are happy to give you a taste of boudin. The musicians come
from all over south Louisiana and they turn up whenever they are
able to take part. Two or three fiddlers, one person on the accordion, a guitarist or two and someone on the triangle round out the
performers, who range in age from twenty to eighty. The session
goes on for a couple of hours, with performers dropping in and out
of the mix.

One night, the Savoy family was to star in a performance at the
Liberty Theatre in Eunice, the highlight of the town's Mardi Gras
celebrations. All day on the closed-off main street of Eunice, other
Cajun musicians cranked out their music as people ate, danced,
watched and wandered off to enjoy themselves. When the box office
opened at the theatre at 4:00 p.m. to sell tickets to the Savoy show,
the lineup was more than a block long. The show, to be broadcast
on local television, was to begin two hours later, but most of the
audience chose to come inside to watch the members of the Savoy
family rehearse on stage. No one was disappointed. The smooth
sound of the performers and their astonishing ability to switch
instruments showed why this group has such a following. During
the break at intermission, costumed revellers came inside and went
up and down the aisles playing out the Mardi Gras rituals, engaging in mock threats and petulant begging for cash.

Other Cajun musical groups have achieved national fame and
have used their celebrity to keep alive the knowledge of Cajun history. For instance, the memory of Joseph Broussard, seen by the
Cajuns as a freedom fighter against British tyranny, is burnished by
a Cajun musical band that goes by the name BeauSoleil. For more
than a quarter of a century, the professional band, led by fiddler,
singer and songwriter Michael Doucet, has developed the taste for
Cajun music, not only in the south Louisiana heartland but in other
parts of the United States and in many other countries. BeauSoleil,
which played in the events surrounding Jimmy Carter's presidential
inauguration in 1977, has appeared at the Super Bowl and has won

a Grammy Award. The band decided that its musical roots were Cajun and that it would stay true to its origins, making its base the Cajun country of south Louisiana and refusing to change that as fame was won. Singing in both French and English to American audiences, BeauSoleil has been credited with developing the growing craze for Cajun music. And in Louisiana, where it has been much harder than in New Brunswick to keep a francophone heritage alive, bands that sing in French have played a critical role. Doucet, who was born in 1951, sees himself as a member of the last generation of Cajuns who "could look before them and see the culture before it got totally enraptured by television, by the oil boom."[5]

The enormous popularity of Cajun music has fostered commercial success for local artists, and it attracts waves of tourists to the region for Mardi Gras and for music festivals. But the Cajun revival is driven by much more than commercial appetites. Over the past several decades, there have been numerous cases in the United States of powerful assertions of ethnic identities. The long-held supposition that America is a melting pot and that everyone in the United States is thoroughly Americanized is being re-examined. The assertion of Cajun identity, in part through music, can be understood in that context. On the other hand, this line of thinking can be pushed too far. Cajuns are Americans, with views and goals that fit within the broad framework of what is acceptable in the United States. In no sense are they radically at odds with the United States in its global or domestic policies. As an identifiable group within American society, however, they certainly differ in observable ways from the Anglo-American Protestants who inhabit north Louisiana.

The Cajun community of south Louisiana, in population terms, is the largest segment of the Acadian Diaspora. Indeed there are about twice as many Louisiana Cajuns as there are Canadian Acadians. The Cajun culture has been proceeding along its own unique course for over two centuries, at the same time as the Acadian culture in New Brunswick and elsewhere in Atlantic Canada has been evolving. What we observe today, as in other cases of a Diaspora, is the development of societies that remain intensely interested in one another, especially in their ties of blood and history, but which have become quite distinct, and in many respects do not share the values, culture and priorities of their now distant cousins.

Yet, in terms of symbolism, the two cultures have touched each other deeply. In the 1880s, at a time of their renewal as a people, the Acadians adopted a flag of their own: the French tricolor—red, white and blue—with a gold star in the blue stripe. In 1964, a Lafayette lawyer, Allen Babineaux, who was a Cajun cultural activist, paid a visit to the town of Caraquet in northern New Brunswick. There, as he recalled, "At every corner I saw this flag flying." Intrigued by it, he inquired and learned that it was the flag of the Acadians. When he returned to Louisiana, he proposed that the same flag be used in 1965 at a cultural event whose purpose was to serve as a sequel ten years after the bicentennial commemoration of the deportation of the Acadians. From this suggestion, the idea grew—initially proposed by Dean Thomas Arceneaux of the University of Southwestern Louisiana—that a new flag, depicting the history of the south Louisiana Cajuns, should be devised. Arceneaux himself, borrowing from his university's seal, came up with a design for the new flag. The flag is divided into three fields. On the top field, with a blue background, are three white fleur-de-lys, symbolizing the pre-revolutionary France from which the Cajuns left for the New World, the symbol that dominates the flag of Quebec. The bottom field features a gold castle on a red background, to symbolize Spanish Louisiana, which gave succour to the Acadians following *le Grand Dérangement*. In a triangular field on the left, with a white background, there is a gold star, meant to represent Our Lady of the Assumption, the patron saint of Acadians. In its Louisiana setting, the gold star also symbolizes the participation of Acadians in the American revolutionary war, as soldiers fighting under the Spanish flag. The new flag, launched in 1965, became ubiquitous in south Louisiana in 1968, a year when Cajun cultural renewal and pride were strongly evident. Today, the flag flies in front of many businesses, schools and government buildings.[6]

In the summer of 2004, thousands of Cajuns travelled to Nova Scotia to celebrate the Congrès Mondial Acadien. They took part in huge family reunions that brought them together with men and women who were their distant relatives from Acadie. They visited the lands once owned by their ancestors and they made journeys to Grand Pré to experience the shrine to the Acadians there. Many Cajuns related how deeply satisfying it was to make these journeys and many are already looking forward to the next Congrès Mondial Acadien to be held in Caraquet, New Brunswick, in 2009.

An issue that has much absorbed the attention of the Cajuns of south Lousiana in recent years, and came to the attention of the world in the aftermath of Hurricane Katrina in the late summer of 2005, is the environmental crisis that has been threatening the entire southern coast of the state along the Gulf of Mexico. The southern coast of Louisiana, the bayou country, is a flat terrain that merges along its edge into the waters of the Gulf. The terrain has been formed over thousands of years out of the rich alluvial soil washed down the Mississippi River to the delta. This mysterious landscape, with its swamps, live oaks, alligators and slow-moving bayous, has been home to a unique culture developed by its Cajun inhabitants. Fishermen who built their own wooden dwellings along the bayous earned a living from the shrimp, crabs, oysters and fish in the region, the whole billion-dollar annual industry dependent on the survival of the vast marshlands. At one time there were small communities in the bayou country that were accessible only by water. In their isolation, the Cajun residents continued to speak French in their daily lives after the majority of Cajuns in south Louisiana had largely switched over to English.

What has already wiped out the livelihoods and communities of the bayou-dwellers has been an environmental crisis that threatens this delicate coastal region, an area about as large as the state of Connecticut. The survival of the delta depends on an intricate balance in which additions of soil from the Mississippi offset the loss of soil being washed out into the Gulf. That balance has been lost so that every ten months a land mass the size of Manhattan Island is washed out to sea. The levees that protect New Orleans and the banks of the lower Mississippi—which proved so inadequate in the face of Hurricane Katrina—contribute massively to the problem by establishing a narrow funnel through which the Mississippi flows so that it deposits less new soil to the maintenance of the delta.

For most Americans and for people outside the United States, the shocking aftermath of Hurricane Katrina revealed the vulnerability of New Orleans and the Gulf region as well as the horror of a disaster whose victims were so disproportionately poor and black. But with all the media coverage of the disaster, there was almost no discussion of the wider environmental problem in the region—a subject of which many living in south Louisiana were already painfully aware. A unique terrain in which a very particular Cajun culture had developed is being destroyed, and with it the culture as well.

Two years before Katrina struck, in an eloquent book titled *Bayou Farewell: The Rich Life and Tragic Death of Louisiana's Cajun Coast*, Mike Tidwell warned:

> [T]he massive coast of this watery southern state is vanishing from the face of the earth. . . . It's an unfolding calamity of fantastic magnitude, taking with it entire Cajun towns and an age-old way of life. . . .
>
> [T]he lower Mississippi River, the great creator of land in southernmost Louisiana through thousands of years of flooding and alluvial deposits, is now straitjacketed with flood levees so high—as high as three-story buildings in places—that the river may never jump its banks again. And that, in a nutshell, is the problem. A devastating chain reaction has resulted from the taming of the Mississippi, and now the entire coast is dissolving at breakneck speed. . . . It is, hands down, the fastest-disappearing landmass on earth, and New Orleans itself is at great risk of vanishing.[7]

—

CHAPTER 14

LOOKING FORWARD, LOOKING BACK

IN AUGUST 2004, in a discourse that was refined and polite, a line was drawn to distinguish the identity of the Acadians in the Maritimes from that of the Cajuns in Louisiana. The setting was Clare, Nova Scotia, and the occasion was the Congrès Mondial Acadien, a meeting of people from the far corners of the Acadian Diaspora that is held every four years. The Congrès in 2004 was especially significant because it commemorated the four hundredth anniversary of the first Acadian settlement. That it was held in Nova Scotia could not help but remind people that the following year, 2005, would mark the two hundred and fiftieth anniversary of *le Grand Dérangement*.

Clare is home to the largest share of the 40,000 Acadians in Nova Scotia, who, all told, make up about 3 percent of the population of the province. The municipality of Clare is the only one of Nova Scotia's fifty-five municipalities that conducts its affairs in French. Clare is composed of a string of villages along the sea, where there are numerous small harbours housing fishing vessels. All along the coast in these little communities, as the Congrès was about to begin, the symbols of Acadie were on display: Acadian flags on the grass in front of houses, lawn chairs painted blue, white and red and arranged to form the Acadian flag, hand-hewn figures standing in front of public buildings, attired in eighteenth-century Acadian garb and wearing the mandatory wooden shoes.

Pride of place in Clare goes to the community of Pointe-de-l'Église, where the Université Sainte-Anne is located. With a student population of three hundred, this is Nova Scotia's only French-language university. The school was established on the foundation that had been built by Eudist fathers from France who founded the Collège Sainte-Anne in 1890.[1] At the Congrès, a focal point was a conference in Clare with the title "Vision 20/20." With thinkers invited from all over the Acadian Diaspora, the conference was intended to provide a perspective on Acadie and how it might be expected to develop between now and the year 2020. Just as the Université de Moncton has been a major spur to the development of Acadian New Brunswick, the Université Sainte-Anne has been important to Nova Scotia's Acadians.

Among those who devote themselves on an ongoing basis to the life of Acadie, those who can be described as members of the Acadian "movement," an important polarity has developed. On one side, there is the notion that Acadie and Acadians can be taken seriously only if Acadie is a real society, living in the present in a real place. And that real place, the proponents of this view insist, can only be the Maritime provinces, principally New Brunswick. On the other side, there is the conviction that Acadie is an idea that exists out of time and place, the consequence of the Diaspora, which allows people to dream the Acadian dream and hold on to it as a central part of their identity wherever they are located. This is a tension between homeland and Diaspora. Thinkers in the homeland, the Acadian communities in the Maritimes, especially New Brunswick, insist that they be recognized as living in the real Acadie, a definable space that Acadians inhabit all year round. They say they are not simply dreamers and part-timers who celebrate their Acadian roots while residing elsewhere.

At the Congrès, these two views were dramatically counterposed at the "Vision 20/20" conference. In his opening address on the first full day of the conference, Maurice Basque, the director of the Centre d'Études Acadiennes at the Université de Moncton, put the case for the first vision of Acadie. Tall, thin and energetic, Basque is always impeccably dressed. A historian who specializes in colonial Acadie and in the history of Acadian political culture, he plays a central role in advancing the study of Acadie.

In his address, Basque tackled the central, controversial question: What defines an Acadian today and what will define an Acadian in the future? He recalled his own adolescence in Tracadie in New Brunswick's Acadian Peninsula. When he first saw the Acadian flag, it was merely a curiosity to him, not a symbol of a nation to which he belonged. He spoke of the factors that have shaped the Acadian identity, making it distinct from all others. One factor to which he drew attention is close proximity to, and pressure from, the English, from the very beginning of the history of Acadie. In the only "real" Acadie that exists today, that of the Maritime provinces, most Acadians understand or are able to speak English. In this Acadie, where Basque believes that the key decisions for the Acadian future will have to be taken, an Acadian identity has been shaped. That identity was influenced by the late-nineteenth-century conferences at which Acadian symbols—the flag, the national anthem, August 15 as the national day—were adopted.

Of considerable importance in developing the Acadian culture and identity, says Basque, has been the absorption of new population groups, including Québécois and English-speakers. (A large number of Acadians talk of their Irish and Québécois ancestors.) In the second half of the twentieth century, he asserts, Acadians grappled with the challenges of modernity. Today and in the future, he concludes, Acadie will not be limited to the descendants of the families who experienced *le Grand Dérangement* in 1755, but will include newcomers, who have become a part of Acadian society. He cites the inclusiveness of the annual Jeux Acadiens, bringing young people together each year for athletic competition, as an example of the new Acadie at its best. Basque declares that Acadians are tired of being seen as "cute" by tourists who come to visit in the summer months. This image, he asserts, stands in the way of developing a viable agenda in a society that exists all year long.

Basque's address posed the central question for the Congrès— whether Acadie was to be a living society in a specific physical location—the Maritime provinces—or, alternatively, a more amorphous meta-reality that conceives of Acadie as existing wherever

Acadians are present. He made a forceful, albeit gracious, case for the former.

The alternative argument was made two days later at the conference by Jules Chiasson, a French radio executive for Radio-Canada, born in Cheticamp, Nova Scotia. Chiasson argued that revolutionary communications technologies will provide the key to developing the wider, Diasporic Acadie. After reviewing the history of communications, Chiasson suggested the possibility of founding a "virtual Acadian country" in the coming period, a "country" whose decisions could be made over the Internet, by Acadians, wherever they were located. The audience did not seem mesmerized by this ultimate extrapolation of the romantic notion of Acadie as existing apart from time and space. Perhaps the idea of a virtual Acadie, accessible over the Internet, was too much of a leap for the folkloric wing of the enthusiasts of the Acadian Diaspora, the natural constituency for such a concept. Indeed, the very idea of a virtual Acadie was stoutly rejected in a comment from the floor by a delegate who said that what Acadians should aspire to is the exercise of political power in the real Acadie, in Fredericton and Halifax.

The Congrès Mondial Acadien was held eight months after a symbolic event of great significance for Acadians. In December 2003, the Government of Canada issued a royal proclamation in the name of Queen Elizabeth II recognizing the wrongs the Acadians suffered during le Grand Dérangement. The proclamation followed several years of wrangling on the issue. The Société Nationale de l'Acadie (SNA) had long been on record calling for an apology from the Queen for the suffering of the Acadians at the hands of the British Crown. In 2001, Bloc Québécois MP Stéphane Bergeron, who has Acadian roots, introduced a motion in the House of Commons calling on the governor general to seek an apology from the Queen. Jean Chrétien's Liberals used their majority in Parliament to defeat the motion. In 2003, in reply to a written request from the SNA seeking an acknowledgment of le Grand Dérangement, the office of the Queen replied that Her Majesty would defer to the judgment of the Canadian Parliament. Heritage

Minister Sheila Copps took the lead in convincing the Liberal Cabinet to endorse the idea of a proclamation.

In Ottawa, on December 9, Governor General Adrienne Clarkson signed the declaration, which acknowledged that "on July 28, 1755, the Crown, in the course of administering the affairs of the British colony of Nova Scotia, made the decision to deport the Acadian people." The Royal Proclamation continued: " . . . the deportation of the Acadian people, commonly known as the Great Upheaval, continued until 1763 and had tragic consequences, including the deaths of many thousands of Acadians from disease, in shipwrecks, in their places of refuge and in prison camps in Nova Scotia and England as well as in the British colonies in America."

"We hope that the Acadian people can turn the page on this dark chapter of their history," the text added. Careful to note that the proclamation did not "constitute a recognition of legal or financial responsibility by the Crown in right of Canada and of the provinces," the declaration concluded with the undertaking that each year, beginning in 2005, July 28 would be designated as "A Day of Commemoration of the Great Upheaval."

The most distinguished contemporary Acadian artist, who also happens to be the lieutenant-governor of New Brunswick, has delved deeply into the question of Acadian identity. In his play *Pour Une Fois*, Herménégilde Chiasson (not to be confused with Radio-Canada's Jules Chiasson) places Acadie on the analyst's couch and diagnoses it as more or less insane. Seen through the lens Chiasson brings to bear on it, Acadie is crushed by the weight of its past, a weight so heavy that it has become an obsession that takes away from the capacity of Acadians to cope with the present. For him, a strict presentation of history will not suffice, nor will a mere account of contemporary life in Acadie. *Pour Une Fois* provides a brilliant amalgam of the two.

The central character in the play is a down-and-out Acadian who lives in Moncton. During most of the play, our protagonist sits on his bed in his pajamas, buffeted by the heroic history of the Acadians on one side and the idiocies of his daily life on the other.

He dreams the dreams of the founding of Acadie and suffers the nightmare of the deportation of his people in 1755, all the while dealing with his loutish anglophone landlord, an unpleasant tax collector and the unpalatable fact that it is his wife who is earning the family's small income. Indeed, it is the wife, named Jeanne, a name associated with strength of purpose, who is coping with contemporary realities. From those realities, however, the central character is drawn ever more into the tales of the Acadian past. In the final scene, while he reaches out for the shining, ever receding vision of pristine Acadie, we see behind him the figures of Evangeline and La Sagouine, the female saints of his people's folklore.

Born in St. Simon, New Brunswick, in 1946, Chiasson was raised by a mother and father who were unable to read or write. In one of his arresting writings, he recalls the exact moment in his childhood when he learned to read. The symbols on a commercial notice on the wall of the store that was managed by his mother suddenly took the form of words he could understand. He exulted in the potency of that achievement. His mother recognized that her son had opened a doorway to an arcane realm that was closed to her.

Acadian writing and painting have often evoked the sea, which has always been intimately connected to the life of Acadie. A forested land, mostly of low elevation, snug up against the coast— that was the terrain of the first Acadie, as it is of so much of the Acadie of today. Chiasson recalls his childhood life by the sea. In an essay titled "Evangeline," he tells the story of how, at the age of seventeen, he created his first painting. He came to an agreement, he tells his readers, through which his mother would buy him "a complete set of tubes of oil paint on condition that I would make her a copy of a portrait of Evangeline that showed her looking out over the shore where the Acadians had been forced onto the English ships when they were deported from their land." His portrait was to be rendered from memory from a lost painting of the subject that had been done by his brother. That painting had been based on the cover of a book, also lost, titled *The Touching Odyssey of Evangeline* by Eugene Achard.[2] When he completed the work, he painted a black frame around it and inscribed his name and the year on the bottom.[3]

Herménégilde Chiasson sees Acadians as caught between the weight of history on the one hand and the pull of utopia on the other. Utopian visions, he believes, are sought as a way of somehow reversing the brute facts of history, as though with the wave of a wand *le Grand Dérangement* could be cancelled. That is why, he says, so much of Acadian thinking about the future is utopian. What this mindset denies, and this matters hugely, is facing up to the reality of the present.

When he speaks, he has the attention of Acadians, but they do not always find his message palatable. Contemporary Acadians cannot find sustenance in folklore, Chiasson warns. They need an identity, a culture, a set of guideposts that will allow them to live in the world of the present. It is no good, he thinks, to dwell in Longfellow's fantasy, which gets in the way of coping with the hard facts of a postmodern society. Chiasson is committed to the creation of a contemporary Acadie that can live its life in French, in the workplace, in the schools, as well as in theatres and other centres of culture.

The appointment of Chiasson as lieutenant-governor of New Brunswick by Prime Minister Jean Chrétien on the Acadian National Day, August 15, 2003, created a sensation in the province. It was greeted with enthusiasm by many but also with the sustained anger of a few. The choice of Acadie's leading contemporary artist to fill the post was welcomed by those who believed Chiasson would become a champion of the arts and of the Acadian place in New Brunswick life. On the other side were critics who saw it as no less than a betrayal for Chiasson to accept the role of the representative of the Queen in New Brunswick. How could he, at a time when a fierce debate raged about whether the Queen should issue an apology for *le Grand Dérangement*, take a job that was so freighted with negative symbolism for many Acadians? For months afterwards, the pages of *L'Acadie Nouvelle* ran columns for and against the appointment.

More than two years after being sworn in as New Brunswick's lieutenant-governor, Hermé (as he is universally known) is a little more serious, perhaps a little more careworn, than before. His wardrobe has certainly grown larger, and he is now at home in dark suits that he would have found it odd to wear in the days before his viceregal appointment. He has begun to play golf, the pastime of the powerful, often a sign that someone has become more comfortable in the public realm. His approach has been to accept almost every invitation that has come his way. He has appeared and spoken in every corner of the province. He has been discovering a wider, more diverse New Brunswick than he knew before. Recently he even made a speech to the aging members of the once potent Orange Lodge of New Brunswick, a staunchly Protestant organization whose power in the past was regularly mobilized against Catholicism and French-language rights. Joking that he was undoubtedly the first Acadian ever to address the Orange Lodge, he was accorded a standing ovation by this unlikely audience.

Over a period of a few days, Hermé attended the funeral of the father of a close friend in Moncton and the celebration of the four-hundredth anniversary of the first Acadian settlement on a muddy, rain-drenched field overlooking Île St. Croix. Just before the funeral, Hermé returned from a colloquium at the University of Poitiers in France, where scholars from many places presented papers on Acadian themes. He has the natural grace of a public figure, and where he goes he is noticed. It is reported that even the premier, Bernard Lord, likes to be seen with Hermé whenever possible.

As lieutenant-governor, Hermé now lives in Old Government House in Fredericton, a vast stone mansion, built in the 1820s, that is located right beside the wide St. John River. Like other imperial mansions of the nineteenth century, this one was constructed to be the centre of political and social life in a British colonial outpost. In those days, the British governor was the figure around whom the life of the genteel revolved. Beside the mansion stands an old British military roundhouse that was built to guard against an American invasion, which was a lurking danger in the first half of the nineteenth century. The first floor of the mansion is still a grand setting where important social events are hosted. With its immensely high ceilings and its paintings of New Brunswick landscapes and imperial figures, its state dining room is the most imposing venue in the provincial capital. On the third floor, there is the apartment of the lieutenant-governor, with its kitchen, an intimate dining room and a number of large, well-appointed bedrooms. Here the ceilings are lower, and the view of the river and the towering maple trees at water's edge is memorable. The panorama from this perspective is pastoral. Except for the scale of the river, which is more like the Rhine than the Thames, it could be set in England, which makes the locale so different from almost all of New Brunswick, with its woods, coasts and rough landscapes.

Many of Hermé's paintings hang on the wall here. But his residence in the mansion does not feel much like a home, as he is the first to say. His wife, Marcia Babineau, who is the director of the Théâtre L'Escaouette in Moncton and one of its leading actors, spends three or four days a week at the theatre. She stays during these sojourns at the couple's house, which is located on the sea at Barachois, east of Shediac. When Hermé is on his own in Old Government House, he mostly locks himself up in the snug study just off the living room. In this room, he can focus on his writing and other tasks. As a man who needs only four or five hours sleep a night, this is the one place in the mansion where he feels truly at home.

During one long dinner in the dining room in the apartment, Hermé talks about his experience as lieutenant-governor and his changing view of the situation of Acadians in New Brunswick. He also reflects on the state of the country during a period of political instability with the prospects for the Quebec sovereigntists once more on the rise. More than ever, Hermé is committed to a conception of Acadie that is not rooted in blood but in the living experience of a twenty-first-century society. He sees the Acadians of New Brunswick as midway through a long journey from one definition of what it is to be Acadian to another.

Ethnicity does not matter much to Hermé. What is truly important is identity. Someone who is descended from one of the families of 1755 but who does not speak and live in French is much less an Acadian, as far as he is concerned, than a person who has migrated to New Brunswick and who lives in its Acadian society. For him, Francis, the artist and professor introduced in the opening of this book, who has lived in New Brunswick for almost forty years but was born in Namur, Belgium, is an Acadian. (As it happens, Hermé and Francis have been close friends for thirty years.)

Hermé's broadest concern is still what it was before: to help create among New Brunswick's Acadians a society that can live and flourish in French, a society whose culture is not locked in a museum but is contemporary and relevant. The tensions that arise in that quest are ever-present in his writing, even when he speaks of everyday matters that should be lighthearted. In a piece titled "Achilles Before Besieged Shediac," he writes of a car ride to the seaside for an ice cream. En route, though, he encounters an historic plaque that records the Deportation, and a stream that makes him think of Beauséjour, "where Monckton allowed women to see their captured menfolk for a day." And then in Shediac, where he is trying to buy ice cream:

> but all the ads there were English so it did seem
> Marcia asked whether there was a special knack
> or if only the English could purchase ice cream
> and was that why no French notice was writ down

For him, Shediac is a "schizophrenic village" that is "English on the outside, inside secretly French."

Hermé is full of humour, but he is always serious. He brings to his melancholy such a thirst for life that his writings bristle with tension between these polarities. He is preoccupied by basic questions about life, love, art, culture and history. His relentless pursuit of the basic from a wide range of vantage points can make him disconcerting. In conversation, as well as in his writing, he is that rare individual who pursues two levels of thought in every discourse. There is the immediate and the concrete, vivid and in the present;

interacting with this, there is the pursuit of the broader, deeper themes that are long-term concerns. Connecting these two streams is the artist at work. The weight of the past is always at hand in Hermé's quest for the Acadie of tomorrow. And that weight, that gravity of purpose, directed with good humour in opposition to those who cling to the folklore, has drawn fire from younger writers and artists.

Raoul Boudreau is a professor at the Université de Moncton who specializes in Acadian literature. In his fifties, Boudreau is acutely attuned to how the evolution of a people's literature interacts with its societal evolution. To an extent that would be unusual in larger societies, the struggles in Acadie about identity and social change are fought out by writers, painters, musicians and even by theatre companies. Acadian artists do not speak for themselves alone. They are recognized by others, such as Boudreau, as representing positions in cultural and societal conflicts. For an analyst such as Boudreau, that is the fate of a major artist such as Hermé. He makes the point to me that when Antonine Maillet achieved her literary breakthrough, numerous other writers followed in her footsteps to see what they could achieve using her approach. None of them is remembered. It was only when Hermé, the most gifted of the next generation, came along with his modernist challenge that something memorable was achieved.

Today in the Aberdeen Centre in Moncton, in a building where Northrop Frye attended school nearly a century ago, a home has been established for Acadian artists and writers. Within these walls, Hermé has come under attack from writers of the next generation. And this is natural, just as it should be, Boudreau assures me. Hermé's gravity—the young writers would say his pessimism—has been criticized by those who want to live in Acadie as they find it, without worrying too much about where the project is ultimately headed. For them, the Chiac of Moncton, the local Acadian dialect, is fine, because it comes as naturally to people who live in the city as breathing. Purity of language is not something with which they concern themselves. Hermé does not go as far as to reject Chiac, as long as it is seen as a separate dialect and not as a replacement for French. As a native of the Acadian Peninsula in the north, where Chiac would not be understood, it is natural for him to see this dialect, spoken only in the south-east, as locking its speakers into a rather small universe. "The future may belong," he tells me "to young, well-educated anglophones who have been educated in proper French. The advantage of French is that it is a language spoken widely in the world." But as long as those who speak Chiac can also speak proper French, he has no wish to stand in the way of those who have demonstrated the creativity of the local dialect.

Conflict between generations of writers, Boudreau tells me, occurs in all societies. It becomes perhaps more personally poignant in the Acadian world, where everyone knows everyone else. One is reminded of the intimate space occupied by this artistic world in the Aberdeen Centre itself. Although he spends little time there these days, the physical fact of Hermé's presence is strongly felt. In one of the studios, many of his paintings are stored, lying on long work tables, some of them unfinished, as though the artist is about to walk through the door and go to work. Indeed, there is a small space behind the studio, with a tiny kitchenette beside a wooden bunk, reached by a ladder, where he lived for a time.

Boudreau talks of the crucial role played by Antonine Maillet in moving Acadie from an oral to a written culture. Maillet, who now lives in Montreal, transformed Acadian literature with her play *La Sagouine* and her novel *Pélagie-la-Charrette*. With these two works, Maillet altered the conception of womanhood in Acadian culture from the image of Evangeline, the tragic and passive figure created by Longfellow in the mid nineteenth century, to potent images of action, passion and effectiveness.

In a radio interview on CBC in 2004, Maillet emphasized that having once created the charwoman in *La Sagouine*, her character simply "spoke for herself," employing language that often revived the usage of old forms of speech and phrases from the Acadian past. This is a culture in which forms of language become questions of passionate controversy. Maillet's invention of a written Acadian language created a sensation in France, where she ultimately won the Prix Goncourt for *Pélagie*, a literary award never before bestowed on a writer outside of France. Maillet recalls, with asperity, a conversation she had with a Québécois who suggested to her that perhaps it was inappropriate that an Acadian should win the Goncourt before a Québécois had won the prize.

When Maillet spoke at the Congrès Mondial Acadien at the Université Sainte-Anne in August 2004, delegates crowded into a classroom to see the doyenne of Acadian literature. In her mid seventies, Maillet exudes youthful energy, along with a savvy awareness of the role she plays. Her listeners hung on every word and frequently applauded or burst into laughter. She is Acadie's unquestioned superstar, a symbol of what others can achieve. She used that standing to give a feel-good address. She told her audience that every person has a special and unique perspective to offer to the world. It's not a matter of competing with Shakespeare or Cervantes. Such a thought should never deter anyone. Instead each person should be prepared to offer his or her vision to others.

In her discussion of Acadie's place in the world, she celebrated the fact that Acadie is no superpower, indeed, that it has no state of its own. She related that when Acadie welcomed the heads of state of the Francophonie summit to Moncton in 1999, there was no Acadian king or president to welcome them. Instead, they were welcomed by the Acadian people. Asked what she thought of the project of Quebec sovereignty, she replied that she admires the people who dream of it as a solution for their society, but she stops short of endorsing it. She does not, could not endorse anything of the sort for Acadie. Her conclusion: without great power in the world, Acadie can be a sparkling jewel on the planet.

Later that evening, Hermé turns up at a seafood restaurant in Digby that looks out over the harbour. He is dressed in blue jeans, having a snack before his return on the ferry to Saint John. He is not here in his persona as the head of state of New Brunswick. Instead, he explains, he was at Antonine Maillet's speech in the afternoon. He is making a film about her. What a strange world Acadie is. New Brunswick's lieutenant-governor takes off in civvies for the Acadian conference in Nova Scotia to film the literary figure whose role he has himself challenged.

Despite his choice of Acadie's most famous folkloric figure for his first painting, Hermé was to become the protagonist for modernism and the rejection of the folkloric in Acadian writing. In the late 1960s and early 1970s, Hermé emerged as pre-eminent among a group of artists working in Moncton. While Hermé conceded that Antonine Maillet's contribution to Acadian writing had been indispensable, he believed that she had represented Acadians in a folkloric manner in her work.

Appropriate to the goal of a living Acadie, Hermé recognizes a difference, if not a tension, within the Acadian communities where assimilation has taken a heavy toll, most notably the Cajuns of Louisiana, but also the Acadians of Nova Scotia, Prince Edward Island and Newfoundland. For Hermé, the Acadians are similar to the Jews as a wandering people, a people of a Diaspora. Just as the Jews have searched for a homeland, so too have the Acadians. But, he notes, while the Diaspora has nourished the Jewish homeland, for the Acadians it has been the reverse: the homeland, by which he means Acadian New Brunswick, has sustained the Diaspora.

David Lonergan, a professor at the Université de Moncton, who is originally from Quebec, studies Acadian culture. What interests him especially is that Acadian culture is both dynamic and the culture of a minority people. It is commonly said that New Brunswick is Canada's only bilingual province. He calls New Brunswick a "*diglossie.*" *Diglossie* is the French word for a society in which there are two linguistic communities, one of which speaks both the languages, while the other community speaks only one of them. In this case, of course, it is the French who are often able to speak English while the English rarely speak French. Lonergan, who is highly dramatic and who moves from chair to chair in his office during our conversation, leaps to his feet to do an imitation of an English-speaking store employee encountering a francophone patron. As soon as the first French word is out of the customer's mouth, the employee freezes, as though struck by a lethal virus, and protests that he does not speak French.

Lonergan recalls the days of his youth when he was employed at the main Eaton's store in downtown Montreal. He was required—in that time prior to the passage of Quebec's language law, Bill 101—to greet customers in English. Only if the customer switched to French was he allowed to speak French at Eaton's. Lonergan remarks that he believes the French language remains fragile, not only in New Brunswick but also in Quebec.

A student of both Acadian and Quebec culture, Lonergan understands the ever-present tension between the Acadians and the Québécois. Antonine Maillet's dismissal of the suggestion that it would have been appropriate for a Québécois to win the Prix Goncourt before an Acadian is symptomatic of the uneasy relationship. The relationship is not unlike that between Quebec and France historically. Before the Quiet Revolution, even traditional Québécois, who were highly suspicious of France's secular culture, recognized that they needed the weight of France to help sustain their own culture. It is much the same for the Acadians, who know full well that their cultural products can benefit from a much larger market in Quebec, not to mention France.

While Herménégilde Chiasson is not offended by France's secular culture, his writing exhibits the ambivalence about Quebec that traditional Quebec writing displayed toward France. In his essay "Acadians in Montreal," he talks of arriving at the airport in Montreal: "The only advantage to landing here is the long walk we have to take through the terminal to the exit, which gives us time to wake up and settle into our we're-not-from-Quebecitude. There was a time when this realization caused me a great feeling of frustration, which always brought on a deep sadness. We lend a sort of dignity to our despair by adopting attitudes of irony and stoicism and, sometimes, cynicism."[4]

On this trip to Montreal, Hermé visits an acquaintance who asks him the question: "So, what's happening in Moncton?"[5] Here is a question that, when asked in Montreal, is bound to raise the hackles of an Acadian. Hermé comments: "Happening in Moncton. Happening. Moncton. . . . Jean-Guy Pilon once wrote, in an issue of *Liberté* devoted to Acadie, that 'Moncton is so ugly its ugliness must be deliberate,' meaning that it is inconceivable its citizens could have achieved such a horror by accident. The relationship between Acadie and Quebec has come to the point where either side can find whatever it needs to cobble together a hatred of or sympathy for the other's artistic or collective expression."[6] He concludes: "I am asleep. I'm dreaming of a land where everyone is fulfilled by their differentness, where everyone has given up making comparisons and has banished all similes."[7]

The tension between the Acadian project to which Hermé is committed and the Quebec nationalist project is clear. It is not that Hermé would wish away the creative sparks that fly from the Acadian-Québécois relationship. Two years after becoming lieutenant-governor of New Brunswick, at a time when the fortunes of both the Bloc Québécois and the Parti Québécois are running high, and another referendum on Quebec sovereignty is not unlikely, Hermé is convinced that Quebec will not secede from Canada. The Québécois will push to the limit, he believes, but they will stay in Canada.

Rita Aufrey, a poet who is in her fifties, was born in Moncton. For many years, she was married to a much admired trade unionist of Acadian origin who was raised in Toronto and spoke French poorly, and who died in 2002. Rita's great-great-grandfather emigrated from Brittany to New Brunswick in the 1820s, settling near Memramcook. With her artistic temperament and her long experience of anglophone culture, Rita comes at the question of Acadian identity with some doubts and many questions. She sees the renaissance of Acadian identity as the product of powerful currents within the Church. She regards the great nationalist revival of the 1960s, despite its secularism, as rooted in the teachings of influential clerics. As she sees it, the nationalists of those days carried out an assault on Acadian mythologies only to replace them with an

Acadian folklore that was perhaps more up-to-date but nonetheless misleading in its own way. The nationalists were seeking power, she says, but when they attained it, they didn't know what to do with it. Very large parts of the Acadian population remain poor, she says, but the Acadian elites don't care much about that.

For Rita, who is from New Brunswick's south-east, there is a big difference between her region and the north, especially the Acadian Peninsula. In the south-east, where the Acadians are cheek by jowl with the English, she believes it is natural, and no cause for concern, that the Chiac dialect has developed. While the structure of speech in Chiac is entirely French, English words are often thrown into the mix. Many young people, and some older ones as well, speak Chiac. For nationalists from the north, like Hermé, Rita says, there is a disdain for a dialect that mixes French with English and an emphasis on purifying the French that is spoken. Rita says, though, that ordinary people don't like to be pushed around on matters of language by members of the elite. Ordinary people, according to her, are proud of their dialect, which they see as their own creation. Of course, these days there is a large migration from the north, especially the Acadian Peninsula, which is much more homogeneously French-speaking, to the south-east, where Moncton, two-thirds English-speaking, has become the true Acadian metropolis. While Rita certainly regards herself as Acadian, she writes her poetry in English. Her poetry would never be published by an Acadian publishing house, she says. But why should her work not be seen as Acadian poetry?

While Rita expresses doubts about the visions the elites have concerning Acadian society, or even that there ought to be such overarching visions, Isabelle McKee-Allain, who is a sociologist at the Université de Moncton, has cast a critical eye on the role of women in Acadian society. Born in Bouctouche, the hometown of K. C. Irving, she has done a good deal of work developing the idea that women have played the role of "producers of identity" in Acadian society. This notion can seem to portray women as a conservative force in society, who provide an indispensable service to the elites, which in the past meant the leaders of the Church, by passing on the tenets of traditional culture to the next generation. It's not nearly as simple as that, though, she insists. Those who transmit a culture, and thereby produce an identity for the next generation, may end up passing on ways of being that are not what the traditionalist patriarchy has intended. She tells a story about her grandmother, who raised twelve children, to illustrate her point. In Acadian society, priests played the role of guardians of the faith and of the moral behaviour of their people. An important tool for the guardians was the Index, which listed the books the papacy decided were unfit for reading by good Catholics. McKee-Allain's grandmother was well travelled and very well read. One day when the *curé* dropped over, he saw books on her shelves that were forbidden according to the Index. He made the point to her that these were volumes not fit for her eyes. She replied to him: "If I can raise twelve children, I can handle reading these books."

Pondering the question of the so-called Acadian renaissance of the latter decades of the nineteenth century, McKee-Allain suggests that, as well as being a renaissance, perhaps it was a retreat.

Traditionalism aside, everyone agrees that Acadian women play a powerful role and that they are often strong, matriarchal figures in their families and their communities. Elaine Landry, whose questions about her identity as an Acadian are discussed at the beginning of this book, speaks bluntly about Acadian women, who she says are "witches," a designation that, for her, is entirely positive. Landry has an outlook on present-day Acadie that differs significantly from that of the cultural leaders of Acadian society. Elaine's father, who was born in Saint John and spoke only English, was descended from a branch of the Landry family from Quebec. Her mother is French-speaking. Born in Moncton, Elaine learned French only when she attended school at the age of six. She remembers a period of a few months at school when she was highly annoyed because she couldn't understand what people were saying.

After finishing high school, Elaine attended the Université de Moncton, where she found herself in a much more thoroughly

French-speaking environment. After graduating with very high grades, she enrolled in medicine at the Université de Montréal. At first, she found this a very challenging experience. For the first few months, she could hardly make out what her professors were saying, they spoke so quickly. To make matters worse, her medical texts were mostly in English or in Latin. She did not find the Québécois milieu particularly attractive. While in Montreal, her closest friends were French-speaking Lebanese and Jewish students at the Université de Montreal.

Following the receipt of her medical degree, Elaine and her anglophone boyfriend moved to Winnipeg, where she spent a year working in a hospital. A year there was enough for her. She moved back to Moncton without her boyfriend and now lives in Shediac Cape with her husband and son.

Elaine considers herself trilingual, saying that in addition to French and English she is fluent in Chiac. Her son Pierre, who is thirteen, attends a French public school in Grande-Digue, north of Shediac. She says that in Pierre's schoolyard many of the children prefer to speak English. Her experience—she is a general practitioner in Shediac, where she comes into contact with a large cross-section of the population—is that the effective French vocabulary of many people is quite limited. She observes that people often think their children speak better French than they actually do. On this point, she says that, in general, the people moving to New Brunswick's south-east from the much more homogeneously French north speak better French than those in the vicinity of Moncton. Despite studies that show that the assimilation of French-speaking New Brunswickers is quite low, she believes the process of assimilation is underway, pointing out that many young children are cared for by their grandmothers and that they spend their days watching American television shows.

New Brunswick has the worst early-childcare system in Canada, she insists, and without an improved system, early education of children in French will continue to suffer. Elaine believes that New Brunswickers who do not attend university end up speaking a rather limited French. She also believes that the frequent intermarriages between French-speakers and non-French-speakers tend to propel assimilation, even in cases where the mothers are French-speaking.

She does believe, more optimistically, that the relationship between Acadians and English-speakers in New Brunswick has improved dramatically. While in the past Acadians in Moncton were looked down on, they have made enormous strides, and in many ways they have passed the anglophones in the hierarchy of the city. As a result, a large number of English-speaking adults want their children to learn French, something unthinkable a few decades ago. While she sees the English as representing Moncton's old money, she says that the Acadians are the power-brokers who represent new money.

The matter of Acadian identity is not something in which Elaine is particularly interested. She says frankly that she does not think of herself as Acadian and feels no real connection with the annual celebrations on August 15.

The Acadian Peninsula is the heartland of New Brunswick's francophone population. In the peninsula, unlike the south-east, French is the majority language. In the south-east, when you walk into a store you are met at the cash with an ambiguous greeting that can open into either English or French depending on your reply. But in the Acadian Peninsula, the assumption in restaurants or stores is that you will speak French. In this sense, the peninsula feels a lot more like Quebec than like Moncton and its environs.

The towns and countryside of the Acadian Peninsula were the bastions from which Acadians rebuilt a society where they could live in their own way in the aftermath of *le Grand Dérangement*. Caraquet, on the northern edge of the Baie des Chaleurs, is the cultural capital of the peninsula. It is a town of hard realities and persistent dreams. It is a town of economic and political struggles. While in the south-east Acadians are at close quarters to the English, in Caraquet they feel they have the world on their doorstep across the sea, and they have Quebec not far away across the bay. On the north shore of the Baie des Chaleurs is the Gaspé region of Quebec, in its own way a land of hard realities and persistent dreams, far from the centre of power in Quebec.

For more than two centuries, Acadians have made a life for themselves in the peninsula, a life built on the unstinting labour they poured into the three basic industries of the region: the fishery, the forestry and farming. The fishery was the first salvation for the people of the peninsula who escaped the deportation or who came here as refugees in its aftermath. But the fishery was a hard taskmaster. Most of those who fished here worked for the big fish companies, often based in Jersey, and earned a pittance. Their lives were little better than those of serfs. Today the fishery has made fortunes for a few Acadians who have become millionaires in the quest for lobster and scallops. But the cod fishery is dead here, as it is in the rest of Atlantic Canada, at least for the time being. It was the victim of overfishing by the great factory ships of Europe and Japan that plied these waters and took everything. What was once the fishery that supplied millions of people in distant parts of the world with basic nourishment has been crippled, who knows for how long, by rapacity.

When Michel Blanchard, the artist, musician and dreamer, former student radical of 1968, looks out on the world from Caraquet in the early twenty-first century, he sees hope in a region that has experienced a long economic decline, a region from which many Acadians have left for the jobs and prosperity of the south-east. He still looks young, with his broad shoulders, large blue eyes and his hair in a ponytail, as he gazes out the restaurant window at the bay. He talks of the Acadians of the peninsula in this new age as a people of the sea who travel to many parts of the world to work and then return home to enrich their own society. He also feels much closer, at least in his heart, to the people of the Gaspé than he does to the people of the south-east. His resentment about the rise of Moncton is palpable. He calls Dieppe, the fast-rising, French-speaking town on the eastern edge of Moncton, the "cemetery of the

Acadians." For him, the south-east to which so many Acadians are migrating is a land where they will inexorably be assimilated. The Université de Moncton, he asserts, can never be a true French university because of its location in the south-east.

Despite the many negative things that have been said about the peninsula, Michel Blanchard sees it as a centre of life, a harbinger of things to come in an age of revolutionary technology. His political dream is that a new province can be forged out a union between the Acadian Peninsula and the Gaspé. Reminded that Parti Québécois founder and later Quebec premier René Lévesque, when asked about whether Acadians could join Quebec, had commented that one Gaspé was enough, Blanchard shrugs off this putdown. He has no use for political centralizers of any variety, whether they are Péquistes, social democrats or Liberals, who are his true *bête noire*. He is on the side of the cause of Quebec sovereignty, and, contrary to the opinion of the Acadian elites who fear that the secession of Quebec would marginalize Acadie, he believes it would be a positive development. He is careful to use the word "sovereignty," rather than "independence," believing it would lead to what he calls "reconfederation." To open the door for this transformation and a sovereign Quebec, Blanchard is happy to see the election of an anglophone Conservative prime minister in Canada. Stephen Harper suits him fine.

Michel Blanchard also has a more "far out" perspective, one that leaves questions of political arrangements as minor details. He has confidence that new technology will resolve many things in the twenty-first century, making the great cities of the industrial age and the cultures that go with them anachronistic. He sees Americans as addicted in their musical and artistic tastes to the industrial rhythms that are now dated. With robots to carry out mundane tasks, and the interconnections of the Internet age to create networks wherever people want them, large federal states such as Canada and the United States will disintegrate. In place of representative democracy will come a new age of localism and universalism. People will relate to their immediate surroundings or to the networks on the planet that they choose to join. Seen this way, the Acadian Peninsula, in his eyes, becomes a rooted place, a strong community, a harbinger of the future, a place that can turn its back on the work-centred, sick society of North America. For those who look down their noses at people who collect welfare or employment insurance in the Acadian Peninsula, he laughs and says that it is the North Americans who have little existence beyond their nine-to-five jobs who are the diseased ones, suffering from a malady that makes them unable to comprehend the basic ways civilization is changing.

See it as a pipe dream, or a counsel of despair, or as the product of the bitterness of the north—Michel Blanchard still dreams.

For his part, without turning his back on the Acadian Peninsula where he was born, Hermé and many of his artist contemporaries have sought to achieve a goal that is daring, even revolutionary— Michel Blanchard would say foolhardy—that is, to conceive of Moncton as the centre of their imaginative space. Moncton is a big town, now almost as large as Saint John (greater Moncton, 120,000; greater Saint John, 125,000), New Brunswick's historic metropolis. The town is spread out on both sides of the Petitcodiac River. The Petitcodiac, which empties into the nearby Bay of Fundy, is noted for its tidal bore. High tide on the bay, which has the world's highest tides, propels a wave of water up the river. The wave courses through the centre of Moncton and is something of a tourist attraction, with electronic signs posted by the river announcing when the tidal bore will next occur. A couple of decades ago, a causeway was put into place to moderate the flow of the bore in Moncton. As a consequence, much of its drama has been lost and the phrase "total bore" is often now employed to describe the phenomenon.

With the river at its centre, Moncton has grown up in a huge bowl of land that is surrounded by low, tree-covered hills. The urban area is divided into three distinct parts. There is the city of Moncton itself, about one-third francophone and two-thirds anglophone; across the river is Riverview, which is almost entirely English-speaking; and to the east of Moncton is Dieppe, which is almost entirely French-speaking. When the population of all three components is added together, the greater city remains two-thirds English, one-third French.

Over the past decade or two, the Acadians have been transforming what was an unlovely city into their economic and cultural engine. Moncton was once the rail hub of the Maritimes. Called Hub City, for decades it was home to the CNR shops where several thousand people worked. Now the shops are gone and Moncton has become ever more a white-collar town in which Acadians play an outsized role in both the public and private sectors. During the 1990s, with Frank McKenna as premier of New Brunswick, a great effort was made to attract companies running call-centres to locate in Moncton. The economic upturn, triggered in part by the call-centres, helped draw thousands more Acadians from the economically stagnant north to the more prosperous south-east. While in any conversation with Acadian analysts about the state of the economy the call-centres are quickly mentioned, so too are the less rosy aspects of such employment. The jobs are not high-paying, and they involve the dreariness that is a feature of most of the employment in the high-tech world. Those making calls from the centres are closer to galley slaves than they are to the glamorous personalities who innovate in the fast-changing realm of communications.

There are, in Moncton's private sector, a few small but significant high-tech companies that have been founded and run by Acadians. Pride of place in the private sector goes to Assomption Vie, the insurance company that was founded by Acadians in Massachusetts nearly a century ago and that moved its head office to Moncton not many years later. On Main Street, right in the centre of town, the Assomption Vie building is the tallest.

The rise of Moncton as the Acadian metropolis has been propelled in the public as well as the private sector. Of crucial importance is the Université de Moncton, with three campuses in the province. The main campus at Moncton convenes a critical mass of francophone scholars that has had an immense impact. The university, taking over from where the Catholic colleges left off, is the prime training ground for the brightest young Acadians. It is also an engine for research on the Acadian past and on present-day Acadian society. In the departments of sociology, political science and fine arts, and in the crucial Centre d'Études Acadiennes, scholars are turning out a large body of work on the study of Acadie.

In June 2004, at the university's annual celebration (in that year, the forty-first) of the founding of the institution, hundreds of faculty, staff and students were present for speeches and for barbecued chicken. The celebration began as everyone stood to sing "Ave Maris Stella," the Acadian anthem. It has been pointed out, ruefully by some, that one of the distinguishing characteristics of the Acadians is that they are the only people in the world whose national anthem is sung in Latin. This was followed by a ceremony in which plaques were awarded to faculty members who had served for ten and for twenty-five years. My friend, fine arts professor Francis Coutellier, has been on the faculty for so long, thirty-four years, that there was no plaque for anyone in his category. The ceremony was followed by conversations over lunch. What sets this annual celebration apart from the many university occasions encountered elsewhere is that no one takes this university for granted. Its founding four decades ago, and its existence ever since, has been understood as crucial to the development of Acadian society.

If the Université de Moncton was a crucial launching pad for the new Acadian nationalism of the 1960s and 1970s, it has also been an important base for the support of cultural undertakings. There are now two Acadian professional theatre companies operating in Moncton. The better established of the two, the Théâtre L'Escaouette, has recently moved into a handsome new theatre in the heart of the city, only a few doors down the street from the Aberdeen Centre. The theatre, run as a co-operative, presents the works of playwrights such as Herménégilde Chiasson, and this has made it an integral feature of a living Acadian culture. The play *Pour Une Fois*, for instance, was written for the occasion of the Francophone Summit held in Moncton in September 1999.

Moncton has also become the key centre for French-language broadcasting in the Atlantic provinces. Radio-Canada, the French

CBC, has television and radio stations in the city from which local programming is done. Despite all the gains the Acadians have made in Moncton, however, this still looks like an English-speaking city in its externals. There are more French signs on restaurants and cafés than before, to be sure, but most of the signage is still in English. And the street names in the city are stubbornly English, with a very few exceptions. "If we are going to live together," Hermé has said, "then surely there should be more street signs in French in Moncton." He once had the idea of producing a street map of Moncton with the English street names in red and the French ones in white. The map would be a blaze of red. It frustrates him that the usual argument advanced against changing street names is that this would be too costly. "My God," he says, "we make an effort to do the things we care about. We go into space, the Egyptians built the pyramids. But having a few streets with French names in Moncton, that seems to exceed the limits of the possible." This reminds me of the early sixties in Montreal when my friends in the student movement at the Université de Montréal would ask me about the signs I saw from the window of my train as it rolled into the city. Were they in French or English, they asked. In English, I replied truthfully.

The Acadian regions of New Brunswick have made great progress in some areas of life over the past four decades. Particularly in the north-east, however, the pillars on which the economy rests have been crumbling. This is a time of genuine crisis. The future will either provide new steps forward or a potentially devastating retreat. Forty years ago, the New Brunswick Acadians made use of the political process to engineer a transformation of their position within the province and of basic aspects of their social existence. The reforms of the Robichaud government gave Acadians equality with Anglo–New Brunswickers in health care, education and roads and highways. The consequence of these reforms was the fostering of an Acadian elite, made up of teachers, professors, intellectuals, artists as well as a new entrepreneurial class. Graduates of the university created a base for the launch of a new Acadian professional class. Acadian lawyers and judges are important members of this class. The new professionals are a crucial part of the audience for theatre and other artistic offerings. Graduates of the university have gone on to medical schools in Quebec, Nova Scotia or elsewhere and these graduates return to Acadie to practise medicine. The fashioning of a new elite, closely tied to public sector institutions— schools, the university, hospitals, the CBC, the courts—has helped create the basis for an entrepreneurial revolution in Acadie.

The most established firm in Acadie, Assomption Vie, the life-insurance company that has existed for close to a century, has been important to the takeoff of the Acadians in Moncton and New Brunswick's south-east. New firms, large and small, have also been created by the new Acadian entrepreneurs. The most famous of these, first established in Shediac and now headquartered in Moncton, is Pizza Delight. Small high-tech firms, firms in communications, restaurants and many other ventures have been started by Acadians in recent years. Today in the Moncton area, it is the new Acadian entrepreneurs who are said to be the risk-takers. Along the coast, east of Shediac, at Cap-Pelé and other nearby points, the new Acadian elites are building fashionable houses by the sea. Recently, this coast has seen some of the most rapidly rising real estate values in Canada.

The Moncton "miracle," as it has been called, has caused some economists to rethink the future development pattern of the Maritimes. Saint John, the dominant city in New Brunswick for two centuries, has been shunted aside by upstart Moncton. Seen by some as an "old economy" company town in the hands of the Irvings, Saint John is by no means out of the game. But there are economists who believe the future of the Maritimes will revolve around what they call the "Halifax-Moncton corridor," an axis of economic vitality connected to the anchor cities at either end. The trouble with the idea that everyone else in the Maritimes should move away from their traditional centres to relocate in the corridor is that it would be impossible for politicians to sell this concept, New Brunswick economist Donald Savoie notes. Savoie has watched government development plans for the Maritimes come and go over the decades, almost always with nugatory results. He thinks the takeoff of the Moncton economy can be sustainable. He sees economic development in terms of the rise of metropolitan centres. Understood that way, New Brunswick, in the early years of the twenty-first century, has reached the stage of development attained by Ontario at the end of the First World War, when that province became half urban and half rural. As far as the north is concerned, Savoie also has no use for the idea that the Acadians of the region have been pampered and have grown lazy as a result of Employment Insurance. You try getting up at 5:00 a.m. to go fishing, he tells me. People from Moncton who look down on the people of the north, he says, should remember that many people in Toronto denigrate Moncton in much the same way. If we lose the north, he insists, we will lose Acadie.

For the future, Moncton will have to build on the successes of recent years to provide employment in professional and non-professional jobs in the service sector. Acadians are well placed to benefit if such a broadening of the service sector can be achieved. They are much better educated than in the past. And as a consequence of the institutional networks that have been established in the Moncton area—including the university, the French hospital, broadcasters, artists and those in the tourist sector, including restaurants and cafés—the Acadians can take initiatives and risks that would have been unimaginable a few decades ago. Another relative advantage enjoyed by the Acadians is that while some young Acadians are quite prepared to move to other parts of the country, there is a strong tendency for them to want to remain in Acadie, a tendency that keeps a higher percentage of energetic youth staying while a higher proportion of English-speaking youth in the Maritimes tends to migrate to other parts of Canada. To take advantage of the possibilities, the Acadians will have to engineer a revolution in our time that is at least as daring as, and much more complex than, the revolution achieved during the days of the Robichaud government in the 1960s.

The Acadians are still left with their oldest conundrum, the question of how to define their homeland. What is Acadie, what is its territory, and who is to make decisions for this nation, which in the world of today remains without a state? The Acadians have gained a very considerable share in the exercise of state power in New Brunswick and have been able to parlay that share into guarantees that have been written into the Canadian constitution. With all its uniqueness and cultural ingenuity, Acadie depends to a considerable extent on the success of the Canadian federation, and therefore on Quebec's ability to find an enduring place for itself within the federation.

Meanwhile, the Acadian Diaspora retains its compelling importance. If New Brunswick has emerged as the central homeland of Acadians at the beginning of the twenty-first century, the Acadian fact remains strongly established in Nova Scotia and Prince Edward Island. And then there is the vibrant reality of Acadian-Cajun Louisiana, with its own identity, the product of two centuries of separate development. For the most part, the Cajuns have lost the use of the French language, despite its survival in some places in Louisiana. Today, in the University of Southwestern Louisiana in Lafayette, there is a concerted attempted to strengthen the francophone culture in the region, including the fostering of the French language. Cajuns who have lost the French language remain strongly attached to elements of their cultural nonetheless. The annual celebrations at the time of Mardi Gras go much deeper in the Cajun regions of Louisiana than a strategy for attracting tourists. Acadian food, music, theatre and ways of perceiving the world remain pronounced in Cajun communities determined to maintain their identity. While most New Brunswick Acadians insist on the intimate connection between the use of the French language and Acadian survival, Cajun identity continues even among those who do not speak French. Their presence in the gatherings of Acadians in the Congrès Mondial Acadien will continue. The desire of many Louisiana Cajuns to maintain their ties with those in their families who live in the Maritimes is a potent fact of Acadian identity.

For their part, New Brunswick Acadians are sailing on a vessel that has survived a perilous journey out of the past, but that is well suited to the seas of the twenty-first century. This is a culturally vibrant society that knows what it means to remain true to itself while living in a world with others, without feeling the need to negate those others. These are very considerable survival advantages in a world in which the peoples of the largest states are perennially locked so narrowly in the projects and culture of their own society that they have little capacity to understand other societies. In many ways, the advantage has shifted to those who know who they are but who are driven by necessity to comprehend the larger world. Acadians are such a people. Their vessel can confidently plot a course in the Canada and the world of our time.

ACKNOWLEDGEMENTS

—

I am indebted to the many people in New Brunswick, Nova Scotia, and Prince Edward Island, as well as in the State of Louisiana, who helped me with advice, ideas and personal introductions. A number of faculty members at the Universite de Moncton were generous with their assistance and ideas, including Greg Allain, Raoul Boudreau, Annette Boudreau, Isabelle McKee-Allain, Chedly Belkhodja, Ronald Babin, David Lonergan and Donald Savoie. One person among these must be singled out for special thanks. Without the generous and unstinting encouragement and help of Francis Coutellier, I would not have been able to write this book.

Maurice Basque, Director of the Centre d'études acadiennes at Université de Moncton, kindly shared his perspectives on Acadie with me and offered the resources of the centre to support my research.

I am indebted to Elaine Landry for her encouragement and assistance and to Rita Auffrey for her unique outlook on the Acadians.

Herménégilde Chiasson and Marcia Babineau were a constant source of inspiration for me during the writing of the book.

The staff of the Acadian Museum in St. Martinville, Louisiana were generous with their hospitality and assistance. Thanks to Amanda Lafleur, professor at Louisiana State University for her advice.

Thanks as well to Georges Arsenault in Charlottetown and to film maker Anne-Marie Rocher.

In the summer of 2004, my son Jonathan spent weeks with me in New Brunswick doing research for the book. The following summer, my daughter Emily carried out research in New Brunswick and accompanied me to interviews in New Brunswick and P.E.I.

Thanks to everyone at Doubleday Canada, in particular Maya Mavjee, for their support. I am grateful to Martha Kanya-Forstner for believing in the viability of the book and for seeing it through its initial phase. Meg Masters did a wonderful job on the basic edit of the manuscript. Amy Black ably oversaw the final edit and managed the myriad questions that went into the production of the book.

My agent, Jackie Kaiser, provided whatever tranquility is ever possible when writing a book.

My heartfelt appreciation goes to my spouse Sandy for introducing me to Acadie so many years ago and for offering advice and the value of her company throughout this project.

——

INTRODUCTION

1. Brenda Dunn, *A History of Port Royal/Annapolis Royal, 1605–1800* (Halifax: Nimbus Publishing Ltd., 2004), 2.

CHAPTER 1

1. Sally Ross and Alphonse Deveau, *The Acadians of Nova Scotia: Past and Present* (Halifax: Nimbus Publishing, 1992), 20, 21.
2. N. E. S. Griffiths, *From Migrant to Acadian: A North American Border People, 1604–1755* (Montreal and Kingston: McGill-Queen's University Press, 2005), 54, 55.
3. Yves Cormier, *Les Aboiteaux en Acadie: Hier et aujourd'hui* (Moncton: Chaire d'Études Acadiennes, 1990), 20.
4. John Mack Faragher, *A Great And Noble Scheme: The Tragic Story Of The Expulsion Of The French Acadians From Their American Homeland* (New York: W.W. Norton and Company, 2005), 35.
5. *Dictionary of Canadian Biography*, vol. 1 (Toronto: University of Toronto Press, 1966), 186.
6. Dunn, 3.
7. *Dictionary of Canadian Biography*, 189.
8. Ross and Deveau, 9.
9. Geoffrey Plank, *An Unsettled Conquest: The British Campaign Against The Peoples Of Acadie*, (Philadelphia : University of Pennsylvania Press, 2001), 23, 24.
10. Plank, 24, 25.

CHAPTER 2

1. R. Cole Harris and John Warkentin, *Canada Before Confederation* (New York: Oxford University Press, 1974), 30, 31.
2. Faragher, 65.
3. Jacques Vanderlinden, *Se Marier en Acadie Française: XVIIe et XVIIIe Siècles* (Moncton: Éditions d'Acadie/Chaire

d'Études Acadiennes, 1998), 22, 24, 25, 26.
4. Vanderlinden, 28, 29.
5. Ross and Deveau, 31.
6. Carl A. Brasseaux, *The Founding of New Acadie: The Beginnings of Acadian Life in Louisiana, 1765–1803* (Baton Rouge: Louisiana State University Press, 1987), 151–156.
7. Faragher, 36.
8. Dunn, 23, 24.
9. Faragher, 77.
10. Ross and Deveau, 57–59.
11. Ross and Deveau, 57–58.
12. Faragher, 177, 178.
13. Jean-Marie Fonteneau, *Les Acadiens: Citoyens de l'Atlantique* (Rennes: Éditions Ouest-France, 1996), 135, 136.
14. Plank, 99.
15. Plank, 110, 111.
16. Daniel N. Paul, *We Were Not The Savages* (Halifax: Fernwood Publishing, 2000), 100, 101.
17. Plank, 111.
18. Plank, 112.
19. Fonteneau, 142.
20. Fonteneau, 143.
21. Charles D. Mahaffie, Jr., *A Land of Discord Always: Acadie from Its Beginnings to the Expulsion of Its People, 1604–1755* (Halifax: Nimbus Publishing, 1995), 193.
22. Mahaffie, 207.
23. Mahaffie, 208.
24. Mahaffie, 208.
25. Fonteneau, 143.
26. Fonteneau, 144.
27. Mahaffie, 209.
28. Mahaffie, 214.
29. Mahaffie, 249.
30. Faragher, 228.
31. Mahaffie, 247.
32. Mahaffie, 215.
33. Mahaffie, 217.

34. Mahaffie, 218.

35. Faragher, 240.

36. Mahaffie, 228, 229.

CHAPTER 3

1. Faragher, 291.

2. Plank, 70, 71.

3. Plank, 127.

4. Plank, 129.

5. Faragher, 118.

6. Fonteneau, 166.

7. Fonteneau, 166.

8. Faragher, 246.

9. Fonteneau,167.

10. Plank, 142.

11. Faragher, 287.

12. Faragher, 296.

13. Faragher, 297, 298.

14. George F. G. Stanley, New France: The Last Phase 1744–1760 (Toronto: McClelland and Stewart, 1968), 108–110.

15. Nova Scotia Documents, Papers Relating To The Forcible Removal Of The Acadian French From Nova Scotia, 1755–1768, vol. 2, 259, 260.

16. Papers Relating To The Forcible Removal Of The Acadian French From Nova Scotia, 261.

17. Papers Relating To The Forcible Removal Of The Acadian French From Nova Scotia, 261, 262.

18. Papers Relating To The Forcible Removal Of The Acadian French From Nova Scotia, 265–67.

19. Papers Relating To The Forcible Removal Of The Acadian French From Nova Scotia, 268.

20. Papers Relating To The Forcible Removal Of The Acadian French From Nova Scotia, 268, 269.

21. Faragher, 329.

22. Faragher, 339.

23. Papers Relating To The Forcible Removal Of The Acadian French From Nova Scotia, 271–73.

24. Ross and Deveau, 62.

25. Faragher, 352.

26. Plank,147.

27. Faragher, 361.

28. Faragher, 370, 371.

29. Papers Relating To The Forcible Removal Of The Acadian French From Nova Scotia, 274–76.

30. Papers Relating To The Forcible Removal Of The Acadian French From Nova Scotia, 277, 278.

31. Papers Relating To The Forcible Removal Of The Acadian French From Nova Scotia, 278–80.

32. Stanley, 91.

33. Stanley, 99, 100.

34. Stanley, 105, 106.

35. Welcome to New Brunswick: http://new-brunswick.net.

CHAPTER 4

1. Faragher, 333.

2. Georges Arsenault, The Island Acadians 1720–1980 (Charlottetown: Ragweed Press, 1989), 33–36.

CHAPTER 5

1. Warren A. Perrin, Acadian Redemption (Erath, Louisiana: Acadian Heritage and Cultural Foundation, Inc., 2004), 10.

2. Perrin, 10.

3. Perrin, 12.

4. Perrin, 15.

5. Perrin, 20.

6. Faragher, 350, 351.

7. Perrin, 21, 23.

8. Perrin, 24.

9. Perrin, 25, 26.

10. Perrin, 26, 27.

11. Perrin, 33–35.

12. L'Évangéline, 2 August 1928. (Fredericton: Goose Lane Editions, 1988), 258.

CHAPTER 6

1. Ross and Deveau, 75.

2. Nicolas Landry and Nicole Lang, Histoire de l'Acadie (Sillery (Quebec): Les Éditions du Septentrion, 2001) 127, 128.

3. Ross and Deveau, 74.

4. Ross and Deveau, 74.

5. Ross and Deveau, 75, 76.

6. Clive Doucet, Lost and Found in Acadie (Halifax: Nimbus Publishing, 2004) 50–52.

7. Landry and Lang, 129, 130.

8. Henri-Dominique Paratte, *Acadians* (Halifax: Nimbus Publishing, 1998), 54, 55.

9. Paratte, 49.

10. Paratte, 52.

11. Paratte, 57.

12. Paratte, 199.

13. Paratte, 200.

14. Landry and Lang, 131.

15. Paratte, 51.

16. Landry and Lang, 158.

17. Paratte, 200, 201.

18. Paratte, 201.

19. Maurice Basque, Nicole Barrieau and Stephanie Côté, *L'Acadie de l'Atlantique* (Moncton: Centre d'Études Acadiennes, 1999) 27.

20. Ross and Deveau, 86.

21. Basque, Barrieau and Côté, 28.

22. Sheila Andrew, "More than a Flag of Convenience: Acadian Attitudes to Britain," *History of Intellectual Culture*, vol. 5, no. 1, 4, 5.

23. Basque, Barrieau and Côté, 28, 29.

CHAPTER 7

1. Landry and Lang, 169.

2. Clarence LeBreton, *La Revolte Acadienne* (Moncton: Les Éditions de la Francophonie, 2002), 48.

3. LeBreton, p. 47

4. LeBreton, 50, 51.

5. LeBreton, 56.

6. Le Breton, 62

7. LeBreton, 75.

8. LeBreton, 89, 90.

9. LeBreton, 80, 83, 92.

10. LeBreton, 92, 93.

11. LeBreton, 94, 95.

12. LeBreton, 95, 96.

13. LeBreton, 97.

14. LeBreton, 98, 99.

15. LeBreton, 100, 101.

16. LeBreton, 103, 104.

17. LeBreton, 104, 105.

18. LeBreton, 105–107.

19. LeBreton, 107–111.

20. LeBreton, 112.

21. LeBreton, 117, 118.

22. LeBreton, 129, 130.

23. LeBreton, 130, 131.

24. LeBreton, 131.

25. LeBreton, 131, 132.

26. LeBreton, 125–141.

27. LeBreton, 143–150.

28. Landry and Lang, 170.

CHAPTER 8

1. James Lee Burke, *Black Cherry Blues* (New York: Avon Books, 1989), 49.

2. R. Warren Robison, "Domestic Architecture in Acadiana in the Eighteenth and Nineteenth Centuries," in Glenn R. Conrad (ed.), *The Cajuns: Essays on Their History and Culture* (Lafayette: University of Southwestern Louisiana, 1983), 156–58.

3. Carl A. Brasseaux, *Acadian to Cajun: Transformation of a People, 1803–1877* (Jackson and London: University Press of Mississippi, 1992), 93.

4. Brasseaux, 5.

5. Brasseaux, 45–52.

6. Brasseaux, 55.

7. Brasseaux, 116.

8. Brasseaux, 117.

9. Brasseaux, 118.

10. Brasseaux, 159.

11. Poché Family History Resource Center: http://www.pochefamily.org/ battleofmansfield.htm.

12. Brasseaux, 151.

13. Brasseaux, 157.

14. Brasseaux, 157.

15. Brasseaux, 181.

16. Jim Bradshaw, "Some thought Jayhawker Carrière was really a hero," *Lafayette Daily Advertiser*, 26 August 1997.

17. Bradshaw, *Lafayette Daily Advertiser*, 26 August 1997.

18. Brasseaux, 125, 126.

19. Brasseaux, 126.

20. Brasseaux, 126, 127.

21. Brasseaux, 131.

22. Brasseaux, 136, 137.

CHAPTER 9

1. Naomi Griffiths, "Longfellow's Evangeline: The Birth and Acceptance of a Legend," *Acadiensis*, vol. 11, no. 2, Spring 1982.
2. Barbara Le Blanc, *Postcards from Acadie: Grand-Pre, Evangeline and the Acadian Identity* (Kentville, N.S.: Gaspereau Press, 1984) 62, 63.
3. Le Blanc, 54.
4. Le Blanc, 64.
5. Adam Shortt and Arthur G. Doughty (General Editors), *Canada and Its Provinces* (Toronto: Edinburgh University Press for the Publishers' Association of Canada Limited, 1913), vol. 13, 93, 98.
6. Le Blanc, 56.
7. Le Blanc, 61.
8. Le Blanc, 59.
9. Le Blanc, 65.
10. Le Blanc, 64.

CHAPTER 10

1. Della M. M. Stanley, "Louis Joseph Robichaud: A Political Biography," Doctoral thesis, Department of History, University of New Brunswick, October 1980, 4–6.
2. Stanley, 1, 2.
3. Stanley, 10.
4. Michel Cormier, *Louis J. Robichaud: Une Révolution Si Peu Tranquille* (Moncton: Les Editions de la Francophonie, 2003), 32.
5. Cormier, 33.
6. Stanley, 29.
7. Cormier, 39.
8. Cormier, 40.
9. Cormier, 43.
10. Cormier, 57.
11. Cormier, 69.
12. Cormier, 73, 74.
13. Cormier, 85.
14. Cormier, 85.
15. Cormier, 92.
16. John Edward Belliveau, *Little Louis and the Giant K.C.* (Nova Scotia: Lancelot Press, Hantsport, 1980) 10.
17. Cormier, 92, 93.
18. Cormier, 93.
19. Cormier, 109.

20. Cormier, 110.
21. Cormier, 110.
22. Belliveau, 16.
23. Cormier, 120.
24. Cormier, 152.
25. Belliveau, 51.
26. Cormier, 186.
27. Cormier, 187.
28. Cormier, 197, 198.
29. Cormier, 201.
30. Cormier, 201, 202.
31. Debates of the Senate of Canada (Hasnsard), Thursday, October 19, 2000.
32. Cormier, 208.
33. Belliveau, 78, 79.
34. Chedly Belkhodja, "The Right Responds to Change: Opposition to the Robichaud Reforms in New Brunswick," in *The Robichaud Era, 1960–70* (Moncton: Institut Canadien De Recherche sur Le Developpement Regional, 2001),122.
35. Belkhodja, 132.
36. Belkhodja, 132.
37. Cormier, 205, 206.
38. Cormier, 207.
39. Cormier, 216–218.
40. Cormier, 226–231.
41. Cormier, 240–244.
42. Cormier, 249–252.
43. Cormier, 271.
44. Cormier, 275, 276.
45. Cormier, 277, 278.
46. Cormier, 280, 281.
47. Cormier, 284.
48. Belliveau, 116.

CHAPTER 11

1. Antonine Maillet in Nancy Southam (ed.), *Remembering Richard: An Informal Portrait of Richard Hatfield by his Friends, Family and Colleagues* (Halifax: Formac Publishing, 1993), 130.
2. Geoffrey Stevens, *The Player: The Life and Times of Dalton Camp* (Toronto: Key Porter Books, 2003), 190.
3. Richard Starr, *Richard Hatfield: The Seventeen Year Saga* (Halifax: Formac Publishing Company, 1987), 42.
4. Starr, 42.

5. Starr, 58.

6. Michel Cormier and Achille Michaud, *Richard Hatfield: Power and Disobedience* (Fredericton: Goose Lane Editions, 1992), 129, 130.

7. Richard Starr, *Richard Hatfield: The Seventeen Year Saga* (Formac Publishing Company, Halifax, 1987) p. 61.

8. Monique Gauvin and Lizette Jalbert, "The Rise and Fall of the Parti Acadien," *Canadian Parliamentary Review*, vol.10, no. 3, 1987.

9. Gauvin and Jalbert, "The Rise and Fall of the Parti Acadien."

10. Cormier and Michaud, 134.

11. Gauvin and Jalbert, "The Rise and Fall of the Parti Acadien."

12. Gauvin and Jalbert, "The Rise and Fall of the Parti Acadien."

13. Gauvin and Jalbert, "The Rise and Fall of the Parti Acadien."

14. Gauvin and Jalbert, "The Rise and Fall of the Parti Acadien."

15. Gauvin and Jalbert, "The Rise and Fall of the Parti Acadien."

16. Gauvin and Jalbert, "The Rise and Fall of the Parti Acadien."

17. Cormier and Michaud, 113.

18. Cormier and Michaud, 139. It was the largest Conservative majority in New Brunswick since 1912. The icing on the cake, the reward for the years of effort, was the election of nine francophones, including Simard's re-election, as members of the Tory caucus.

19. Cormier and Michaud, 143.

20. Cormier and Michaud, 142.

21. Cormier and Michaud, 143–45.

22. Gauvin and Jalbert, "The Rise and Fall of the Parti Acadien."

23. Cormier and Michaud, 143–45. Though the Parti Acadien continued its nominal existence for a time, it was a spent force, hardly even noticed, after 1982.

24. Gauvin and Jalbert, "The Rise and Fall of the Parti Acadien."

25. Cormier and Michaud, 50.

26. Starr, 101, 102.

27. Starr, 103, 104.

28. Cormier and Michaud, 160–162.

29. Cormier and Michaud, 171–80.

30. Cormier and Michaud, 186.

CHAPTER 12

1. Donald J. Savoie, *Pulling Against Gravity: Economic Development in New Brunswick During The McKenna Years* (Montreal: The Institute for Research on Public Policy, 2001), 195.

2. Jacques Poitras, *The Right Fight: Bernard Lord and the Conservative Dilemma* (Fredericton: Goose Lane Editions, 2004), 11–22.

3. Starr, 250, 251.

4. Poitras, 237, 238.

5. Poitras, 238–241.

6. Poitras, 298, 299.

7. Poitras, 301.

8. Poitras, 305, 306.

9. Poitras, 306, 307.

10. Poitras, 312, 313.

11. Poitras, 314.

CHAPTER 13

1. Shane K. Bernard, *The Cajuns: Americanization of a People* (Jackson: University Press of Mississippi, 2003), 36, 37.

2. Brasseaux, 153.

3. Bernard, 147.

4. Bernard, 148.

5. Michael Tisserand, liner notes to *Looking Back Tomorrow: BeauSoleil Live*, Rhino Records, 2001.

6. Bernard, 82.

7. Mike Tidwell, *Bayou Farewell: The Rich Life and Tragic Death of Louisiana's Cajun Coast* (New York: Vintage Books, 2003), 6.

CHAPTER 14

1. Basque, Barrieau and Côté, 27, 28.

2. Herménégilde Chiasson, *Available Light* (Vancouver: Douglas and McIntyre, 2002), 31.

3. Chiasson, 33.

4. Chiasson, 63.

5. Chiasson, 64.

6. Chiasson, 65.

7. Chiasson, 68.

—